NEITHER WOLF
NOR DOG

NEITHER WOLF NOR DOG ◆ On Forgotten Roads with an Indian Elder

KENT NERBURN

NEW WORLD LIBRARY
NOVATO, CALIFORNIA

New World Library
14 Pamaron Way
Novato, CA 94949

© 1994 Kent Nerburn

Cover design: Kathy Warinner

Library of Congress Cataloging-in-Publication Data

Nerburn, Kent, 1946–
Neither wolf nor dog : on forgotten roads with an Indian elder /
p. cm.
ISBN 1-880032-37-6 (acid-free paper)
1. Dan, 1915– . 2. Dakota Indians — Biography. 3. Dakota philosophy. 4. Dakota Indians — Social life and customs. I. Dan, 1915– . II. Title.
E99.D1D345 1994
970.004'975--dc20   94-21558
                                                        CIP

First printing, August 1994
Printed in Canada on acid-free paper
ISBN 1-880032-37-6
Distributed by Publishers Group West
10 9 8 7 6

For the silent ones

TABLE OF CONTENTS

Introduction

"Let us put our minds together and see what kind of life we can make for our children." — Sitting Bull

It was on a motorcycle ride, several years before this book was even an idea in my mind, that the seed for it was actually planted.

I was traveling across North Dakota. The August sun was unbearably hot and the land rolled on endlessly before me. As I came over a rise I saw in the distance a forlorn wooden structure with three enclosed sides and a low-pitched roof. At first I thought it was a farmer's abandoned fruit stand or a life-sized creche placed on the roadside by some fundamentalist religious group. But as I got closer I realized that it was a shelter for some kind of historical marker.

I pulled to a stop and walked across the simmering highway toward the enclosure. As I approached, I could see that it contained a large, irregular boulder enclosed in a fence. A plaque nearby explained that this was a buffalo rock of the sort that the Lakota Indians held sacred.

The plaque was fine — very informative — and at great pains to be respectful of the Lakota tradition. If you looked closely, it said, you could see the chippings and markings where the anonymous craftsman generations before had tried to coax a more recognizable form from the rock.

I read the words carefully and then turned toward the boulder

1

itself. Though I could not examine it minutely because of the fence, I could see a few of the chip marks from the ancient craftsman who had tried to enhance its shape. It did, indeed, look like a buffalo. It was easy to see how the Lakota had come to value this rock and invest it with spiritual significance.

At another time, earlier in my life, I might have catalogued the information somewhere in my memory and gone happily on my way, satisfied that I had seen something interesting and pleased that I had learned a little more about Indian culture.

But my eyes have changed. I have had the good fortune to have lived and worked among Indian people. I have sat at their tables, talked with them about their children, played basketball with them in the chill of mission school gyms, helped them bury their dead. I have seen how they love each other and fight each other and chide each other and respect each other. I have been part of their lives.

Because of this, I saw something else in that sweltering roadside enclosure. I saw a piece of the earth — a huge and silent rock — enclosed in a pen like an animal. I saw the living belief of a people reduced to a placard and made into a roadside curiosity designed for the intellectual consumption of a well-meaning American public. In short, I saw one of the most poignant metaphors for the plight of the Indian people that I am likely to confront in my entire life: the spirit of the land, the spirit of a people, named, framed, and incarcerated inside a fence.

And I wasn't the only one who had seen something more than a history lesson in that roadside enclosure. On the top of the rock, insignificant to anyone who didn't understand, some previous passerby had placed a few broken cigarettes. In an act as simple and caring as a Catholic's genuflection before the Blessed Sacrament, that person had placed the sacred gift of tobacco on the rude image of the buffalo, and in so doing had paid homage to the animal that is the physical embodiment of the universe in all its bounty for the Lakota people. And more than that, he or she had paid homage to

Wakan Tanka, the Creator, whose immutability and eternal steadfastness is seen as incarnated in the character of every stone.

To that anonymous passerby that rock was not an artifact; it was not even a metaphor. It was a living, spiritual presence. And nothing that the highway department or the historical society or a thousand well-intended anthropologists could do or say with their plaques and enclosures would ever hallow that stone as much as that simple gift of tobacco laid by an unknown hand.

At that moment, as I stood there in the searing August heat on a lonely stretch of North Dakota highway, I made a solemn and private vow. Though I could never experience the sacred presence of the land in the way that it was experienced by the Indian people, neither could I ever again look at the lives and works of my Indian brothers and sisters as object lessons for my education and edification. I had a human obligation to try to bridge the gap between the world into which I had been born and the world of a people I had grown to know and love.

Neither Wolf nor Dog is my attempt to fulfill that obligation.

I realize that there will be a great many Indian readers who will be skeptical about my decision to undertake this task. You have seen your people misinterpreted, misrepresented, and unconscionably exploited by white writers of both good and bad heart.

To you, my friends, who feel this way, I can say only that you should judge me by what I do.

I believe you will see that I am neither a white exploiter who traffics in Indian themes because they are popular, nor a blue-eyed wannabe who has miraculously discovered a Cherokee grandmother somewhere in my distant past. And, most of all, I believe you will see that I am not one of that most pernicious breed of white writer who claims to have met some wisdom-bearing elder who has unaccountably decided to share his or her innermost cultural secrets and teachings with me.

No, if I have done my task well, I believe you will see that I am simply a person of honest heart who has had the good fortune to know and value Indian people, and who has happened upon the opportunity to create a book that can give voice to the thoughts and feelings of a very special man. This opportunity is, to me, a gift, and I take it seriously.

Dan, whose story I tell and thoughts I reveal, has sworn me to secrecy. "Cover my tracks like I am being hunted," he told me. I have done so, changing what needed to be changed, obscuring what needed to be obscured. But his words are as true and as honest as I can make them. If there is good in what he says, it belongs to him; if there is error in the way it is presented, that belongs to me. I have done my best, with honor and humility, and I offer it as my gift to you.

And to you, my white readers, I say read with an open mind and heart. The land you walk upon, whether it be city streets, country lanes, or suburban cul-de-sacs, is Indian land. There are echoes beneath your feet that are there to be heard if you are willing to still your mind and listen to your heart.

But those echoes are not to be found in the myths and false images upon which we have been raised. The drunken Indian, the vicious savage, the noble wiseman, and the silent earthmother are all products of our historical imagination. We do the Indian people no honor by dehumanizing them into such neat and simple packages.

The real Indian people laugh, cry, make mistakes, honor their creator, get angry, go to stores, raise children, and dream all the same dreams as you or I. And it is in the real Indian people, not in the myths and images, that the true voices of our land can be heard.

Dan is such a person. He will not fit your images. He is like the buffalo rock — rough-hewn, elemental, and born of the earth. But, like the buffalo rock, he is also possessed of a deep spirituality for those who have the eyes to see.

Listen to him. Learn from him. Come along on our journey and share our story. You will learn as I have learned, and you will be the better for it.

In the last analysis, we must all, Indian and non-Indian, come together. This earth is our mother, this land is our shared heritage. Our histories and fates are intertwined, no matter where our ancestors were born and how they interacted with each other.

Neither Wolf nor Dog is one small effort to help this coming together. It is not an attempt to build a fence around a man and his people, but to honor them with the gift of my words. I have done my best, and I place this book before you, like the tobacco before the buffalo rock, as a simple offering.

May you receive it in the spirit with which it is offered.

Kent Nerburn
Bemidji, Minnesota
Spring, 1994

Chapter 1

An Old Man's Request

I got to the phone on the second ring. I could hear the scratchy connection even before the voice spoke.

"Is this Nerburn?"

It was a woman. I recognized the clipped tones of an Indian accent.

"Yes," I responded.

"You don't know me," she continued, without even giving a name. "My grandpa wants to talk to you. He saw those 'Red Road' books you did."

I felt a tightening in my chest. Several years before I had worked with students on the Red Lake Ojibwe reservation collecting the memories of the students' parents and grandparents. The two books that had resulted, *To Walk the Red Road* and *We Choose to Remember*, had gained some notoriety in the Indian community across North America. Most of the Indians had loved them for the history they had captured. But some found old wounds opened, or familial feuds rekindled.

Occasionally, I would receive phone calls from people who wanted to challenge something we had written or to set the record straight on something their grandfather or grandmother was supposed to have said.

"Sure," I answered. "Let me talk to him."

"He doesn't like to talk on the phone," the woman said.

I had grown accustomed to Indian reticence about talking to white people, and I knew there were still a few of the very traditional elders who didn't like to use the telephone or have their picture taken.

"Is he upset?" I ventured.

"He just wants to talk to you."

My nervousness was growing. "Where is he?"

She told me the name of a reservation. It was a long way from my home.

"What does he want?"

"Could you come and see him?"

The request took me aback. It was a strange request on any terms, coming as it did from someone I didn't even know. But the distance involved made it even stranger.

"I guess it's important for me to know if he's angry," I said.

The woman betrayed no emotion. "He's not angry. He just saw those books and he wants to talk to you."

I rubbed my eyes and thought of the travel. When I had left the oral history project I had made a silent promise that I would keep using such skills as I had for the good of the Indian people. I had never enjoyed a people so much and had never found such a joyful sense of humor and lack of pretension. But more than that, I had felt a sense of peace and simplicity among the Indians that transcended the stereotypes of either drunkenness or wisdom. They were simply the most grounded people I had ever met, in both the good and bad senses of that word. They were different from white people, different from black people, different from the images that I had been taught, different from anything I had ever encountered. I felt happy among them, and I felt honored to be there.

Sometimes I would stand on the land in Red Lake and think to myself, "This land has never been owned by the United States. This land has never been touched by the movement of European civi-lization." It was as if I were feeling a direct link to something ele-mental, something beneath the flow of history, and it was powerful beyond imagining. Though I was a white man, and all too aware of the effects of well-intentioned white people on the well-being of the Indian people, I wanted, from within my world, to help them retain the goodness in theirs.

Now, a voice had come to me from a place far away, asking me to come back to that world and hear what an old man had to say.

"I'll come," I said, half hating myself for my hesitancy, half hat-ing myself for agreeing at all. "It won't be right away, though."

"He's pretty old," she responded.

"Soon," I said.

"Just ask at the store in town. He doesn't go anywhere much. He really wants to talk to you." She gave me his name and hung up.

And so this book began.

I t was several months before I could make the trip. I packed a few clothes in the truck and made my way across the bleak land-scape of America's northern tier. Scrub pines gave way to fields. Morning mist rose over rolling prairies. Small towns, signaled in the distance by towering grain elevators or church steeples, shot by on the side of the highway, unnoticed, unvisited, undisturbed.

The radio came in and out, offering moments of rock or classi-cal music before disappearing into static. I switched from FM to AM. Farm reports, local ads for hardware stores, specials on rakes and fertilizer and feed.

I checked the map and marked my progress. The reservations were defined only by slightly off-color squares surrounded by dot-ted lines. I tried to imagine an America seen from within these tiny islands in a sea of invading cities and farms. I thought of how a mild sense of discomfort overcame me whenever I crossed one of these borders into a reservation, and how I felt vaguely alien, unwanted, even threatened. How must it be for the Indians themselves, traveling across great expanses of country, feeling that same threat and alienation until they could reach the protective confines of one of the tiny off-color squares that were so few and separated on the vast map of our country?

I arrived on the old man's reservation shortly after dark. The clerk at the local store was a heavyset Indian girl. She eyed me suspiciously when I gave her the name. Three young boys who were standing at the video rack stopped talking and watched me quietly.

"Over there," she said, pointing toward the west. "He lives about three miles out. It's kind of hard to find."

I assured her that I was good at directions.

She drew a tiny map on the back of a napkin. It was full of turns and cutbacks and natural landmarks like creekbeds and fallen trees. I thanked her, bought a pack of Prince Albert tobacco, and set out.

Her map was good, better than I had expected. I soon found myself bouncing up a rutted path with weeds growing in its middle. The headlights formed a vague halo in the darkness. The eyes of small animals would gleam for a second on the side of the road, then disappear as shadowy forms made their way into the underbrush.

The road made a quick turn, then opened into a clearing. My headlights were shining directly onto a small clapboard house. Two cars sat outside. One was up on blocks. Three wooden steps made their way up to the front door. An old, low-bellied dog lay on the top stoop. When I opened the car door she came running toward me, barking and wagging her tail.

The front door opened and a figure emerged, silhouetted against the light inside the house.

"I'm Nerburn," I said.

"Yeah. Come on in," came the reply, as if he had been expecting me. The voice was old but warm. Suddenly I felt more at ease. There was that Indian sense of humor and grace — almost a twinkle — in its tone.

The dog continued barking. "Get away, Fatback," the old man yelled. The dog fell silent and scrabbled her way under the car that was sitting on blocks. "Damn thing. Just showed up here one day. Now she thinks she owns the place." The old man turned and walked back inside. He was slow and deliberate, hardly lifting his feet as he walked.

I made my way up the steps and into the door. The matter-of-fact way he accepted my arrival had me confused.

The house was full of man smell. Fried food. Stale cigarettes. Old coffee.

Dishes stood in the sink. One wall was covered with photographs — a 1940s-vintage sepiatone of a young man and woman standing in front of an old car; a department-store posing of a little girl in a taffeta party dress; a graduation photo of a solemn young man in a mortarboard. An old *Life* magazine photograph of John F. Kennedy stood framed on an end table.

"Sit down," the old man said. He beckoned to a yellow Formica table that stood in the middle of the kitchen. "Do you drink coffee?"

I told him I did. "Good," he answered, and poured me a cup of thin brown liquid from a white enamel pot he kept on the stove. Then he padded over and slid into a seat across from me.

He must have been almost eighty. His face was seamed and rutted, and his long grey hair was pulled back into a ponytail. He had on a plaid flannel shirt over a white T-shirt. His pants were held up by suspenders and he wore sheepskin-lined slippers. One eye was clouded over, but there was a twinkle in his look that matched the twinkle in his voice.

I reached into my pocket and handed him the Prince Albert. My days in Red Lake had taught me that the gift of tobacco was the gift of respect among Indian people.

The old man looked at it.

"Hmm," he said. He reached across the table with a hand twisted by arthritis. He took the packet and shoved it into the breast pocket of his shirt. "You wrote those 'Red Road' books."

"I helped the kids."

He folded up the newspaper on the table. *To Walk the Red Road* lay underneath, as if it, too, had been awaiting my arrival. Small notations were written all over its cover.

"They're pretty good."

"We tried our best."

He spit once into a coffee can he kept by his chair.

"I don't like white people much," he said. He was looking straight at me.

"That's understandable."

"Did they?"

"Who?"

"The old folks at Red Lake."

"Not all of them."

He picked up a can of snuff from the table and slid some behind his lip.

"What about you?"

"You mean, did they like me?"

He didn't answer.

"I think so. Some didn't. They thought I was a pushy white guy. But what could I do?"

"You did okay." He tapped the cover of *To Walk the Red Road*. "Now, let me ask you something else. Do you know why they let you?"

I smiled a bit and took a sip of my coffee. "I think so. I think it's because I like people and they could tell that. That I wasn't going to screw them. That the kids thought I was okay so they decided to trust me."

"No, I don't think so," he said. "There's something else. You don't try to be an Indian."

I smiled at the compliment and let him continue. He was clearly a man who formed judgments quickly.

"White people that come around to work with Indians, most of them want to be Indians. They're always wearing Indian jewelry and talking about the Great Spirit and are all full of bullshit."

"Yeah, I know the type," I said.

He peered around the side of my head. "You got no ponytail. That's good. You don't have any turquoise rings on, do you?" I held up my hands. They had no rings, no watch. "Good," he said wryly.

He picked up his train of thought. "Or else they think we need some kind of white social worker telling us what to do. Some of them come here because they can't find a job anywhere else and end up out on the reservation. We got them here, all of them."

I nodded my head.

He leaned over as if to tell me a secret. "You aren't like that, are you?" he asked.

There was a kind of conspiratorial hush in his voice. I wasn't sure if it was a question or a joke.

"I try not to be. But I'd be lying if I said I didn't like Indian people."

"That's okay. It's good that you like Indian people. I like them too. But how much do you like white people?"

The question seemed strange.

"I'm not much thrilled with the culture we've created."

"Yeah, okay. But how about white people?"

I didn't know what he was driving at.

"I like white people just fine," I said. "I mean, after all, I am one."

"That's what I mean," he chuckled. "That's good. That's good. If you hate your own people you can't be a very good person. You have to love your own people even if you hate what they do." He gestured toward the mug on the table. "Here. Drink your coffee."

I took a gulp to placate him. It tasted like something brewed from twigs and rubber tires. "No, I don't hate white people," I said. "Sometimes I'm embarrassed by us. But white people are okay."

He waved his gnarled hand for silence. He was done toying with me. He fixed me with a solid stare.

I was suddenly intensely aware of my whiteness and my relative youth. I wanted to know what this was all about, but I had learned through hard experience that Indians make their own choices and take their own time. The old man would come to the point when he wanted to.

He pointed to a picture on the wall. "That's my grandson," he said. "When he graduated from Haskell."

Haskell is an Indian junior college in Kansas. The people I knew who had gone there looked upon it with a great sense of pride.

"Did he like it?"

"He's dead now," the old man answered. "Got killed."

"He was a good-looking boy," I offered, unsure of what else to say.

"Yes. He drank too much. Would have been about your age." He fixed me again with that hard stare. "I want you to help me write a book."

The abruptness of the request left me speechless.

"I'm seventy-eight," he continued. "This is a hard life. I want to get all this down."

"All what?" I asked.

"What I have in my mind."

I thought he wanted me to write his memoirs. "You mean, like your memories?"

"No. What I have in my mind. I watch people. Indian people

and white people. I see things. I want you to help me write it down right."

He got up and went into his bedroom. When he came out he had a sheaf of loose-leaf papers in his hand.

"I've been writing some things down. My granddaughter said I should do something with them."

I was shocked and excited and nervous. I didn't know whether I wanted to see the pages or not. The old man might be a crackpot full of wild religious theories. But there was always the chance that he was one of those rare chroniclers of life who had managed to catch the living, breathing sense of the times he had lived through.

He handed me the pile of papers. "Read them," he said.

After two pages I knew that I was in the presence of someone extraordinary. The old man was neither the crackpot I had feared nor the chronicler I had hoped. He was a thinker, pure and simple, who had looked long and hard at the world around him.

His work wasn't polished. It wasn't even finished. Pages were filled with disconnected observations and long unpunctuated paragraphs. Thoughts were scrawled on hunks of napkins and the backs of envelopes.

But beneath the fragmentary disorder lay a level of insight that was as deep and as clear as a mountain lake.

"I'd be honored to help you with this," I said.

"Good. I want it all fixed. I want things to sound right."

"It sounds good now," I told him.

"No, not the way I want. I've been thinking about this for a long time. There are things you white people need to hear. I want them to sound good so people don't say, 'Oh, that's just an old Indian talking.'"

"Well," I laughed, "You are an old Indian talking."

Instantly I could feel I had made a mistake. He turned and looked away from me. Without looking back at me he spoke very slowly. "White people have always tried to make us into animals.

They want us to be like animals in a zoo. If I don't sound good, like a white person thinks sounds good, you just make me into another animal in the zoo." He got up and walked to the sink. He kept his back toward me. "I'm tired now. I'm going to bed."

My cheeks burned. I knew I had offended him.

Once more I had been a white person who had talked before I had thought. But I had seen enough of his writing to believe that it was more important than my feelings, or even his.

I tried one more time.

"I'm sorry," I said. "I hope I didn't offend you."

"I'm going to bed," he said without turning around. He padded into the bedroom and shut the door.

I sat there in silence, listening to the erratic buzzing of the fluorescent light over my head. I didn't know what to do. I thought of writing him a note, but that seemed stupid. I got up and turned off some of the lights. Then I put the tattered pages of the old man's writing under my arm, and went out the door.

I got almost no sleep that night. The motel bed was lumpy and the trucks roaring by on the highway outside shook the walls. But it was my own anguish that kept me awake.

I had never before done anything like taking those pages. The old man hadn't offered them to me. It was a gift for him to even show them to me. Then I had gone and stolen them. I felt like the worst white man who had ever lived, gaining the trust of an Indian then using it to my advantage.

But I kept telling myself there was more to my action than that. I wanted to show the old man that I could be trusted, and the only way I could do it was to take a chance on his trust.

All night I pored over the writing. I rearranged paragraphs and corrected grammar. I tried to link up themes and organize chapters around ideas. Then I tried to write it in a way that sounded like the old man's voice. By 4:30 I had created one chapter that felt right. I wrote it out in longhand and fell asleep just as the sun was beginning to color the edges of the curtains.

I awoke around 7:30. I was afraid the old man would be up and find the manuscript gone. I washed and got dressed and made my way out to the house without stopping to eat.

There was another car parked next to the house.

I waited by my car until someone came to the door. It was a younger woman — the old man's granddaughter. She gestured me in.

I went up the steps and found the old man sitting at the table. He was eating oatmeal and bacon. I immediately put the tattered pages down beside him. He didn't look at me.

"I tried to make a chapter sound like he might want it to," I said to the woman. With every fiber of my being I wanted to keep talking — to explain myself and justify myself. Most of all I wanted some kind of response from them. But I knew I had to keep quiet.

"Read it, Wenonah," the old man said.

I sat there in silence while she read my words in her soft, lilting voice. They sounded stilted to me — not good at all.

When she had finished the old man tapped the table with his crippled finger. "Have some coffee," he said.

I could barely suppress a smile. I knew I had passed some kind of test, but I didn't know how or why.

She poured me a cup from the big enamel pot.

"That's what I wanted you to do," he said. "Make it sound like that. Make it sound like I graduated from Haskell."

Chapter 2

Burnt Offerings

It was several months before I was able to make the drive back out to the old man's reservation. I had gone home with a pile of tattered notebook sheets and several shoe boxes of notes scribbled on everything from napkins to cash register slips. One of the boxes had contained a selection of clippings from newspapers that the old man had collected over the years. Some of them were obituaries of friends. Others were articles on subjects ranging from Indian affairs to politics. There were several Ann Landers columns and a few advertisements. I had been unable to discern any pattern to them, or to divine any reason why he had chosen to collect them in a shoe box, much less to send them home with me.

But I had not asked questions.

In the months that had passed I had spent many hours laying out pieces of paper and cobbling phrases and notations together into thematic unities. As I drove up the pathway to his house, I was excited but apprehensive. I had crafted a few good chapters, or so I thought. But still, it seemed artificial and vaguely unsatisfying, as if it were more my work than his. I was anxious to see how he would receive it.

Fatback was lying in her usual place on the stoop. She barked once, then scuttled off into the dirt hollow she had dug beneath the junk car. I could hear laughing inside the house.

Soon the old man appeared at the door. He gestured me in with a flap of his wrist. "Haven't been around for a while," was all he said. For all his surprise and sense of ceremony, I might have been gone only fifteen minutes.

Three men were sitting around a table, playing cards. They were all old, but none so old as the old man himself. The house was filled with cigarette smoke. The TV was blaring in the corner.

One of the men looked up and said, "Who's that? Grizzly Adams?" It was said with good humor and directed at the old man, as if he, not I, were responsible for explaining my presence. The other men laughed a bit and nodded, then turned back to their cards. Other than that, no one paid any attention to me. The old man didn't introduce me or offer me a place to sit.

One of the men threw three cards on the table. "Son of a bitch," said another, and they all burst into laughter. I had my packet of Prince Albert to offer the old man, but it seemed strange and inappropriate. I stood silently, holding my computer printouts and listening to the buzz of the fluorescent light over my head.

"*Wasichu* play cards?" one of the men said to the old man. I recognized the Lakota term for "white man."

"Don't know," he answered. He pointed toward me with the ash of his cigarette. "Hey, Nerburn. You play cards?"

"No," I answered. "I never really learned."

One of the men grunted. I was no longer significant. He began dealing a new hand while I stood awkwardly in the doorway, disregarded and forgotten.

Suddenly, as if he had been waiting, the old man said, "Well, read one." The others kept talking among themselves and smoking cigarettes.

"Now?" I said.

"Hell, yes. I might not make it until tomorrow."

There was a general round of laughter. I wanted to leave.

I stepped further into the room and started paging through the neatly stapled packets, trying to find one in which I had confidence.

"Just pick one. It don't matter," said the old man.

I grabbed the one sitting on the top. It was one of the most beautiful, I thought, and it was the one that had come to me most fully crafted. Unlike the others, this one had been meticulously printed in ballpoint pen and sealed into a separate envelope. I was not even sure he had written it alone.

I had improved the grammar and changed a few words. But the phrasing, the cadences, and the thoughts were exactly as I had received them.

I cleared my throat like a schoolboy and began:

> Hello, my friends.
>
> I am going to speak to you now. I have thought about this for many years.
>
> I have always tried to follow the ways of my grand-fathers. In my ears I have heard the words of Sitting Bull, telling me that white people are not to be trusted. But I have also heard the words of Black Kettle, who told us to reach out a hand of peace.
>
> I have carried them both in my heart.
>
> Now that I am old I have decided to speak.
>
> There are many of my people who would have me keep silent. They feel we must continue to hide ourselves from the white man. They say that every time we have offered our hand we have been destroyed.
>
> But there is no more place to hide. The white man controls the air we breathe and the water we drink. He comes among us for good and for ill. Our numbers are small, but we are strong in heart. We must meet together,

red people and white, one final time before it is too late. Perhaps our strong hearts will be heard this time. If they are not, what does it matter? Then our time is done either way.

I choose to believe otherwise. The Creator did not put our people here to be destroyed and forgotten. We are part of the great circle of creation. The voice of our people needs to be heard.

If I remain silent, our voice is silenced by one. So I choose to speak.

If at times my words seem angry, you must forgive me. In my mind, there is great anger. No one who has seen the suffering of our children and the tears of our grandmothers cannot be angry. But in my heart I struggle to forgive, because the land is my teacher, and the land says to forgive.

If the mountain can forgive the scarring and the mining, and can cover over her gashes with the fresh grasses of summer, should I not, too, be able to cover over the gashes with the fresh grasses of kindness and understanding?

If the forest can survive the murder of all her children, and rise again once more in beauty, should I not, too, be able to survive the murder of my people and once again raise my heart toward the sun?

It is not easy for a man to be as great as a mountain or a forest. But that is why the Creator gave them to us as teachers. Now that I am old I look once more toward them for lessons, instead of trying to understand the ways of men.

They tell me to be patient. They tell me I cannot change what is, I can only hope to change what will become. Let the grasses grow over our scars, they say, and let the flowers bloom over our wounds.

If I have spoken too much, or spoken wrongly, may others speak out to make it right. If I have spoken truly, may others hear the words and take them to their hearts.

I am only a man. I was not given a seat at the head of my people and I was not raised up to speak for them. I say these things because I believe they must be said. Others may come who can say them better. When they do, I will stand aside.

But I am old, and I cannot wait. I have chosen to speak. I will be silent no more.

When I was done, one of the others looked at the old man. "Did you write that, Dan?"

The old man was impassive. "That one's okay," he said.

"What the hell you doing?" the man with the cards said.

"Just making some little talks."

"Jesus. You making a book?"

One of the other men spoke up. "I think it's damn good."

The third man had remained silent. "I don't know," he said. As if on some inaudible cue, he got up to leave. The other two stood up, also.

"Don't forget the card up your sleeve," the old man said. The others laughed and filed out the door.

"Did I do something wrong?" I asked.

The old man took out a cigarette. "Nah. They just decided to go home. Let me hear that one you just read me again."

I reread the chapter. It sounded strange and stilted in a room full of playing cards and cigarette smoke. The old man could see my puzzlement.

"You white boys don't understand," he said. "Come back to-morrow morning and I'll show you something." He spit something into the coffee can by his chair. "Be sure to bring some tobacco."

♦ ♦ ♦ ♦

Morning dawned with a wet and heavy air. Mosquitoes buzzed against the screen and a foggy haze rose from the fields outside the motel window. Somewhere nearby a semi sat idling with its refrigeration unit on. The low diesel rumble pulsed and droned against the motel wall.

The enigmatic nature of the old man's response had set me on edge. It was a long drive and an expensive trip to come out and visit him. I wanted some greater sense of purpose out of these encounters — a thank-you, a level of excitement and anticipation, anything. But all I was getting were nods and grunts and people coming and going with no discernible purpose.

"Stay calm," I told myself. I remembered what a man I respected, a tribal leader of the local Ojibwe, had said when asked about Indian time. "You know what Indian time means?" he had responded in a session with local college students. "It means, 'When I'm damn good and ready.'"

The old man was operating on Indian time. I was still operating on a clock and a paycheck.

I showered quickly and pulled on a pair of blue jeans and a T-shirt. I had driven out in my sandals, but they seemed embarrassingly citified. I took the old pair of workboots out of my duffel bag and slipped them on over some grey cotton socks. I took a quick glance in the mirror. With my blond hair and rapidly greying beard, I guess I could easily be seen as looking like Grizzly Adams to an old Indian. There were worse things they could have called me.

The old man was waiting when I arrived. Once again, his granddaughter was cooking him breakfast. I began to wonder if this was a daily ritual, and where she emerged from every morning. She was frying smoky strips of bacon on an old cast-iron griddle, then pouring the bacon grease into a big pot of oatmeal.

"You hungry, Nerburn?" she asked, stirring the grease into the oatmeal with a large metal spoon. Her familiarity took me aback, almost as much as the breakfast she was concocting.

"A couple of strips of bacon and a cup of coffee would be great," I said. I remembered her brew; it had at least shown some promise. It was more twigs and less tire than the old man's. And I was willing to endure anything to avoid the mephitic gruel she was brewing up on the stove.

The old man tapped the table with his arthritic finger. "Did you bring the tobacco?"

I nodded. "I had it along last night, but it didn't seem like the right time to give it to you."

"Suit yourself," he said. His granddaughter glanced over at me out of the corner of her eye, but turned her gaze away when I saw her looking.

Soon another car came rumbling up the driveway. Fatback raced out from her hollow and started barking.

"Aw, shut the hell up," came a voice from outside. Three car doors slammed and I heard footsteps clomping up the wooden steps. The screen door opened and the three card players from the previous night came in. They nodded to me, and pulled up chairs. One of them wandered over to the old man's granddaughter and put his arm around her. "You can cook my bacon anytime," he cackled. Wenonah gave him a playful push. "You got no bacon left to cook, Grover," she said. The others roared with laughter.

Grover came over and sat down at the table. I had not paid much attention to him the night before, except to notice that he was the one who had seemed to take offense at what I had written. He was probably in his late fifties and had the wiry body of a one-time athlete or street tough. He wore a pair of jeans, cowboy boots, and a sparkling white T-shirt that looked as if it had just come from a laundry. The sleeves had been carefully rolled up to reveal an eagle tattoo on his right bicep. He wore his hair in a crewcut that was the color of cigarette ash. I had the distinct sense that he had been in the Navy once; he had the rolling gait and personal carriage of a sailor.

Wenonah brought me the bacon and a tin cup full of coffee. "Treating this white boy pretty good, Wenonah," Grover said.

"He's not an old goat like you."

Grover bleated several times and let out a hearty laugh.

"I suppose you want to eat, too," she said to the men.

"Nerburn here's got something for you," the old man interrupted. He glanced at me and gestured with his eyes toward my pocket. I fumbled quickly and pulled out the tobacco.

"Here," I said, offering it to Grover. "Mr. . . ." I didn't know how to refer to the old man. I knew his name was Dan, but that seemed too intimate. I settled for avoidance. "I was asked to come out here to help with this book. I consider it a great honor and I want to do it right. I would consider it a great honor if you would help me, too."

The men sat silent, impassive. No one said anything for what seemed like minutes. The whole mood in the room had changed. Finally, Grover took the packet of Prince Albert. "If Dan wants my help I will give it." The others nodded too. Wenonah kept her back to us and said nothing.

Grover had taken on a look of seriousness. He stared at the floor as if in contemplation. Then he got up and went out the front door.

The old man mopped at the dregs of his oatmeal with a piece of limp toast. The other two men sat on a torn floral couch against the wall. The silence seemed to bother no one but me.

Grover said something through the screen door that I did not understand. The old man answered him in the same language, then got up and went outdoors. Wenonah dropped two pieces of toast onto my plate. "You'd better eat," she said quietly.

One of the men on the couch got up and turned on the television. An insistent announcer's voice was describing the benefits of some dishwashing detergent. Outside the screen door I could hear Grover and the old man talking in Lakota. I could tell nothing about the nature of the conversation from the tone of their voices.

The screen door slammed abruptly behind me. The old man came over to the table and gestured me outside with a turn of his head.

"Grover thinks it's too white," he said. "The way you wrote it."

I looked at him, puzzled. "They're your words. I just scrubbed them up a little."

He gestured me forward with that strange pawing motion I had noticed before. "Come on out."

Grover was sitting on the stoop with his elbows on his knees. His hands were cupped around a cigarette to keep it from burning too fast in the wind. He was staring straight ahead, away from me.

"Something ain't right," he said, still looking straight ahead.

My cheeks flushed a bit. "You mean it sounds wrong?"

"Naw, not exactly. It sounds alright. But it just don't sound real. It sounds too much like movie Indians."

"I'm not sure what you mean."

Grover shifted on the stoop. He looked over at the old man. "You remember that New York woman?"

Dan broke into a loud laugh. "I sure as hell do. You damn near scared her to death with all that coughing of yours."

"Tell Nerburn the story." Again, their presumed familiarity with me took me aback.

Dan sat down on an old car seat that was propped up next to the stoop.

"There was a woman that came out from New York one time. She was writing a movie about some white man who did something good for the Indians — I don't remember his name. She wanted to talk to Indians so she could see how we talked.

"She was all dressed up in new jeans and cowboy boots and had a bandana around her neck. She looked like she was going on a safari. I think her clothes cost more than my car. It was just funny to see her. She had to look at everything before she sat down or walked or anything. She was more worried about getting dirty than anything else.

"A couple of us said we'd talk to her. I guess we thought maybe we might make a few bucks or something. Besides, we wanted to know what she was all about. You know, there's a lot of people coming looking for Indians since that 'Dances with Wolves' movie.

"Anyway, I had some books with me. I had one of your 'Red Road' books and some other books that tribes have done where people tell stories. I thought maybe they would help her.

"She tried to ask us questions, but I could see that the other fellows didn't like her. So they didn't say anything. They just sat there and watched her get nervous. It was pretty funny.

"I let her read those books I had. She looked at them real quick. Then she said that they weren't any help because the people sounded 'flat and uninteresting.' That's what she said. I remember those words. She said that they sounded 'flat and uninteresting.'

"Those were real people's voices written down. But they weren't good enough for her. They didn't sound like how she wanted Indians to sound. She didn't give a damn how Indians really sound. She just wanted to have us sound the way she thought we should sound.

"I told her maybe there were some Indians in Greenwich Village who sounded better. She didn't know if I was serious or not, so I kept on telling her how maybe New York Indians sounded better because they had been part of that Iroquois Confederation and had been a lot more used to giving speeches.

"She wrote it all down and went away. I think she was really glad to go. Grover here kept clearing his throat all the time and she kept thinking maybe he was going to spit or something. The more nervous she got the more he cleared his throat. Got so rattly in there I thought he was going to drown. I damn near split in half trying to keep from laughing."

Grover was nodding his head silently. His cigarette ash was almost an inch long. "That's the way it is, Nerburn," he said. "White people don't want real Indians, they want storybook Indians."

I was embarrassed and hurt. "I hope I didn't make . . ." I paused again, confronted by the need to use his name.

But the old man came to my rescue. "Hell, call me whatever you want. My name's Dan, but lots of people just call me the old man, or grandpa. I don't care."

"Okay," I continued, turning to him. "I hope I didn't make you sound like a storybook Indian. But you told me to make you sound like you went to Haskell."

The old man smiled. He wanted me to know that what I had done was fine. But Grover still had something on his mind.

"Here's the problem," Grover said, directing his attention toward me. "That thing you wrote was okay . . ."

"I think it's pretty damn good," Dan interrupted.

"Yeah, it is," Grover said. "It's too damn good. You should send it to that New York woman."

I was watching the old man closely. Even with my own minimal involvement I was feeling attacked and wanted to defend what I thought was a beautiful passage. But the old man just sat back with a bemused look on his face and drew heavily on his cigarette.

"Here's what I think," Grover continued. "That speech is good. But it's dangerous as hell."

"Dangerous?" I said.

"Yeah. Let me ask you something. What am I doing?"

"You mean, what are you trying to tell me?"

He shook his head like a frustrated school teacher. "No, no. I mean, what am I doing? What am I doing right now?" He held his cigarette toward me, a clue for the slow-witted.

"You're smoking a cigarette."

"Right. Now, what's this cigarette made out of?"

"Tobacco."

"Okay. You know how we talk about tobacco being sacred, right? You just gave me tobacco, right? So, is this cigarette sacred?"

Dan was grinning. He sensed where Grover was going. I was completely confused.

"I don't know," I said.

Grover took the short white butt from his mouth and crushed it theatrically on the stoop. "Nope. It's just a casual smoke." He reached into his breast pocket and took out the packet of Prince Albert I had given him. "Now, this is sacred, because you gave it to me sacred. Do you follow me?"

I smiled weakly. He continued. "Sometimes things are sacred and sometimes they're not. It's not sacred when the guy at the store hands me a pack of cigarettes because he's just handing me a pack of cigarettes. Do you see? But when you hand me that tobacco, you're making it sacred because you're offering it to me."

"Okay," I said. The purpose of the discussion still eluded me.

"But it's still tobacco, am I right?"

"Yes," I said, thankful for a question to which I knew the answer.

"It's the same with Indians," Grover stated, as if the connection were obvious. "Sometimes we're sacred, sometimes we're not. But we're always Indians. If you write only the sacred stuff, it's like that New York woman. Just write it all. The old man will try to trick you, but you've got to be smart."

Dan was enjoying himself immensely. He puffed on his cigarette and emitted a series of little "heh, heh's" as Grover talked.

"So what are you saying?" I asked, truly confused.

"Look over here," Grover directed. "Look at old Fatback there. Watch her close."

Fatback was snuffling in the brown fieldgrass. She sneezed several times, yawned, scratched herself, urinated on a bush, dug violently on a patch of dirt, then turned around several times and laid down.

"What did you see?" Grover asked.

I told him.

"Did it all make sense?"

"It was all dog stuff."

"But if you were writing a story about dogs, you'd put all that in."

"Sure. As much as was necessary."

"Well, you're writing a story about Indians. But you're writing like a white guy. You want everything all neat. Put it all in. Just write it the way it is."

I turned to Dan. He was digging at the ground with a stick. Grover spoke again. He wanted to emphasize his point. "This old man's seen a lot. You ought to write everything, not just like speeches."

I had a sense of what he was driving at. But I was beginning to get angry and frustrated. I had done what the old man had asked, and I had done it well. I had done it with no promise of reward and not even a thank-you. Dan had seemed satisfied. But now he was sitting silent, letting Grover tell me it was all wrong. I was beginning to feel like I had felt so many times before working with Indians. Nothing you ever did was enough. Nothing was ever acknowledged. You just worked and worked until someone perceived some slight or some wrong in what you did, then you were shown the door. A burr of indignation rose up inside me. This time I was not going to be shown the door. If the time came, I was going to walk through it myself.

Dan raised his hand slowly. It was a deliberate gesture, calling attention to his desire to speak. He chose his words carefully. "I've been listening here," he said. "You're right, Grover. It's the white man's way to try and make everything neat. I guess I wanted a white man's book."

Grover was gratified. His point had been taken. "You do it all like that thing Nerburn read," he said, "and it's going to be like that New York woman's clothes — all ironed and neat." Then, to me, he counseled, "You can't be afraid to get things dirty."

Dan sat hunched over in thought. He bit on the edge of his cigarette and spit out several strands of auburn tobacco. "Yeah," he said slowly. His thoughts were still forming. "I guess we should do it the Indian way."

I didn't know what "the Indian way" was. It sounded ominously unformed, and I had invested a great many hours in the shoe box and its contents. I started to protest. Dan silenced me. He turned and began walking slowly up the steps. "Listen to Grover," he said.

Grover picked up the cue.

"Forget the speeches," he said. "You'll get speeches. The old man is always giving speeches. Has been ever since I've known him. Get the rest of it." He stopped on the top step and spit once into the dust. "Think about Fatback." He nodded his head toward the dog and grinned.

Fatback kicked twice in the throes of some dog dream, let out a blubbery wheeze, and settled contentedly into her hollow of dirt.

"That's how you should write it," he said. "Just tell the story."

It took me a while to get over my anger at Grover's airy dismissal of my literary method. I had worked too hard, too long, to take it in stride. Still, Dan, who had spent years collecting those shoe boxes full of thought fragments, seemed decidedly indifferent to our change in direction. I tried to tell myself that if Dan could absorb the idea of a whole new direction, I should be able to as well. I decided to ask him about it.

The opportunity came in an unexpected fashion. The next morning as I drove up the path to his house I noticed a thin haze of smoke lingering in the air. When I turned the corner into his yard I saw him standing in front of his stoop tending a small fire with a stick. He was chanting under his breath and throwing something onto the small patch of flames. I drove in cautiously, afraid that I might be interrupting some private ritual. But he grinned and beckoned me over with a hurried gesture.

"Come on. Come on," he said as I climbed out of the truck. A sweet fragrant odor came from the flames. "Here." He reached into a small leather pouch he was holding and pulled out a pinch of something. "Put this on the fire."

"What is it?" I asked.

"You're too late for the pipe. I did that alone."

He sprinkled some more of the substance on the fire. The rich odor rose and filled the air.

"It's sweetgrass, Nerburn. You've heard of sweetgrass?"

"Yes," I answered, though I was not acquainted with the intimacies of its usage.

"The Creator loves the smell of sweetgrass. If you smoke the pipe and pray and then put sweetgrass on the fire, he will listen to you."

I wanted to be involved, but I felt uncomfortable entering into his spiritual reality.

"I'm doing this for you," he said.

"For me?"

"Yeah. That you will write a good book."

Things started connecting in my mind. "What are you burning?" I asked, unsure if I wanted the answer.

"All the stuff I wrote," he said. Then he lifted a small chant into the air.

"You mean all the notes in the shoe boxes?"

"Yeah. I saved some of the good things from Ann Landers. But I burnt all my own stuff."

I thought he might be joking with me to see my response. But there was no twinkle, no nuanced pauses, in his manner. He was intent upon his mission. "Come on," he said. "Here." He sprinkled a little more sweetgrass on the fire and beckoned me to do the same. "You're going to need the help, Nerburn. Come on."

I sprinkled the green leaves on the fire. The flames bit at them, then swallowed them into a haze of sweet smoke. Dan chanted a few more words. I felt a knot in the pit of my stomach. Those pages had been my book and that book had somehow been my hope. I stared into the fire, numbed, like someone whose house had just burned down.

Dan was positively cheerful. "This is good," he said. "Grover was right. This will be better."

I didn't answer. What I saw in my mind's eye was the loss of several months worth of work. And worse, the whole burden of the project now fell on me. Dan's words no longer existed, except insofar as I could extract them from him and get them down in a meaningful fashion.

Dan must have been following my thinking on his own. "It's not the end of the world, Nerburn. You're a good writer." He sprinkled more sweetgrass on the fire. The wind blew the smoke around my legs like a playful kitten. "Here. Put some more on. We need to make a strong prayer."

Halfheartedly, I dropped more sweetgrass into the diminishing flames. Cheap metaphors of dying embers of hope filled my mind.

"You're thinking, not praying," he said. He raised his voice in a lyrical, rhythmic chant. I stood silent, watching the crumpled edges of several stubborn pieces of paper as the flames crawled their way up and curled them into ash.

I waited what I hoped was an appropriate time before speaking. "So what do we do, now?" I asked.

"Grover was right. It's all inside of me. We'll do it the Indian way. I'll make talks and you watch and listen. Then you just write it down."

"Oh." It didn't seem that simple to me. But Dan was as lighthearted as a child. I had a sense of the burden those boxes must have been to him, filled with the best and deepest of his own thoughts, closeted away in a dark corner of his house from which they might never emerge except to be burned in an anonymous fire in the event that he died before finding a way to give them voice.

Now he had burned them himself. Now I was the box. Now he was going to fill it again.

Chapter 3

Talking for the Grandfathers

"Here. Smoke with me," Dan said. We were sitting on his front stoop listening to the larksong and the keening of the morning wind.

I had always been uncomfortable taking the pipe when it was offered to me by Indian people. It was not that I didn't want to smoke with them. I wanted to do so desperately. But it somehow did not seem to be my place. I was so attuned to the "wannabe" syndrome that I tried to stand back, putting myself last at the table, as it were, so I didn't seem to be feeding hungrily at the trough of Indian values because of the emptiness of my own inner life.

"Here," he said again, holding the stem toward me. There were just two of us. It was a private, intimate act; he did not have to offer it if he didn't want to. I took the pipe.

I smoked several puffs, cupping the smoke with my hand as he did, forcing it toward the ground, then the sky, then around my head. Then I handed it back.

He puffed several times more before it went out.

"You need to understand this, Nerburn," he said. All levity was gone from his voice. "You're not a good liar."

"No, never have been."

"I know, because I see how bad you lie."

34

I flushed a bit. I didn't think I had lied to him. And old people always scared me when they made observations like that. It was as if they had a second sight that allowed them to see more clearly.

"Have I lied?"

"Not in words. Only by silence."

"By silence?"

"Yes. Silence is the lie of the good man, or the coward. It is seeing something you don't like and not speaking."

"I don't understand," I said.

"You were mad the other day when I burned those words of mine. You were angry at Grover, too. You thought you had done good work. You didn't think Grover knew what he was talking about."

"You're right," I said. "I guess I'm easier to read than I thought."

"You are. So don't lie to me again."

His manner was authoritative and final. I felt like a small child being scolded. I waited for him to say more, but he had spoken his peace. I was left with the echo of his reproach floating like smoke around my head.

He occupied himself with emptying and disassembling the pipe according to some private rituals. It was as if he no longer knew that I existed. I sat there next to him, half watching, as he wrapped it gently in a pouch of some soft animal hide.

When he was finished, he spoke again. His tone was formal. "We have smoked together. It is not a joke. You have made a promise to me not to lie with your words or your silences. It will not be easy for you, because you think you aren't a liar. You will have to watch closely. That's why we have tobacco. It makes us look hard for the truth.

"Remember when I told you to bring tobacco and to offer it to Grover? Did you see how he changed?"

"Yes," I said.

"The tobacco was why. The tobacco is like our church. It goes up to God. When we offer it, we are telling our God that we are speaking the truth. When Grover took the tobacco from you, he was telling the Great Spirit that he would do the best he could.

"Wherever there's tobacco offered, everything is *wakan* — sacred, or filled with power. When you gave Grover the tobacco, he had to stop bullshitting. Now he's promised the Great Spirit that he will help. It doesn't have to do with you or me. It's a promise he made to the Creator.

"It isn't important that you didn't like what he said. I didn't like it either. He knew that. But he didn't care. He had made a promise to speak the truth."

I felt sheepish and ashamed. The simple rectitude of Dan's words made my concerns about wasted work seem tawdry and fraught with self-interest. But Dan was no longer concerned with redirecting me. His thoughts had taken wing, and he was ruminating on larger issues.

"You know," he said, "That's a lot of why we Indians got into trouble with the white man's ways early on. When we make a promise, it's a promise to the Great Spirit, *Wakan Tanka*. Nothing is going to change that promise. We made all these promises with the white man, and we thought the white man was making promises to us. But he wasn't. He was making deals.

"We could never figure out how the white man could break every promise, especially when all the priests and holy men — those men we called the black robes — were involved. We can't break promises. We never could."

He picked at a loose splinter on the side of his step.

"It's really kind of funny," he continued. "We didn't always agree with the religion the white man brought. But there were things in it we could really understand. Like the Communion, how that made something sacred whenever it happened. That was just like our tobacco. And the way there were vows, like for marriage.

We had vows, too. We had them for everything. A lot of them were private — we didn't need a priest to make them happen. But they were real. They were promises to the Creator to do something.

"So we thought we were seeing the same thing from the white man. Especially when he swore on the Bible or used the name of God to make a promise.

"But I guess it was a lot like their church. It was only important on some days. The rest of the time it didn't matter."

Dan cradled the pipe bundle on his lap like a baby.

"Listen, Nerburn. I'm not trying to say bad things about you and your people. I'm just trying to tell you how it was for us. I hope you don't get mad." He seemed to have completely forgotten his concern with my veracity.

"No, Dan," I said. "I'm not mad. I'm just listening. You've got every right in the world to be mad."

"You're a good boy," he said. "That's the trouble. Our whole people were ruined by your whole people. But there are good people in the middle. There always have been. We used to help settlers. They would help us. We thought we could all live together. But we were so different."

A hint of melancholy had crept into the old man's voice. He fingered the bundle on his lap and began staring past me as he talked.

"When I make a promise, I see my grandfathers looking over my shoulder. If I break my word I disgrace them. Do you see what I mean? How could I do that? They're in the spirit world. It's up to me to act for them here. That's why I want to speak now. That's why you're here.

"I want to try to say things right. I know it's hard for you to figure out, how one minute I can be bullshitting with Grover, then do spirit talk. It's because, with Grover, I'm just talking for me. When I say these other things, I'm talking for my grandfathers. I'm talking in the way they passed down to me."

I sat quietly, waiting for a sense of what the old man wanted next. I wanted to honor his words and accord them their proper respect. He stared blankly into the ground. He seemed to be falling asleep. I wondered whether I should take the pipe to keep it from falling. Suddenly he jerked his head up and cocked his ear, as if listening.

"I want to show you something," he said. "You got gas?"

"Sure," I answered.

"Let's go for a ride," he responded. He was already up and shuffling toward the truck.

"Where we going?" I asked.

"Bring that tape recorder of yours. You'll see."

I helped him into my truck and started to back down the path. Fatback had scuttled out from beneath the junk car and was limping alongside and whining.

"Put her in the back," Dan said. The old dog was wagging her tail feverishly.

"Come on, Fatback," I said, hoisting her into the pickup bed. She licked my face with her wet, fetid tongue and took her place against the tailgate.

"That's a good dog, that Fatback," Dan said as I climbed back into the cab.

"She should brush her teeth a little more often," I said.

Dan let forth a happy cackle and settled back into his seat. Something had changed in him. The pensive, melancholy drift had been replaced with a sense of purpose.

"Go down this road here," he said. The "road" was nothing more than two tire ruts through an old wash and up over a hill. A few bumpy miles later the trail met up with another set of ruts that snaked their way up a ridge.

"Take a left," Dan said. He held the pipe bundle tightly on his lap.

My truck was a four-wheel drive. But I had mainly gotten it to deal with northern Minnesota snows. I wasn't much for off-road driving. Dan started laughing. "You're on a reservation highway, Nerburn," he said. "We want to give the cows a fair shake."

We bumped and juddered our way up the ridge. The truck's suspension was groaning from the unfamiliar jostling. "White boy's truck," Dan offered. "My car likes these roads."

I thought back to the old automobile carcass sitting up on blocks in front of his house. "Your car's a little short of wheels," I said.

Dan chuckled. "Yeah, that's why I made it into Fatback's house."

I ground the truck down into its lowest gear. We inched our way up the final rise. It was steeper than anything I had ever driven on before. Yet the ruts were well traveled and the prairie grass was crushed down from frequent use.

"Stop here," Dan said.

I pulled to a halt on the top of the ridge. The wind buffeted the truck and whipped the antenna back and forth with its force. Beyond us to the west, the ridge dropped off into a panorama of undulating hills and draws. The prairie grasses bent and moved in the distance like waves on the sea.

Dan stepped out and walked to the front of the truck. He took out a small buckskin pouch of tobacco and started sprinkling it in all four directions. I could hear him singing, a low, melancholy song. The words were in his language, but the heart of the song was universal. It sent a shudder through me. When he was finished, he squatted down on his haunches and stared out to the west. He somehow seemed younger, more alive, more at home.

Fatback made her way over the tailgate of the pickup and ambled up to Dan's side. The old man idly stroked the old dog's ears. I stood behind, uncertain if I was part of this or if I was intruding upon a private moment. Finally, the old man spoke. "Nerburn, come here. It's time for you to learn something."

I approached him tentatively. "Sit down," he ordered. It was a gentle command, but firm.

I sat down quietly.

"Turn on that tape recorder," he said. Then he began to speak.

"Let me tell you how we lost the land. Let me tell you the real story.

"The white people surprised us when they came. Those of us out west had heard about them. Some of our elders had told prophecies about them. But still they surprised us.

"We had seen other strangers before. But they were just other people like us — other Indians — from different tribes. They would come and ask us to pass through our land. If we wanted them to, we would let them. Otherwise they couldn't.

"But, you see, it wasn't our land like we owned it. It was the land where we hunted or where our ancestors were buried. It was land that the Creator had given us.

"It was the land where our sacred stories took place. It had sacred places on it. Our ceremonies were here. We knew the animals. They knew us. We had watched the seasons pass on this land. It was alive, like our grandparents. It gave us life for our bodies and the life for our spirits. We were part of it.

"So we would let people pass through it if they needed to, because it was our land and they knew it. We did not wish them to hunt or to disturb our sacred places. But they could come to our land if they needed to.

"You need to understand this. We did not think we owned the land. The land was part of us. We didn't even know about owning the land. It is like talking about owning your grandmother. You can't own your grandmother. She just is your grandmother. Why would you talk about owning her?

"So when the first of your people came, they just wanted to go through. They were strange to us. They wore strange clothes. They smelled different. But they had many powers we had never seen. They were part of the Creator's plan, we thought. It was not our place to deny them, because it was not our right to control them.

We were just living our lives.

"They promised they would not do any damage. They were like a new kind of warrior with guns and different weapons. They were strange because they were always searching. We thought they would just come and go. We let them come among us, and we fed them and helped them. They were like raindrops that fell out of the sky, then stopped and were gone.

"But soon other strangers came. This time they were like a stream. They came with horses and wagons. They went on paths through our lands. Still, it did not bother us except that it scared the animals and that these people did not know what was sacred. But we knew they had to eat, so we did not mind when they shot the buffalo.

"I have heard that it was the same for other tribes with other animals. They tried to help these people. They were worried that the animals for the hunt would be scared away. But these people brought guns and that made hunting easier for us. So we did not mind.

"But then these strangers shot animals just to kill them. They left them lying in gullies. They made paths through the lands that were heavier than our paths. These people became like a river through the land.

"We had never seen the kind of things they did. For us, the earth was alive. To move a stone was to change her. To kill an animal was to take from her. There had to be respect. We saw no respect from these people. They chopped down trees and left animals lay where they were shot. They made loud noises. They seemed like wild people. They were heavy on the land and they were loud. We could hear their wagon wheels groaning in the next valley.

"We tried to stay out of their way. But they made us angry. They made hunting hard for us. They took food from our children's mouths. We did not want them around. Still, they were on small paths and we were free. We tried to leave them alone, except for the young men who were most angry.

"And we did want their rifles.

"Then something strange happened. These new people started asking us for the land. We did not know what to say. How could they ask for the land? They wanted to give us money for the land. They would give us money for the land if their people could live on it.

"Our people didn't want this. There was something wrong to the Creator in taking money for the land. There was something wrong to our grandparents and our ancestors to take money for the land.

"Then something happened that we didn't understand. The people who came said that we didn't belong here anymore. That there was a chief in Washington, which was a city far away, and the land was his, and he had said they could live here and we could not.

"We thought they were insane. The elders said to be careful because these people were dangerous. Most of us just laughed — at least this is what the elders told me when I was young. These people would ride across the land and put a flag up, then say that everything between where they started and where they put the flag belonged to them. That was like someone rowing a boat out into a lake and saying that all the water from where he started to where he turned around belonged to him. Or someone shooting an arrow into the sky and saying that all the sky up to where the arrow went belonged to him.

"This is very important for you to understand. We thought these people were crazy. We thought we must not understand them right. What they said made no sense.

"And here is what was really happening. They were talking about property. We were talking about the land. Do you see what I mean? Your people came from Europe because they wanted property for their own. That was what they needed to farm and raise the food to live. They had worked for other people who had claimed all the property and took all the things they raised. They never had anything because they had no property. That was what they wanted more than anything. That is what was behind the whole idea of America as a new country across the ocean. To get property of their own.

"I don't know. Maybe long, long ago, Europe was just land, too, like this land was for us. But that was so long ago that no one remembered. It had all been turned into property. If people didn't have property they didn't have very much control over their lives, because everyone believed that whoever had a piece of paper saying they owned the land could control everything that happened on it. The people that came across the ocean believed this, too. They came here to get their own property.

"We didn't know this. We didn't even know what it meant. We just belonged to the land. They wanted to own it.

"And here is something that I think is important — your religion didn't come from the land. It could be carried around with you. You couldn't understand what it meant to us to have our religion in the land. Your religion was in a cup and a piece of bread, and that could be carried in a box. Your priests could make it sacred anywhere. You couldn't understand that what was sacred for us was where we were, because that is where the sacred things had happened and where the spirits talked to us.

"Your people did not know about the land being sacred. We did not know about the land being property. We could not talk to each other because we did not understand each other. But pretty soon your people were not like a stream or even a great river any more. They were like a great ocean. This ocean washed us back upon each other. It washed us off our land.

"Some of us wanted to fight. Some of us wanted to run away. There were old chiefs who said we should make the best deals we could so we could keep our most sacred lands for ourselves. There were even Indians who saw all the things white people had and thought we should give up our way because the Creator wanted us to try this new way.

"We did not know what to do. You were everywhere. You were killing all the animals. The buffalo were gone. The birds were gone. You put two rails across the country that the buffalo would not cross. Then you rode by on your trains and shot the buffalo as you passed. You left them to rot in the sun. You would not let us hunt. You gave us blankets and whiskey that made our people crazy. We were put in little pens of land that were like tiny islands in your sea.

"The worst thing is that you never even listened to us. You came into our land and took it away and didn't even listen to us when we tried to explain. You made promises and you broke every one.

"First you said we could have our sacred lands, but then when you wanted them you took them. That is what happened with the Black Hills.

"Then you said we could have enough land to hunt and fish on. But when you wanted it you made it smaller or took it away and sent us somewhere else.

"Then you said we could always hunt and fish on the lands you took for your people, but then these new people said we couldn't.

"You did something we did not think was possible. You killed us without even taking our lives. You killed us by turning our land into pieces of paper and bags of flour and blankets and telling us that was enough. You took the places where the spirits talked to us and you gave us bags of flour.

"This is what you have to understand. To us the land was alive. It talked to us. We called her our mother. If she was angry with us, she would give us no food. If we didn't share with others, she might send harsh winters or plagues of insects. We had to do good things for her and live the way she thought was right. She was the mother to everything that lived upon her, so everything was our brother and sister. The bears, the trees, the plants, the buffalo. They were all our brothers and sisters. If we didn't treat them right, our mother would be angry. If we treated them with respect and honor, she would be proud.

"For your people, the land was not alive. It was something that was like a stage, where you could build things and make things happen. You understood the dirt and the trees and the water as important things, but not as brothers and sisters. They existed to help you humans live. You were supposed to make the land bear fruit. That is what your God told you.

"How could we people ever talk together when we each believed our God had told us something different about the land? We couldn't and we never did.

"But you were stronger. There were more of you, so your way won out. You took the land and you turned it into property. Now our mother is silent. But we still listen for her voice.

"And here is what I wonder. If she sent diseases and harsh winters when she was angry with us, and we were good to her, what will she send when she speaks back to you?

"You had better hope your God is right. That is all I have to say."

I sat, stunned. The eloquence and the heartbreak had caught me unawares. I felt tears in my eyes. This was the man I had met in the notebooks.

Dan said nothing. In all the time he had spoken he had never once looked over at me. Now he stood up and walked off along the ridge. I could hear him chanting that strange, tragic dirge again. Fatback trailed behind him, limping and panting, until the two of them were but small dots in my vision and his song had blended with the howlings of the wind.

Chapter 4

One Wily Old Indian

I didn't bring up the subject of our conversation for a few days. I figured that the old man would say more when the time was right. But I knew now that Grover had been right. The old man had an orator's eloquence that could never be captured by piecing together notes from a shoe box. I needed to stay with him, live with him, follow him, and listen. It was my pen and my tape recorder that were going to be my most precious assets.

Dan really did live his life like Fatback. He got up when he wanted, lay down when he wanted, spoke when he wanted, stayed silent when he wanted. Unlike white people, he never explained his actions, or announced when he was going to do something, no matter how abrupt it might seem. I might be sitting and speaking with him, and he would suddenly stand up and go into his bed. Or he might stop in the middle of a sentence and start watching the television, which droned perpetually from the corner of his living room. Sometimes there were reasons. Other times it made no sense that I could understand. He was responding to some inner promptings that were not mine to know.

The days passed in this relaxed and enigmatic way. Little of purpose was actually accomplished. We mostly spent the time driving around in my truck and sitting in his kitchen or on his porch.

I became increasingly aware of how old and fragile he really was. It was as if he had etched a strength into his body over the years, and he now could call upon it when he needed it to act. But the effort was great, and there were times when he would just sink into a reverie and then gradually slide into a fitful sleep. If I happened to speak he would open his eyes and answer, but I could see that I was calling him back from some faraway place. So I soon learned to occupy myself in silence while he slept.

One time Wenonah drove up while I was sitting there waiting for the old man to awake. She gestured me to her car. "You don't have to sit there and wait for him, Nerburn," she said. "He won't mind if you go."

"It feels disrespectful to me to leave when he falls asleep," I answered.

"Don't worry about it. That's the Indian way. When you are here, you are here. When you are gone, you are gone. It isn't a problem to be gone, so long as you are really here when you're here."

"That's a nice Zen sentiment," I offered.

She just smiled and shrugged. "He likes you. That means you can do what you want to. He will respect it."

"I'd rather sit and wait. I'd feel better."

She smiled and walked up the steps. "I've got to cook him some dinner."

As soon as the screen door slammed, the old man was awake and alert. "Been waiting for you," he said.

"You're one wily old Indian, Grandpa," she retorted. He responded with something in his own tongue and the two of them broke into gales of laughter.

The old man saw me still sitting on the stoop. He called me in. "You're getting to be like Fatback, Nerburn. That's how she started, just hanging around."

"Maybe you should start sleeping under the car," Wenonah said. "It's cheaper than that motel."

The two of them laughed again. Dan seemed wide awake and

in a good mood, so I ventured a question: "Do you mind being called an Indian, Dan?" It seemed appropriate, since his granddaughter had just referred to him as an Indian, and it was a question that always lurked just below the surface when I was involved in conversations with Indian people.

"What the hell else would you call me?"

"Oh, Native American. I don't know. Something. Anything other than Indian."

The old man took a deep breath, as if he had explained this many times before.

"It doesn't bother me. It bothers a lot of our people, though. They don't like that the name we have was a mistake. Just because Columbus didn't know where he was, we have to be called Indians because he thought he had found the East Indies. They think it takes away our pride and our identity."

"That seems like a fair sentiment to me," I said. The old man waved his hand in front of his face to silence me.

"I guess I don't mind because we have taken the name and made it our own. We still have our own names in our own languages. Usually that name means 'first people,' but no one would ever call us that. So we let people call us 'Indians.'

"Does that tell you something about us?"

I wasn't sure what he was driving at. "It tells me you are willing to accept a certain level of injustice."

He nodded vigorously. "Sure. What if you called black people Russians or Chinamen? Do you think they'd stand for it?" He laughed at the thought. "Hell, they change what they want to be called every few years.

"I don't blame them, though. They've been called some pretty bad names. And being called by a color is almost as strange as being called by a place you never lived. But the point is that our people mostly don't care so much about something like a name. We're pretty easygoing about things.

"There is something we don't like, though. It's when people call us Indians and then start calling sports teams and other things Indians. If we're going to have a false name, at least let us have it and then leave it alone. Don't start putting it on beer bottles and ice cream cartons and making it into something that embarrasses us and makes us look like fools. And don't tell us it's supposed to be some honor to us. We'll decide what honors us and what doesn't."

The old man was getting agitated. The subject obviously brushed against a nerve.

"See," he said, "this is all part of the way it has always been since the white people first came to our country. No one will leave us alone and let us be who we are. First we were told who we are, then we were told how we should be. Now we are being told how we're supposed to take it when someone wants to define us in a certain way. No one ever asks us. No one ever listens to us when we speak. Everyone knows what they want and we're supposed to let them think it. If we don't agree with it, we're called radicals or troublemakers.

"You remember a few years ago? Some Indians decided they would rather be called Native Americans. It's an okay name; it's more dignified than 'Indians.' But it's no more real than Indians, because to us this isn't even America. The word America came from some Italian who came over here after Columbus. Why should we care if we're called Native Americans when the name is from some Italian?

"It's like if someone took over this country now and called it, say, Greenland, and then they said that those of us who were already here are going to be called Native Greenlanders. And they said they were doing this out of respect. Would you feel respected? Would you care a whole hell of a lot if they called you that or something else?

"That's the way it's been for us. It's what we put up with every day — people calling us a bunch of names that aren't even real and aren't even in our language, then asking us if one name is better than another. Hell, it doesn't even matter. If some of us want to be called Native Americans, you should call us Native Americans. If some of us want to be called Indians, you should call us Indians. I know it makes you kind of uncomfortable, not ever knowing which one is right. But I think that's good. It reminds you of how uncomfortable it is for us — we had our identity taken from us the minute Columbus arrived in our land."

The old man turned toward Wenonah. "Go get that magazine with the map on it." Wenonah went into the bedroom and came out with an old *National Geographic*. Dan spread it out on the table. "Look at this," he said. It was a map of various tribal areas in North America. He tapped his finger on the Bering Straits. "That's the problem, right there."

I shrugged my shoulders and gestured for him to continue. But he wanted me to respond. He tapped the map again. "Tell me, Nerburn, what is an Indian, anyway?"

I was wary of the question. I didn't want to anger him, but I knew I had to answer.

"It's one of the people who was here originally," I said, knowing full well that wasn't a satisfactory answer.

"Okay. Where did we come from?"

"A lot of people say you were part of a migration across the Bering Straits."

"Ha!" he spat. "See, you don't have an answer, either. You're afraid to say we started here, that the Creator put us here. You come out with that damn Bering Straits idea, just like this magazine."

"Well," I said, "Nobody knows."

"What do you mean, nobody knows? We know. But nobody believes us. We know in our hearts who we are. We have the stories from our ancestors. But we can't prove anything. If we say we are the first people, the ones who are from here, some damn archaeologist will jump up and tell us we came over through Alaska on a land bridge. They want to make sure that we're immigrants, too. Just that we got here earlier.

"If we say that our ancestors tell us we started here, some

anthropologist will pull on his beard and tell us that is just a myth.

"Then if we don't even try to talk about where we came from, but just say we are part of a tribe, no one will believe us without proof. We say we have the proof in our stories, but that's not good enough. We are told it must be written down. But the people who wrote down the tribes were all white people or Indians who worked for white people and they made all kinds of mistakes.

"And what about the Indian people whose tribes were destroyed and don't exist any more? Are you going to say that those people aren't Indians because they aren't members of a tribe that the government recognizes?

"You see how it is? We have a false name, someone else tries to tell us about our history and says that the history we know is wrong. Then the government tries to make its own rules about who we are and who can be part of us."

"It's a sad situation," I said.

"Sad? I'll say it's sad. Then there's another thing. There were times when the government let white people move onto our land and claim it for their own. Lots of white people moved onto Indian lands and later if there were treaty payments, they said they were Indians so they could get part of the treaty payments.

"And then there was a lot of intermarrying between our races, and sometimes there were rapes, so nobody really knows who is an Indian anymore, or even what it means."

Wenonah had been leaning against the sink, listening placidly. She obviously enjoyed seeing her grandfather like this. She placed a cup of coffee on the table in front of him and gave me a sideways wink. "Take it easy, Grandpa," she said. "You'll give yourself a heart attack."

The old man waved her away. "The hell with the heart attack. These are things I need to say."

He turned back to me. "You'd better be getting this down."

I pointed at the tape recorder. He nodded his approval.

"This can get real confusing to us, Nerburn. Real confusing. The

Europeans really did exterminate us, you know. They did it with guns and they did it with laws and they did it with all kinds of censuses and regulations that confused who we were.

"They mixed us up with white people. They took away our language. They took our kids away to schools and wouldn't let them learn about the old culture. They herded us onto reservations and rewarded Indians who acted just like white people. They created a generation of Indians who didn't even know who they were."

He leaned over to me so close I could hear his chest wheezing. "Now, don't get me wrong on this. But you've got to understand that we are still at war. It's not like we are fighting against America or the American people, but we are still defending who we are. It's a war to us, because if we don't fight for who we are we will be destroyed. We'll be destroyed by false ideas and phony Indians and all the good intentions of people who think they are helping us by making us act like white people."

"Grandpa," Wenonah interjected.

The old man shook his head. "No. Let me finish. I'm almost done.

"Think about this. Do you ever hear white people saying that they are part black or part Mexican? Hell, no. But the world is full of people who say they are part Indian. Usually they'll say it was their grandmother or their great grandmother. It's never a grandfather. You wouldn't want an Indian man in your background. He might have had a tomahawk or something. You want some old blanket Indian woman who taught your family wise ways. And they're never a Potawatami or a Chiracahua or a Tlingit — usually it's a Cherokee. Something about the Cherokees is more romantic. I bet I've met a hundred white people who say they had a Cherokee grandmother. And you know what? They believe it! They want it to be true so much that they make themselves believe it.

"Mostly they leave it at that. But some of them don't. They grow their hair in braids and go to some powwows. Maybe take a class from some phony medicine man, and presto! we've got a new

Indian. Pretty soon they're spouting Indian philosophy and twisting up the idea of the Indian even further.

"I'll tell you Nerburn, being an Indian isn't easy. For a lot of years America just wanted to destroy us. Now, all of a sudden, we're the only group people are trying to get into. Why do you think this is?"

I told him I didn't know.

"I think it's because the white people know we had something that was real, that we lived the way the Creator meant people to live on this land. They want that. They know that the white people are messing up. If they say they are part Indian, it's like being part of what we have."

Wenonah had been hovering around the outside of the conversation. She had been watching the old man carefully, monitoring his anger and his exertion like a nurse watching a patient. It was clear that she loved him dearly. I let her take the lead in how to proceed.

Soon she walked over behind him and put her arms around his neck. She nestled her head against his and spoke softly into his ear. "That's enough, Grandpa. That's enough."

The old man nodded. He slumped back in his stiff wooden chair. An impassive look settled over his face. Wenonah took the *National Geographic* off the table and returned it to the bedroom. From the half darkness of the back room I could see her looking at me. She raised her hand to her lips, as if to say, "He's had enough."

The old man's exhaustion was palpable. He seemed to be turning to stone before my eyes. His stare did not vary and he didn't move a muscle. It was as if he had gone inside to a place of tears and memory.

"I'll come back tomorrow," I said. Wenonah nodded, obviously pleased that I had understood her message. I took one last look at the old man as I pushed open the screen door. Wenonah was standing behind him, stroking his hair with the side of her hand and humming softly like a mother hums to a child.

Chapter 5

A Land of Dreams and Phantasms

It had been several weeks since I arrived on the reservation. The weather was starting to take a slight autumn turn. Great roiling cumulus clouds rolled like tumbrels across the sky. The light seemed filtered, the ground animals more industrious.

As a child of the woodlands, I had never had much of a sense for the plains and the prairies. But now, as the days passed, the hypnotic power of the land had overtaken me. I felt like a man on an inland sea. The billowing, waving prairie grasses were symphonic in their ebbs and swells; the marching cadences of the passing clouds transfixed the eye. Sound was magnified, as if echoing against some vast, celestial vault. Thunder would roll in from beyond the horizon; the buzzing of insects would seem to be inside your head. It was equal parts peace and dread — a land of dreams and phantasms.

Sometimes at night I would spread out a sleeping bag in my pickup bed and watch distant flashes of lightning illuminate the inside of giant, looming thunderheads six or seven miles high. The earth itself had ceased to be the prime element in my consciousness. This was a land of the sky, and every turn, every action, lifted the eye upward.

Dan had noticed my growing fascination. We had taken to visiting his favorite hilltop almost every day. He never said anything, but I could see him watching me as I would stare out over the plains. We would sit for hours, oftentimes without speaking. The only sound would be the endless rushing of the wind and the rustling and snuffling of Fatback as she burrowed around in the tall prairie grasses.

Sometimes the old man would make a passing comment, like the time he told me that his father had brought him to this spot when he was a child, and many things had happened to him here that he couldn't talk about. Other times he would begin singing, keeping his song low and private, as if meant for no one to hear. One time he looked at me and nodded. "Your eyes are different, Nerburn," he said. "You are looking farther." He didn't elaborate or say another word, but that phrase, with all its cryptic meaning, buoyed me like nothing else he had ever said.

When we were on the hill, I would pass my time thinking of my family, or wondering about God or any number of other topics that fill the mind when confronted with vast, empty spaces. Never having been much for examining flora or fauna, I found little of interest in the profusion of tiny flowers and plant life that seemed to occupy so much of Dan's attention. For me, this was a land of poetry — sparse, singular, with lyricism written on the wind.

One day Dan startled me with a full sentence. "You're getting better with silence," he said.

"I am?"

"I watch you."

"I know."

"You're learning. I can tell because of your silence."

I sensed that he had something to say. Dan did not make small talk when he was on his hill.

"We Indians know about silence," he said. "We aren't afraid of it. In fact, to us it is more powerful than words."

I nodded in agreement.

"Our elders were schooled in the ways of silence, and they passed that along to us. Watch, listen, and then act, they told us. This is the way to live.

"Watch the animals to see how they care for their young. Watch the elders to see how they behave. Watch the white man to see what he wants. Always watch first, with a still heart and mind, then you will learn. When you have watched enough, then you can act."

There was a silence.

"That's quite a bit different from our way," I volunteered, hoping to prod him into further conversation.

"Yes," he said. "With you it is just the opposite. You learn by talking. You reward the kids who talk the most in school. At your parties everyone is trying to talk. In your work you are always having meetings where everyone interrupts everyone else and everyone talks five, ten, or a hundred times. You say it is working out a problem. To us it just sounds like a bunch of people saying anything that comes into their heads and then trying to make what they say come around to something that makes sense.

"Indians have known this for a long time. We like to use it on you. We know that when you are in a room and it is quiet you get nervous. You have to fill the space with sound. So you talk right away, before you even know what you are going to say.

"Our elders told us this was the best way to deal with white people. Be silent until they get nervous, then they will start talking. They will keep talking, and if you stay silent, they will say too much. Then you will be able to see into their hearts and know what they really mean. Then you will know what to do."

"I imagine it works," I said. I knew full well it did; my students had used the same trick on me, and it had taken me months to catch on.

"It works, all right," the old man said. "But it causes problems, too. I remember as a little boy in school. When the teacher would call on me I would sometimes want to think about my answer. She would get nervous and tap her ruler on the desk. Then she'd get angry at me and ask me if maybe I didn't hear her or if the cat got my tongue.

"How was I supposed to think up my answer when I could see her getting upset and nervous and knew that the longer I waited the worse it would be? I'd end up saying one word or, 'I don't know.' I'd say anything to get her away from me. Pretty soon they said I was stupid.

"I remember one teacher telling me I needed to learn how to think. She really didn't care about my thinking. She just wanted me to talk. She thought talking meant thinking. She was never going to be happy unless I started talking the second she called on me. And the longer I talked, the happier she would be. It didn't even matter what I said. I was just supposed to talk.

"I wouldn't do it. I thought it was disrespectful to talk when I didn't have anything to say. They said I was a bad student and that I was dumb.

"Now I see the same thing happening to my little great grandchildren. Their teachers say they don't pay attention because they don't look at the teacher's eyes all the time and they say they aren't very smart because they don't talk all the time.

"I know what they are really doing. They don't look at the teacher's eyes because they are trying to form their thoughts. They are just being respectful in the way we teach them, because for us it is respect to keep your eyes down when someone more important is talking. If the teachers would give them time to form their thoughts and let them do it inside their own minds, they would see that my great grandchildren are very smart. But the teachers don't think like us. They want everyone connected to everyone else by words and looks. They don't like silence and they don't like empty space."

"Like the pioneers didn't like the empty space of the land," I said. Dan brightened perceptibly. "Exactly! You're starting to understand." I glowed inwardly and kept listening.

Dan continued. "This is a lot of the reason why we Indians make white people nervous, Nerburn. White people like to argue. They don't even let each other finish sentences. They are always interrupting and saying, 'Well, I think . . .'

"To Indians this is very disrespectful and even very stupid. If you start talking, I'm not going to interrupt you. I will listen. Maybe I will stop listening if I don't like what you are saying. But I won't interrupt you.

"When you are done I will make my decision on what you said, but I won't tell you if I disagree with you unless it is important. Otherwise I will just be quiet and go away. You have told me what I need to know. There is nothing more to say.

"But this isn't enough for most white people. They want me to tell them what I think about what they are thinking, and if they don't agree with me, they want to talk more and try to convince me.

"You don't convince anyone by arguing. People make their decisions in their heart. Talk doesn't touch my heart.

"People should think of their words like seeds. They should plant them, then let them grow in silence. Our old people taught us that the earth is always speaking to us, but that we have to be silent to hear her.

"I try to be that way. I taught my children to be that way."

He swept his hand out across the panorama in front of us. "Do you hear the sound of the prairie? That is a great sound. But when I am talking I can't hear it.

"There are lots of voices besides ours, Nerburn. Lots of voices."

I smiled at his gentle lecture. "You make good sense, old man," I said. He nodded in quiet acknowledgment. I think we both felt a sense of pride at how things were progressing.

He picked up a handful of loose earth and looked at it. "What do you do in your mind while we are up here, Nerburn?" he asked.

"Oh, I think about my family. Sometimes I make little prayers or look for shapes in the clouds. Mostly, I guess I'm just in some kind of reverie."

"Do you know what I do?" he said. "I listen to voices. For me this hill is so full of life I can never be quiet enough to hear all the voices."

I wanted to press him on this, but gently. I didn't want to break the spell. "Do you mean real voices, or sensations that seem to have meaning?"

"I mean real voices. They're not all people. They're not all speaking our language. But they are voices. Listen."

I heard the buzzing of locusts and the distant, rhythmic call of some kind of bird.

"Do you hear that bird?" asked Dan.

I told him I did.

"Do you know what he is saying?"

"I don't speak 'bird'," I answered.

"You should," he twinkled. "Learn a lot. The birds are 'two-legs', like us. They are very close to us. He is calling to another. He is saying it will rain soon."

"You can tell that?"

"Yes, and I can tell that the wind is switching to the north and we will soon have colder weather."

"How do you know that?"

"I just do," he responded cryptically. "It's in the voices I hear. I can understand all the trees. The wind. All the animals. The insects. I can tell what a color of the sky means. Everything speaks to me.

"There," he said, pointing to a patch of scrubby grass in the distance. "What do you see?"

"It looks a little greener than the rest of the hills," I answered. "At least in a few patches."

"Good. Now why is that?"

"I don't know."

"Look closer."

I squinted my eyes. There was nothing to be seen except the short green grass.

"I don't see anything," I said.

"Look closer."

I squinted again. There seemed to be some kind of movement, but it was too small to make out.

"Something is moving," I said.

"Good. Do you know what it is?"

I admitted I didn't.

"*Pispiza*. You call them prairie dogs."

"Okay," I acknowledged.

"That's why the grass is green. Our brother prairie dogs dig under the ground to make their homes. They dig up the earth so the rain can go deeper and the roots of the grass can grow stronger.

"Where the grass is richer, the bigger animals come to feed. If we sit here quietly, in the morning, when the antelope are hungry, we will see them and we could hunt them. It is all because of our brother prairie dog. Where he lives, we can live.

"These are the kind of things I see when I look out here. They are things my grandfathers taught me. I hear them, too. My grandfathers. I hear their bones under the ground."

I looked at the clump of dusty earth he held in his hand.

"You think I'm lying, don't you? Or just a crazy old fool. I can't explain it. But I know where the dead are buried. I hear them. They speak to me in some ancient tongue. It's a gift I have.

"You've read about those people who can find water by using a forked stick? They walk along with the stick above the ground, and when they get above water the stick just points down.

"That's the way it is with me. When I get over one of the graves I have a feeling inside me. It's like a shiver. My grandmother had it, too. She said that our ancestors gave it to us, and that I should always listen.

"That's why I come up here, Nerburn. Out there is where my people are buried. This is where I come to listen."

"I believe you, Dan," I said. And I did. Once, many years ago, I had taken a great deal of peyote. I had thought nothing of it at the time — it was just one of those acts that went along with life in the sixties. Within hours I was lying on my back under the midnight sky listening to the springs flow under the ground. It was a rushing sound, as if they were all speaking to each other. I felt like I was overhearing a conversation in the earth. Then, as I walked to a certain spot that sat like a plateau overlooking a valley, I felt a cold shiver come across me. "There are graves here," I had said to myself. I knew I believed it, but I had never been sure whether it was the peyote talking or whether I had been opened to some deeper realm of meaning. I had never forgotten that moment, though I seldom shared it with anyone.

Now, this old man was telling me the same thing, but for him it was not some drug-induced awareness, but a part of everyday reality. I wondered what it must be like to have that sensitivity every moment of your life.

He saw my curiosity. "Here," he said, "Watch this." He sat back on his haunches and cupped his hands over his knees. Nothing seemed to be different. I sat silently beside him, wondering what it was I was supposed to see. Suddenly, Fatback came rustling through the tall grasses wagging her tail.

"Good dog," he said, and ruffled the scruff of her neck. Fatback wagged her tail furiously, then pushed back off through the weeds.

I raised my eyebrows and gave Dan a little half smile.

"See," he said.

"You called her over here?"

"Want me to do it again?"

"No," I answered, though I truly wanted to challenge him on this. But I knew that, on some level, everything was a test, and I did not want to appear the skeptic. My job was to record what I saw as he wanted it told, not to get involved in some ersatz anthropological research. All I could think of was what one tough old woman had said to me when I first arrived on the Red Lake reservation to begin the oral history project. I had gone over to her office to request her assistance in identifying elders who might be interested in participating. She stared at me with a hard glare, then stated, simply, "If you think you're going to come up here and do one of those goddamn white anthropology projects, you can just get on your pony and ride." Then she turned back to her beadwork and never said another word.

As much as I wanted Dan to prove that he had called Fatback, it seemed too close to a "goddamn white anthropology project." So, I just said, "That dog's got good hearing," and let things go at that.

Dan chuckled knowingly. "You're a good boy, Nerburn. Let's go get some lunch."

Chapter 6

Junk Cars and Buffalo Carcasses

On the way back down the hill, Dan suggested that we go visit Grover. "He makes a mean baloney sandwich," he said.

I was more than happy to agree. I had come to value Grover greatly. He was a tough and crusty character. But he spoke his mind. Ever since I had given him the tobacco, he had taken on the role of Dan's protector. He did not trust me totally. He had seen enough *wasichus* come and go, bearing good intentions, sycophantic fantasies, and simple greed. He was not willing to give an easy assent to any white person who claimed to want to work or live among Indians. As he had put it to me one time, "Most of you white people don't even know what it is you want. But you want something, and you're using us to get it."

Until proven otherwise, I was just one more in this long tradition of exploiters who had come among the Indian people to fulfill some personal agenda, whether spiritual, material, or otherwise. But he knew the old man had asked me to come, so he was willing to work with me. He just wanted to make sure I kept what he called "a good heart."

Grover's house was on the other side of the village. I had not yet gone through the village itself — Dan's house was nearer the highway. A visit to Grover would give me a chance to see more of the reservation without feeling like a white intruder.

We bounced our way back down the hill, then turned onto a gravel road that skirted a dusty, amber wash. Houses were set back from the road about a half a mile apart. They all had the look of prefab postwar bungalows gone to seed. Doors hung by one hinge. Windows without screens were covered by blankets. The front yards were nothing more than spotty patches of dirt with kids' bicycles and old appliances lying randomly on the ground.

Everything seemed to have just been left where it was dropped: there was no sense of order or indication of effort to keep things clean. One house had an old spool table sitting in front of it with a pile of oily car parts on it. Another had a large frame made out of telephone poles with an engine block hanging from it by a heavy logging chain. Beneath the engine a rusty beige Chevrolet with no front wheels sat on heavy timbers, its hood open as if the engine had just been extracted like a tooth.

It was a world of half-efforts. Nothing had been brought to a conclusion. The only sign of industriousness was the inevitable line of laundry flapping behind each house in the ceaseless prairie winds. The white sheets seemed like flags of defiance in a landscape of despair.

I had always been mystified by the willingness of people to live in squalor, when only the simplest effort would have been required to make things clean. Eventually, I had come to shrug it off to the old sociological canard that it reflected a lack of self-esteem and a sense of hopelessness about life.

But, in my heart, I knew that this was too facile, too middle-class in its presumptions. But it certainly was preferable to earlier explanations — that people who lived like this were simply lazy and shiftless. I wanted to ask Dan. I was sure he'd have a point of view. But I hesitated: the question seemed to run to the heart of the contemporary Indian life.

I needn't have worried, though. The old man saw me glancing around and came right to the point himself.

"Bothers you, doesn't it," he said.

We passed a house with a burnt-out station wagon lying on its side in the front yard.

"Yeah. I guess so," I answered. "I just don't understand it."

"I've been waiting for you to ask. But I guess you figure I got forever." He gave me a mock blow on the shoulder. "I'm damn near eighty, Nerburn. You've got to work faster."

I grinned at his humor. "Sorry, Dan. I'm on white man's time."

He chuckled several times and pointed at another of the passing houses. The top of an old Plymouth protruded from a patch of weeds. "What do you see when you look out there?"

"Do you really want to know?"

"I asked, didn't I?"

"I see lack of concern for the land that you claim to revere."

"You mean, you see a bunch of shit, right?"

His candor was liberating. "Yes."

"That's what all white people see. You drive through our reservations and say, 'Look at all the junk cars and all the trash.' What do you think we say when we drive through one of your cities?"

"I really don't know."

"We say the same thing. Just because you have everything scrubbed down and in order doesn't mean anything. What is bigger trash, a junk car or a parking ramp? We can tow the junk car away. The parking ramp has to be torn down with bulldozers and wrecking cranes. The only reason you don't see it as trash is that you still use it. When you don't need a building anymore, or it is too expensive to fix, then it is trash. To us it looks like trash all the time.

"If Fatback lives in my car, is it trash? To you it is because it isn't being used the way you want it to be. If a car is new and shiny and goes down the road, then you say it isn't trash. If it is old and can't go, then it is trash. It really isn't any different on the earth whether it moves or not. You just think it is. When it comes time for the earth to take it back, it is going to be just as much trash as the car sitting in my yard."

"Still, it wouldn't take anything to clean it up."

"Maybe we're still using it. That was the Indian way. Use every part of the buffalo. Make ropes from its hair. Make drumsticks from its tail. Some of these people are making one car out of a lot of them. I'm making a dog house out of mine."

This was the closest I had ever come to a confrontation with Dan. Usually, I had just acceded to his point of view. This time I wanted to challenge him to see where it would lead.

"Junk cars aren't buffalo carcasses."

"Same thing."

"That's bullshit."

"Bullshit!" he exploded. "I'll tell you what is bullshit! White people's attitude toward possessions is bullshit!"

"Okay," I said, "Tell me."

He shifted himself in the truck seat so he was squinting right over at me. "Owning things is what white people's lives are about. I watch TV, and every ad I see tells me something is 'new'. That means I should get it because what I have is old and this is new. That's no reason to get something, just because it's new. Your way teaches people to want, want, want. What you have is no good. What you don't have is new and better.

"From the first you are told, 'This is mine, this is yours;' 'Don't touch that, it doesn't belong to you.' You are taught to keep away from things because of ownership, not because of respect. In the old days we never had locks on our doors. There was no stealing, but if someone was hungry, they could go in your house and get food. That was all. Why didn't people take things? Because of respect.

"You build fences around your yards and pay money for people to measure the ground to tell you if your neighbor's fence is one inch too close to your house. You give nothing away unless you can get something in return. Everything is economic.

"Your most powerful people don't even hide their thinking on this matter. If you ask for something, they don't ask whether you need it; they say, 'What's in it for me?'"

"I'm afraid that's America, Dan," I said.

He hammered the air with his gnarled fist.

"I know it. And a lot of our people have started to act like that, too. Not all, but enough. This kills the old Indian way, where everything was shared. We believed that everything was a gift, and that a good man or woman shared those gifts. Next to bravery, generosity was the most important.

"Now we have been turned around. We think that good people should be rewarded, just like the white man thinks. Can't you see how much better it was when good people thought they should give, not that they should get?

"We didn't measure people by rich or poor. We didn't know how. When times were good everyone was rich. When times were bad everyone was poor. We measured people by how they shared."

"I believe you," I said. "That's one of the things I admire so much about your way of life. But what does it have to do with junk cars?"

"I'm trying to tell you," the old man said. "But you interrupt too much. Let me finish."

I settled back and concentrated on the road ahead. Dan sat silent for a moment to gather his thoughts. He was still irritable and angry. Then he began again:

"Listen. Look at us now. We have rich Indians that don't even know what to do with their money. They just get more and more and keep it. They will get a new car or a good rifle or something, but they don't go buy a new suit every week or a huge rich house. Look at this reservation. There are people here who have a lot more money than some of the other people. But they still live in a simple way, because the idea of possessions is so strange to them.

"What it is, Nerburn, is that things are important when we need them. If we don't need them, they're not important. You think this is just some old-time philosophy about the way things used to be. But it's not. I've thought about this."

He pointed toward a brushy hillside we were passing. "Look. Do you see that bike?"

There was a black dirt bike lying on its side in the field. No kids seemed to be around anywhere.

"What does that look like to you?"

"It looks like a bike some kid lost. Or maybe he is off playing somewhere. I don't know."

"White eyes, Nerburn. You've got white eyes. The boy probably left it there. This is what I mean. Watch our little children. They might get a bike and ride it, then just leave it somewhere, like that. You say they are irresponsible. They are just being like their ancestors who believed that you owned something only so long as you needed it. Then you passed it to someone else.

"Wenonah's little boy comes home from school and the teachers call and say he left his book somewhere or didn't bring a pencil. I try to tell them that he didn't need the book right then and that he will get another when he needs it, but they don't understand. They would have him get big bags and boxes and fill them with everything and never let anyone touch them. They want him to keep papers when they are finished and graded. They want him to keep everything.

"No wonder white people need such big houses. They aren't to live in, they are to store things in. I have been in some houses where the closets are as big as the rooms because the people want to store so many things. If all the buildings and all the rooms you use to store things were used for people, everyone in the world could have a place to live."

"Buffalo carcasses and junk cars, Dan," I prodded.

"You're getting me angry, Nerburn," he said. "I know what you're up to." He leaned over close to me and lowered his voice. "Okay. I'm going to tell you a secret. All of this — all these cars and stuff — makes me proud."

"Proud?"

"Yeah. It means we haven't lost our traditional ways."

The anger had faded from his face and been replaced with a placid smile. "We have to live in this world. The Europeans killed all the animals and took all our land. We can't live our way anymore. We have to live your way. In our way, everything had its use then it went back into the earth. We had wooden bowls and cups, or things made of clay. We rode horses or walked. We made things out of the things of the earth. Then when we no longer needed it, we let it go back into the earth.

"Now things don't go back into the earth. Our kids leave pop cans around. We leave old cars around. In the old days these would be bone spoons and horn cups, and the old cars would be skeletons of horses or buffalo. We could burn them or leave them and they would go back to the earth. Now we can't.

"We are living the same way, but we are living with different things. We will learn your way, but, you see, you really don't understand any better. All you really care about is keeping things clean. You don't care how they really are, just so long as they are clean. You see a dirt path with a pop can next to it and you think that is worse than a big paved highway that is kept clean. You get madder at a forest with a trash bag in it than at a big shopping center that is all clean and swept.

"It all comes back to possessions. You want to have everything and you think that is fine as long as it is put in piles or in rooms or in boxes with labels. We don't have very much and we leave it when we don't want it or need it.

"If I lived in a big house and had rooms full of different things, if I had big cars and a library full of books, if I had pulled out all the flowers and medicine plants and made a lawn that looked like a rug, people would come to me and ask me about everything because they would say I am a 'good' Indian. All it would mean is that I am an Indian with lots of possessions, just like a white man. That would make me good and important in your eyes. Admit it.

"Every once in a while I would have to go to a powwow and put on some feathers so you could believe I was a real Indian. But other than that you would think I was smarter and more important if I lived in a big house and owned lots of things. That's just the way white people are. It's the way you are trained.

"Here," he said abruptly. "Turn here." A rutted path ran up a little rise toward a beige trailer. "This is Grover's place."

The trailer sat exposed on a treeless hill. A perfectly ordered woodpile stood in the yard to the left. Each log seemed to have been cut to an identical length, and they were piled in a crisscross fashion, with each layer running perpendicular to the one below and above.

A small patch of earth to the right of his stoop had been cleared of brush and raked smooth. Two lawn chairs sat evenly spaced against the skirting of the trailer. There were no junk cars, no engine parts, no kids' bicycles — just Grover's old Buick parked in a spot marked off by a frame of fist-sized rocks arranged in a perfect rectangle.

Dan glanced over at me. The twinkle was back in his eye. "Goddamn reservation Indian," he muttered. "Lost his culture."

Then he sat back and let out a long rolling laugh that seemed, like prairie thunder, to come from the beginning of time.

Chapter 7

Rooting for the Cowboys

Grover was sitting on an old brown couch in his living room watching a black-and-white cowboy show on his television. He didn't even turn toward us when Dan opened the door.

"Hey, Grover," Dan shouted. "How come you don't have any junk cars in your yard?"

Grover didn't move a muscle. "Don't have a dog," he answered. The two men roared with laughter, as if this were part of some longstanding joke between them.

Grover made an elaborate charade of looking out the window toward the sun. "Must be about lunchtime."

He gestured me toward a brown wooden chair with green tweed cushions. It was like the chairs in a cheap motel, with a slanted back and flat, foam rubber cushions. I lowered myself into its sagging seat. Dan was already at the refrigerator.

I stared blankly at the scratchy image on Grover's television. A group of cowboys were riding as fast as they could through some nondescript sagebrush. They were leaning over the fronts of their horses, waving their guns as they shot as if they were throwing the bullets out of the barrels. The sound track of tinny music, thundering hooves, and gunshots echoed off the walls of the trailer. I wanted to reach over and turn the sound down, but knew I didn't dare.

Dan shuffled over with a loaf of white bread, a half-full cellophane pack of baloney, a jar of Miracle Whip, and a bottle of ketchup. Grover laid a butter knife and three light-green melmac plates on the coffee table in front of the television. Dan fumbled with the little red wire tie that held the bread bag closed and finally managed to get the bag open. The two men started rummaging around and constructing their sandwiches.

"Better get on with it, Nerburn," Grover said. "The old man can really pack them away."

Dan made a grunt of acknowledgment and piled a third slice of baloney on his bread. Then he hammered the bottom of the ketchup bottle until a large blob splotted onto the meat.

"Damn!" Grover said. "I hope I can eat like you when I'm eighty." He reached across and turned up the volume on the television.

"Here, watch. Pretty soon they'll go by a rock and an Indian will jump on them."

The gang of cowboys rumbled across the countryside, dust flying and music blaring. Soon the camera switched to a shot of a rocky cliff. The music changed to some ersatz Indian melody with a heavy tom-tom beat, and a group of suspiciously Italian-looking Indians emerged, like sphinxes, to stand on the top of the rock outcropping. They were bare-chested except for vests, and had big scarves tied around their heads.

"Too high," Dan said. "They won't jump from there."

He was right. The Indians saw the oncoming bustle of cowboys and said something to each other in a guttural approximation of an Indian language. They ran to their horses — all pintos — and vaulted onto their backs from behind, like gymnasts mounting a pommel horse, and rode off yipping and hollering.

The scene shifted back to the cowboys. One of them held up his hand and the others all reined to a stop. "There," the lead cowboy pointed, "Comanches!" The pack surged off to the left in hot pursuit, hooves pounding and guns blazing.

"My God," I said. "How can you watch this? Doesn't it make you crazy?"

"Hell," Grover said. "I used to go to the movies as a kid and root for the cowboys. I probably even saw this one."

"Yep," said Dan. "In the old show houses everyone used to cheer and boo at movies. We all booed the Indians; cheered when the cavalry came. I really liked John Wayne."

I had heard this same story many times from the older Indians. It seemed astonishing to me. But always, the response was the same: we didn't even feel those were Indians like us. We cheered the cowboys and booed the Indians just like the white kids.

"So it doesn't bother you?" I asked.

"A lot of things bother me," Grover answered. "This isn't worth the effort."

"It bothers me a lot more now than it did then," Dan added.

I slipped a rubbery pink piece of baloney onto my white bread. "Why's that?"

"Well," said Dan, "When we were kids we didn't see a lot of white kids. Those we saw were just like us. Poor as hell and just kids playing in the dirt. Their folks might have had it better than our folks, but the kids seemed just the same. We never thought of ourselves as any different. Cowboys and Indians was just a game, like cops and robbers. It didn't have anything to do with our real lives.

"I mean, nobody had any cars. We didn't get to any big town except maybe once or twice a year. There wasn't any TV. It wasn't until after the war, when the soldiers came back and told us what it was like out there, that we even knew that anyone lived different from us."

"Yeah," Grover said. "That's when it hit me. When I got back from Korea. All the other guys in my unit called me 'Chief', and I kind of liked it. But when I got back and lived in the city for a while,

I started to hear white people talk about Indians for the first time. The things they said were so damn stupid. That's when I started to get mad about those cowboy movies.

"See, it never bothered me about the way those movies made Indians look. But it bothered me about the way they made us look to white people — like a bunch of savages who just rode around faster than hell on horseback shouting and hollering. Made white people treat us bad."

Dan swallowed a mouthful of sandwich. The television gun-shots were blaring in the background.

"You know where all that stuff came from?" he asked me.

I had done some reading on the subject, but I wanted to hear his thinking.

"Buffalo Bill's Wild West Show. You heard of it?"

"Yes."

"Good," Dan said. "Then you know a little bit. Buffalo Bill had this show that traveled all over, to New York and to Europe and everywhere. He sort of made it up after he had killed all the buffalo and the U.S. had pretty much destroyed us all. He thought he could still make some money on Indians. It was right after we had taken care of Custer and all the newspapers were writing about Indians as bloodthirsty killers. Buffalo Bill figured people wanted to see real live Indians."

"Like animals in a circus," Grover cut in.

"Right," Dan said. "Only we were the animals. He put together this show. Sitting Bull even was in it for a while, although I'll be damned if I know why he let himself do it. Anyway, it had Indians riding around on horseback hollering and killing people, just like white people wanted.

"People came to see that show from everywhere. I think even the Queen of England saw it. I know some Indians met the President. It was in all the papers. It was really a big thing."

"Yeah," Grover echoed. "That was all people knew — what

they saw in Buffalo Bill and what they read in the papers."

"No, there was another thing," Dan said. "There was that poem of Hiawatha. 'By the shores of Gitchi-gumi.' What the hell is Gitchi-gumi, anyway?"

"I think it's Lake Superior — up my way," I offered.

"Maybe," continued the old man. "But that's the other idea white people had of us. Moccasin Indians sneaking through the woods and paddling canoes. Buckskin Indians in the forest, while we out here were the war-paint Indians.

"That's what white people thought Indians were like. Then when movies came, and TV, they just kept making us look the same. Sometimes you'd even have some Indian sneaking through the woods in his fringy buckskin shirt in one scene — paddling around in a canoe and stuff — then in the next one he's covered with war paint and wearing some little towel while he's riding a horse across the prairie and shooting arrows at white men. It was so damn dumb I can't even imagine it."

"There!" interjected Grover. The Italian Indians in buckskin pants were racing along on their pintos shooting arrows and brandishing tomahawks.

"At least they're not wearing those damn little towels," Dan said. "Think about it, Nerburn. You live up in the woods. You should know how it is. Do people from New York and California ever come up there? I bet if they made a movie about where you live, it would just be a joke, too."

"They have," I said. "And it was."

"Then think about us. We're Indians. We live out here in buffalo country. All we ever see are little tiny planes going over our heads between New York and California. They don't stop here. Those people don't want to stop here."

"Except that New York woman," Grover said.

Dan nodded and continued. "That's the way it's always been. All the settlers either stayed in the East or they went straight across to California, and most of us Indians ended up in the middle. We were where no one else wanted to be. That's why they let us be here.

"But all the movies and all the books came from either California or somewhere out East, so they didn't know a damn thing about Indians except what they wanted to know. That woman that came from New York was just another one of them. She was just the new version. She's probably back there right now writing some script where all the Indians talk like wise people. She'll find some scriptwriter who has read some Indian speeches and then she'll have the Indians talk like that. She won't even know that we speak different when we are giving speeches. She won't even care.

"And you know what? When you get right down to it she'll have the hero be a white person. The Indian will offer advice to the white person and that will make the white person better, but it will really be a movie about white people and how they become wiser when they add Indian wisdom to their white lives.

"I don't even know what the hell the movie is, but I'd bet everything that it will be like I say. They all are these days. We see them on video. We know what they're like. Can't have savages anymore. Now it's the wise Indian — you know, at one with the earth and all — who makes white people get better by teaching them Indian ways, so they add Indian values to their whiteness."

"Like that 'Dances with Wolves'," Grover said.

"Yeah, exactly," Dan said. "That was at least pretty good. They paid some real Indians and the Indians were pretty good. But the white guy got wise. He was the hero."

Grover had gone to the refrigerator for a carton of milk. "I wonder what that New York woman's movie will be?" he asked.

"'Old Indian That Cleared His Throat,'" Dan said.

Grover laughed. "Well, I sure as hell wised her up, I know that. I better start watching for it on TV."

"That's the trouble," Dan answered. "Whatever the hell she

does, it'll be on TV. Kids will see it. White kids, Indian kids. They'll all see it and think that's what Indians are like. They'll see what some white woman who almost peed in her pants thinks Indians are like, and they'll believe it."

Dan stuffed the last bite of sandwich in his mouth. The TV was showing a woman spraying a garbage can with some air freshener. He pushed his plate away. "Give me some of that milk," he said. Grover handed him the carton. He took a gulp directly from the spout.

He handed it across to me. "No, thanks," I mumbled.

Grover turned toward me. "You better not write some book like that, Nerburn."

His voice was not threatening, but it left no doubt that he was serious.

I shook my head. "I pee in the toilet," I said.

Dan raised his hand and wagged his head, as if scolding me. "You got to pee on the earth, Nerburn. You got to pee on the earth."

Chapter 8

Taking Maize from Squanto

I couldn't get to sleep that night. Something about the afternoon with Dan and Grover had left me unsettled and uneasy. Though I had been treated well and had felt honored that Grover had shared his home and table with me, the sense of the distance between us had somehow grown, not diminished, in the course of the day. Maybe it had been the easy intimacy of the two men; maybe it had been some deeper cultural gulf that I would never be able to cross. All I knew is that I had come back to my hotel room feeling more distant and alien than at any time in any of my visits. For the first time I felt like the dreaded anthropologist — an observer who pretended to participate, an outsider for whom the natives felt compelled to perform.

I lay back against the hard motel pillow and flicked on the television set. The late-night talk shows had just begun, and the various hosts were doing their stand-up routines. I watched them parade and preen — mugging and smirking and rolling their eyes while they told jokes about current events and political figures.

Their humor was hard, their audiences raucous. They thrust their hands in their pockets and rocked back on their heels, like smart-aleck college kids making fun of people dumber than they were.

I turned off the volume and watched them in pantomime. They seemed a million miles away.

Dan's image of the jets flying overhead between the coasts kept haunting me. How often had I been a passenger on one of those jets, peering down into the midnight darkness at a tiny cluster of lights and wondering who had chosen to live there, and what kind of lives they lived.

Now I was one of those lights.

I rolled onto my side and stared out the window. The great vault of the sky was ablaze with stars. High among them I could barely make out the rhythmic blinking of a passing plane.

I imagined the passengers dozing to the drone of the engines or staring down at the darkened landscape far below. I wanted to wave, or signal them somehow, to let them know we were alive and well, and that this landscape was not empty, but full of life and stories and dreams. But the blinking lights kept moving and soon disappeared over the horizon, leaving only the twinkling silence of the sea of stars. I turned back to my room and my silent TV. The funny men were still strutting around their respective stages, gesticulating and making faces. If I, who had been raised in cities and was a part of their culture, now found myself disconnected from their raucous energy and frantic antics, how far removed was someone like Dan, who had been born in a land of endless spaces and had been raised to hear the voices in the wind?

Yet it was entirely possible — indeed, very likely — that at that very moment Dan was watching David Lettermen read a top ten list, or staring at some phony crime re-creation full of screeching sirens, jumpy camera work, and hysterical scratchy rebroadcasts of 911 calls.

What did this all mean? And how could I make sense of it?

Gradually, I was coming to wish I had never undertaken this project. There was no way I could do it right. As much as I respected Grover, he was forever watching over me, monitoring my intentions with a ceaseless vigilance that had begun to feel suffocating.

Dan himself wanted so much from me, yet he was unable to articulate just what it was I was supposed to accomplish. "Make it sound like I went to Haskell." "Don't make it sound too white." Every instruction was a contradiction. And the only stylistic advice I ever received was to observe the comings and goings of a mangy old dog.

Then, on the other side, I could already hear editors and publishers saying, "The old man is too crusty and ornery. Make him nicer. And couldn't you make him a little less ordinary and a little more wise?"

I was weary of the entire enterprise. I was sick of living in a motel room and listening to screen doors slam and toilets flush in the next unit at two in the morning. I was running short of money and I missed my family. I had no guarantee of a publisher, and no idea how this series of conversations and simple daily occurrences was ever going to take form.

The story of the buffalo carcasses and the junk cars had been the last straw. I wasn't sure if Dan had been toying with me or if he was serious. There had been such a mock theatricality about the way he had leaned over and lowered his voice when he spoke; he could as easily have been entertaining himself as educating me. The only certainty was that I would be judged on whether or not I had gotten it right.

I had not come out here to be given an endless series of tests in cultural sensitivity, or to become the butt of some deep and private jokes. Even if the old man didn't realize it, I was doing him a favor, and at great cost to myself and my family. I was willing to play his Boswell, but I was not willing to play his patsy. And I surely was not willing to have my every action judged, critiqued, and used as the basis to decide if he was going to let me pursue this any further.

At that moment I made a hard and painful decision. I decided to give up and go home.

Perhaps it had been the stress of the day; perhaps the phantoms of the nighttime imagination just overtook me. But, whatever, the

decision eased my mind considerably. I would take what I had written so far and mail it all back to him along with an explanatory
note. It wasn't the noblest option, but I wanted to explain myself
on my own terms. That was likely to be impossible if I tried to do it
in person. I could just see him getting that blank look on his face
and turning away from me, or padding off into his bedroom in the
middle of one of my sentences, leaving me sitting at his table as if I
were some kind of leper or tainted piece of meat.

No, if I wrote a note he might not respect me, but at least he
would understand me. He would be unable to resist reading it, so
he would hear what I had to say. After all, he had raised a family.
He had made hard choices in his life. I wanted him to hear me say
my peace.

It was even possible that sometime in the future, when we
both had our motives clearer, we could undertake the project
again. Or perhaps he could find an Indian to serve as his chronicler,
who understood more deeply the shadings of his actions, and was
less likely to be seen as a potential betrayer who had to have his
every act judged as a measure of the purity of his character. I even
let myself entertain a thought that had been unthinkable up to
now: that no one except a few Indians and a few Indianophiles
even gave a damn about the old man and what he had to say, and
that it wasn't really that important, anyway.

I went to my bag and took out a sheet of paper. The motel
room had no desk, so I propped some pillows against the wall behind my bed and made a writing surface out of the Gideon Bible.

"Dear Dan," I began. "I wish to speak to you honestly and from
the heart. You have given me a great honor by asking me to write
your thoughts for you. But with each day I am . . ."

Out of the corner of my eye I could see Arsenio Hall waving his
hand over his head like a lasso and doing some kind of a cakewalk
across the stage. I grabbed for the remote and tried to shut him off
before I lost the rhythm of my thoughts.

I slammed at the button with my thumb, but only succeeded in changing channels. The Atlanta Braves were playing the L.A. Dodgers or San Diego Padres and something of consequence had just happened. The camera panned the fans and came to rest on three shirtless white men with great fishbellies who were wearing headdresses and waving giant rubber tomahawks. Next to them sat a woman with a little girl about two years old.

The fishbellies gestured wildly to the woman and pointed at the camera. She looked up, excited, then lifted the little girl's sleeping head so the camera could see that her face was painted in red and white stripes. Then the woman stuffed a tiny rubber tomahawk in the little girl's hand and began making chopping motions with her arm. Soon the five of them were facing the camera and making synchronized tomahawk chops, with the little girl still sleeping, the mother grinning, and the three shirtless men beating their beefy hands over their mouths in an imitation of a war-hoop.

I looked down at the paper on my lap. Slowly, methodically, I crumpled it up and tossed the wadded ball off the wall into the wastebasket.

"See you tomorrow, old man," I said with a sigh, and clicked off the TV and the light. The only answer was the dull thunking of beetles against the screen door, and the low, insistent drone of a plane passing somewhere far overhead.

It would be far from the truth if I said I met the next dawn with joy and enthusiasm. A patina of shame had been added to my feelings of alienation and indignation.

I had the terrible feeling that Dan would know I had considered leaving. At the same time, I had tasted — if only for a moment — the sense of relief that would come from being free of this project. I had allowed the image of my wife and children to flood in upon me and transport me back to my home, and that image echoed in my mind as I showered and dressed for another day.

I decided I had to confront the old man on some level. If this was to be my project, it had to be on my terms — not his, not Grover's, not some ancient dog's. Too much had to be done to leave everything to serendipity.

I had too many notes. My method and purpose were unclear. My truck had begun making an odd, vaporous smell during our trip up the rise yesterday, and was long overdue for a servicing.

Today I would set everything in place. I would clarify my task and the old man's expectations, then leave for home with my notes, my tapes, and a better sense of my ultimate intentions. I would spend some time with my family, get my truck checked out by a mechanic I trusted, and allow everything to gestate into some kind of meaning and order. Then, when I had a clearer picture of where I was going, I would come back with a series of specific tasks and hammer this whole thing into form.

It was the only way. None of these people knew what was involved in producing a book. None of them had experienced that need to get control of a project so you could bring it to a meaningful conclusion. For them it was an endless exercise of niggling and criticizing and saying, "Why didn't you do this?" or, "You should have mentioned that."

When all was said and done, this was my book and I had to give it form.

I had to take charge. I just had to.

It took me only a few minutes to pack. I had become accustomed to traveling light, and everything I owned went easily into the green canvas aviator's bag that had become my suitcase of choice.

The woman at the front desk didn't even look up as I checked out. Her eyes were glued to a small black-and-white television that was propped on the ledge of the sign-in counter. She scribbled a haphazard receipt and slapped it on the counter with exasperated indifference. She didn't even count the bills I had given her.

The knowledge of my plan buoyed me as I drove out toward Dan's house. A violent thunderstorm had passed overhead late last night and drenched the prairie with a short but nourishing rain. The earth exuded a smell of sweet nectar, and the swaying grasses were alive with buzzings and flutterings. I rolled down my windows and breathed deeply. White butterflies were hovering near the tall grasses and doing crazy dances against the azure sky.

It was a day to savor.

I bounced my way through the ruts leading to the old man's house. Fatback scrambled out from beneath the dead Chevy and barked and wagged. Wenonah's car was parked in the driveway, as I had expected.

I hopped out, gave Fatback a tousle, and walked to the steps. It was my habit to wait outside until invited in.

Soon Wenonah appeared at the door and peered through the broken screen. "He's not here, Nerburn," she said.

"That's okay," I said. "I'll just walk up the hill and sit a bit."

"He won't be back for quite a while," she continued.

"Like, how long?"

"I don't know."

The news startled me. "Where'd he go?"

"He just said he was going on a little trip."

I shook my head in amazement. He could have told me yesterday. Then I could have started for home last evening and saved the cost of another night in the motel. There I was, anguishing over my decision to leave, and he had no trouble just getting up and going without even telling me.

Wenonah must have seen my disgust.

"He didn't tell you to come back today," she said.

Something snapped inside me. "Damn it," I said. "I know he didn't tell me to come back. But I'm doing this book for him. I drive hundreds of miles on my own time and money to do a book to help him have his peace at the end of his life, and you're standing there acting as if I have no right to be upset when he just up and disappears without telling me.

"I'm sick of this crap. I have no right to be upset about anything, but you and he and Grover can be upset if I tie my shoelace wrong or use the wrong adverb. How come nothing that I think is important matters?"

Her voice was calm and composed. "Maybe we're tired of having everything you think is important matter. Maybe that's the way it's been ever since your people got here, and maybe we're sick of it. Nobody asked your people to come over here. Nobody asked you to give us blankets full of smallpox and to kill our old people so you could take over the whole continent and build highways and shopping malls.

"Maybe you drive 500 miles to see him. Big deal. He fights to stay awake and fights back pains and memories you can't even imagine to give you the story you think you want.

"You should be thankful he talks to you at all. It's a privilege when an elder shares with you. You don't even appreciate it."

She turned around and walked back into the darkened room.

"Hey, Wenonah," I shouted. "You can't just walk away like that."

There was silence from the house.

"I know you can hear me, and I'm going to say what I have to say. I've had it with this honorific shit. I know it's a privilege, and I appreciate it. But it's a privilege for him to have someone care enough to do this thing, too.

"I've got a wife and a teenage daughter and a young boy who I die for every day being away from them. I'm sleeping in a fleabag motel room filled with the stink of whiskey from the endless drunks who stay in the next room. I'm spending money I don't have, and I'm being watched like a goddamn hawk by Grover and everyone else to make sure I don't make a false move.

"I didn't give anyone smallpox blankets. In fact, I think I'm probably sleeping on some of them in that damn motel. I didn't sail on any damn Pinta or Niña or Santa Maria, and I didn't take any maize from Squanto or ride with General Custer.

"I'm just a decent guy who is trying to do his best for a man I respect. And all I want is a little respect in return."

Wenonah's shadow reappeared in the doorway. She opened the door and stepped out onto the wooden stoop. There was a tattered manila envelope in her hand.

"Come here, Nerburn," she said.

I walked up the steps. She was holding a jumble of stiff sepia photographs. She handed me one. It was of a little boy in a military suit with a pair of heavy black shoes. He looked like a little Civil War or Spanish-American War soldier.

"You know who that is?" she asked. "It's my grandfather," she said without waiting for an answer.

"You know what he's wearing? A little wool suit made out of U.S. Army uniforms.

"You know why he's wearing it? Because he was kidnapped from his parents and taken to a boarding school where they cut off his hair and burned the leather leggings and moccasins that his mother had made for him with her own hands.

"And you know why his parents didn't come and get him? Because his dad was arrested when he complained about the police taking his son away to school.

"You think you know everything, Nerburn. But you don't know anything."

She handed me another photo. It was a big white wooden barn-like building. "Do you know what that is?"

"It looks like a dormitory, or old boarding school," I said.

"It's the place where they made him kneel on marbles and hold his arms out to the side for a half-hour if they caught him speaking his language. It's the place where they made him line up with all the other kids and open his mouth for a dentist who took pliers and

pulled out every tooth that didn't look right, and never gave anyone any Novocain. It's the place where he started wetting his bed
and the matron tied the skin on the end of his penis shut with fish-
line every night until he got an infection so bad that he almost
died."

She shoved the photographs back into the envelope and folded
it shut. "He doesn't do what white men want anymore, Nerburn."

She stood up and walked into the house. I looked at Fatback,
who was engrossed in chewing on her own rectum.

"Christ," I said, and climbed back into the safety of my own
truck.

Chapter 9

Jumbo

I must have raced out of the driveway too fast or perhaps accelerated too hard, because by the time I got to the main road the vaporous smell was back. A steamy haze was starting to come into the cab through the air conditioner vents. "Come on, Baby," I said to the truck. "You can do it."

But she couldn't. Within a half a mile there was a loud pop and a great fluttering sound from the engine. Something between smoke and steam started to fill the cab.

I hopped out and opened the hood. A wall of white vapor engulfed me.

"Damn! Damn! Damn!" I bellowed. It had to be a head gasket. There was no hope, and only a little time. I jumped back in the cab and hit the gas. A great cloud of steamy smoke poured from the tail pipe. The engine roared and flapped and spewed billows of steam from under the hood. The truck inched forward. It wouldn't go more than five miles an hour.

I headed for the center of the reservation. Cars full of Indians passed me in rez-mobiles, honking and waving. Agonizingly, glacially, I popped and roared down the incline toward the few buildings that passed for a town.

As I thundered onto the central street, I searched frantically for any indication of a gas station or auto repair shop. The temperature gauge had buried itself in the red zone. Kids on bicycles were circling around me and laughing and pointing. One little fellow pedalled in front of me and waved for me to follow. I didn't know where he was going, but I was in no position to ask.

He zoomed around a corner beckoning me with his left hand. He skidded up in front of a low, run-down concrete building with a white garage door. A piece of weathered plywood was nailed above the entrance. On it had been scrawled, "Broke Car's and Stuff 'fixed.' Not running 'ok' Jumbo."

I turned off the key and coasted into the dusty area in front of the garage door. The engine dieseled and chugged, then wheezed to a stop.

I sat in my truck collecting my thoughts. Whoever he was, Jumbo was going to have to save me. This truck was not going another foot further.

The little boy on the bike ran into the shop. Soon the door opened and he ran outside again. He stood in front of the truck, staring toward the shop in anticipation. I started to get out when a shadow emerged in the doorway. At first I thought it might have been a car being moved inside. But the door pushed open, and out stepped the hugest man I had ever seen. He must have weighed well over four hundred pounds. His head was the size of a basketball and just as round. He had a shaggy bowl haircut and chestnut brown skin. From what I could see he appeared to have few, if any, teeth.

A dirty white T-shirt hung like an umbrella over his midsection, which in turn hung like a flour sack over his belt buckle. From the front, the origin of his pants was invisible beneath the great pendulous girth of his belly.

He wore filthy white high-topped tennis shoes with no laces, and when he walked he kept his arms out at his side like a man trying to balance himself.

"Jumbo?" I said, trying to contain my astonishment.

He didn't even look at me. He just walked over to the front of the truck and popped the hood.

He stuck his head into the billowing steam, like a man placing his head in the mouth of a dragon. He pulled on a few things, then slammed the hood shut.

"Car's fucked," he said.

The diagnosis was not sophisticated, but it seemed accurate.

"Can you fix it?"

He bent over slowly and squinted at the grill.

"What kind is it?" he asked. His voice rumbled like thunder in a well.

"A Nissan," I answered.

"Never heard of it."

Then he turned like a great battleship and walked back toward the door.

I slumped against the steaming fender. This was more than defeat. It was total devastation. I knew I had felt slightly out of place with my tidy little Japanese truck. But now, as I thought back on it, I had not seen one other foreign car or truck on the entire reservation. The vehicles of choice seemed to be huge Fords or Chevys of the early seventies vintage, and beat-up pickups that all looked like they had been rolled over or beaten with sledgehammers.

I thought of the endless automotive carcasses baking in the prairie sun throughout the reservation. There was no way I was going to be able to communicate the desperation of my situation to a man who lived in a land where cars were as disposable as tin cans or a pair of cheap shoes.

I was about to climb back into the cab and begin rummaging around for the title when I heard a scraping sound behind me. I turned to see the white garage door going up to reveal a dark, oily cavern of space with a greasy pit in the middle of the floor. Jumbo was looming behind the pit and gesturing toward his feet.

At first I didn't realize what he meant. Then it dawned on me that he wanted me to get the truck into the garage. I climbed back in the cab and tried to start the engine. It whirred and chuffed, but would not fire. Several of the young boys who had been swirling around on bicycles ran behind the truck and threw their shoulders against the pickup gate. I stepped out and pushed from beside the driver's door. Slowly we coaxed the car into the stall while Jumbo directed it first a bit to the right, then to the left, to make sure that the tires didn't fall into the grease pit.

When we had it inside Jumbo walked around to where I was standing.

"Looked it up. Can fix it."

I glanced at my shiny black truck. Then I looked around at the greasy benches piled with tools and oily hoses and old filthy air filters. I felt like the New York woman in her million-dollar clothes.

"You sure?" I asked.

"Yep."

"How long will it take?"

"Don't know."

"Any idea? A few days? A week?"

"Don't know."

I was going to ask how much, but things were beyond hope.

"But you're sure you can do it?" I said one more time, more in an attempt to get him talking than to reassure myself.

"Yep."

I reached behind the seat and grabbed my aviator's bag. I was about to detach the truck key from the other keys on the ring, but I realized that was an absurdity. No one here knew where I lived, or cared. Besides, it might give Jumbo the impression I didn't trust him, and that was the last thing I wanted to do.

I shrugged and looked over at the great shadowy figure who held my fate in his hands. He had lumbered off into the blackened recesses at the rear of the shop and propped himself against a pile of tires, legs spread, belly hanging. He was eating a sandwich. The soft, white bread had greasy finger marks all over it. It looked like a soda cracker in his massive ham of a hand.

"I'll stop back later to see how it's going," I said.

"Yep," he answered.

I turned and started to walk out the open garage door. Standing behind my truck, silhouetted against the noonday sun, was a hunched figure with its head cocked to one side. It was Dan. I breathed a deep sigh of relief and almost ran over to him.

"Wenonah said you were off on a trip," I said, forgetting my anger and frustration at his untimely disappearance.

"Grover had to make some sandwiches." He nodded toward Grover's barge-like Buick that was idling in the street. Grover waved at me from the rumbling vehicle. He had on a large cowboy hat with a turquoise hatband. Fatback was sitting up like a vigilant grandmother in the back seat.

"Figured you needed me," the old man said.

I gave him a quizzical look.

"Saw the smoke signals from your truck. Old Indian signal of distress," he cackled.

He walked slowly around the side, shaking his head and surveying my hissing vehicle as if it were the steaming carcass of some freshly expired elk or buffalo.

He ran his finger delicately along its side.

"Real shiny," he said. "Would make a nice dog house."

"Come on, Dan," I said. "This is no joke. I've got to get this thing going."

Jumbo grunted something from the shadows.

"Jumbo here will fix it. He's good at fixing stuff," Dan said. The giant form in the back of the garage moved the sandwich toward its mouth and another chunk of white disappeared.

"Yeah, but how long?" I said to the old man.

"Hard to say. That's up to Jumbo. He's pretty busy."

I peered into the junk-filled darkness at the hulking figure propped up against the tires masticating the sandwich. There was no vehicle in the building other than my truck.

"Oh," I said.

The old man shouted in at Jumbo. "How long this going to take, Jum?"

The voice from the back was slow, dark, and deep. "Don't know."

I grabbed Dan by the sleeve of his shirt. "Ask him if it's a day or a week," I whispered.

"What do you think? A day or a week?" Dan shouted.

Chewing sounds emanated from the darkness. "Could be," came the voice. "Car's fucked. Shoulda got a Chevy."

Chapter 10

Ponytails and Jewelry

I slumped morosely next to Fatback in the back seat of Grover's big green Buick as we made our way up over a ridge toward the main highway. I should have been happy at the good fortune of getting to go on "a little trip" with Grover and the old man. But all I could think of was my meticulously engineered little truck sitting in the darkness of Jumbo's garage. Images of those piles of greasy wrenches alternated with thoughts of hospital-clean Japanese factories full of intense, fastidious men in white coats, adjusting micrometers and making marks on clipboards.

Jumbo's laconic comment — "Can fix it" — kept echoing in my head. That's probably what those plier-wielding dentists at the boarding school had said before ripping into the kids' mouths and extracting the nearest available tooth.

I slumped even lower. There was no doubt in my mind that I had seen the last of my beloved truck. It was all too clear: I was staring at twenty-six hours on a Greyhound full of squalling babies and pathetic old women in head scarves. My truck was destined to become a forlorn monument in the dusty field behind Jumbo's garage, while happy Indians rode around on its new hundred-dollar tires and listened to powwow tapes on its recently purchased two-hundred-dollar tape deck. I was lost in a sea of private despair.

Dan and Grover were laughing in the front seat. My plight — if indeed they even saw it as a plight — had not dampened their enthusiasm. I knew I should just give myself over to the moment, but I needed a little more reassurance.

"Grover?" I asked. "Do you know Jumbo?"

"Known him since he was a kid."

"Do you think he can fix my truck?"

"Fix it or kill it," Grover answered. Dan laughed.

Grover turned his head and looked at me slumped morosely against the rear passenger door. "Nah. Jumbo's a good guy. He'll get it fixed or else he'll tell you," he said.

"'Course, if he fixes it he won't have to tell you," Dan chimed in. The two men broke out in laughter again.

I didn't have the faintest idea what they were talking about. If it was humor, it eluded me. If it was information, it was unimportant to me. I just wanted to go back to the motel and sleep until this whole thing was over.

"Come on, Nerburn." It was Grover again. "Forget about it. Nothing you can do, anyway. This little trip will be good for you. You worry too much, anyway."

I realized he was right, but I couldn't shake my sense of depression. An hour ago I was on my way home in my mind. Suddenly I was aiming in the opposite direction, toward an unknown destination, while a great hulk of a man who ate grease-covered sandwiches tore apart my computer-designed car with a set of pipe wrenches.

Still, the constant use of the phrase "little trip" was beginning to pique my fancy. It was as if this were some kind of ritual exercise that had a significance for Grover and the old man. Perhaps there was more to be learned here than I expected. I did my best to put my truck out of my mind. Grover was right: There was nothing I could do, anyway.

Grover slowed to a stop, then wheeled the car onto a major

highway. He was what one would charitably call a "leisurely" driver, seldom exceeding forty-five miles per hour. Eighteen wheelers shot past us with horns blaring. Grover paid them no mind. Other Indians with out-of-state plates surged past us in conversion vans and station wagons. Some had God's-eyes in their back windows. Others had old bumper stickers that read, "Pow Wow Power" or "Custer had it coming." One banged-up Econoline had a cow skull wired to its roof and a garish version of Frederick Remington's *The End of the Trail* airbrushed across its side.

Grover and Dan lapsed into Lakota. The old tires of the Buick thumped rhythmically against the seams in the pavement. I had nothing to do, nothing to contribute to the conversation, and nothing good to think about, so I soon fell into a deep sleep.

How long it lasted was uncertain, but by the time I awoke the shadows had lengthened and the hills were tinted with a deep, burnished gold. "About time you woke up, Nerburn," Grover said. "Time for supper."

He gestured to a sign advertising a truck stop at the next turnoff. "We'll stop there."

He wheeled the lumbering Buick into the truck stop parking area. Ten or fifteen semis were parked in a row at the back of the lot with their engines running. The seismic rumble from their throbbing motors echoed against the golden hills.

Grover pulled up next to an old green school bus with Idaho plates. The windows were covered with heavy red curtains, and a stovepipe stuck out of the roof a few feet in front of the rear door. A heavy platform, like a balcony on an old politician's train car, had been welded out from the rear of the bus. It was piled high with old bicycles and coolers and canvas tarps. A dream catcher hung from the center of the rear window.

"Trouble," Dan said.

"Not for me," Grover laughed. "Just you. It's that damn ponytail," he said. He rubbed his hand once across his ashen crewcut. "You should shave her down, like me."

Dan just grunted.

The restaurant did not look inspiring. It was a typical nonde-script highway truck stop with a restaurant on one side and a gas station that catered to truckers on the other. We wandered in through the gas station door. Dan went to fill a coffee can with water for Fatback while Grover and I proceeded into the restaurant.

A row of booths with orange vinyl tuck-and-roll upholstery lined the window wall and looked out over the parking lot. The center area was filled with a row of square tables covered with red-and-white-checked tablecloths that hung like skirts around their shiny chrome pedestals. A counter faced the cooking area, which was visible through an open area where the cooks slid the plates of hot beef sandwiches and red plastic baskets of burgers and fries when they were ready.

A few truckers sat slumped at the counter drinking coffee and eating pie. Most of the booths were full of men in faded T-shirts and baseball caps. It was clearly a roadhouse that catered to the over-the-road driver; there was hardly a local to be seen.

"Where are we?" I asked. So much truck traffic indicated we must have been on a major cross-country route.

Grover just shrugged. "We've gone a few miles," was all he vol-unteered.

In the booth nearest the door sat a family that was immediately apparent as the owner of the bus. The man had a gaunt, hollow face and a long braided ponytail held in place by a beadwork-and-porcupine-quill barrette. The woman was wearing a T-shirt and a floor-length tie-dyed skirt. She had three turquoise rings on her right hand. Across the table sat three blond-haired kids ranging in age from about three to twelve. They were patiently sucking on ketchup-covered french fries and drawing designs on placemats. As we passed them the sweet, pungent odor of patchouli oil rose from their booth and mingled with the heavy restaurant air of sweat and fried onions.

Grover and I took a seat in one of the empty booths. No one

paid us any mind. Soon Dan came through the entryway and into the restaurant. He squinted a bit against the bright golden light that was filtering in through the windows, and finally spotted the two of us across the room. He cast a sideways glance at the couple and shuffled his way over to us.

He was shaking his head and hissing through his teeth as he slid in next to Grover. "See those people?" he said, nodding toward the family.

"The old hippies?" I asked.

"Yeah. What do you think of them?"

It was clearly another test, and I was in no mood for tests. "If I had made a few more left turns in my life, that might have been me," I said.

The old man just sat. He wanted me to say more. I considered the wisdom of matching his silence with a silence of my own, but thought better of it. There was nothing to be gained by making an issue out of anything at this point.

"They seem decent enough," I continued. "They're a couple. They seem to care about each other. Their kids are well behaved. In the larger scheme of things they seem harmless enough — not throwing grannies out on the street in the name of corporate progress, or anything like that. They're probably just sixties dreamers who got caught up in a time warp, and still hold to some vision of a better world. Probably moved out into the woods of Idaho, built a house, grow some vegetables and dope, and want to be left alone."

Grover nodded his head and chuckled. "You're pretty good, Nerburn. You should try writing."

"Thanks," I said. "I'll keep it in mind."

Dan wasn't quite so light-hearted. He kept looking down at the table, as if trying not to be seen. He was clearly agitated about something.

I didn't feel it was my place to say anything, but I was curious as to what was bothering him. I looked over at Grover, but he, too, was sitting impassively. Finally I asked.

"What's wrong?" I said. I knew it was a "white" question: no Indian I knew would violate the inner feelings of another by demanding to be let in on them. But I was a captive audience and I had nothing more to lose. This uneasy consternation was something I had never seen before from the old man.

"I don't want to talk to those hippies," Dan said.

"Why should you have to?" I asked.

"Because they always want to."

"Want to talk to you?"

"Yeah. They're wannabe's. Trying to be Indians."

"Why do you think that?" I probed.

He nodded his head toward the couple. "Look at the jewelry. That quill thing in his ponytail. They're wannabe's. Probably following the powwow trail. Damn!"

"You don't like white people at the powwow?" I said. The amount of out-of-state Indian traffic on the highway had convinced me that there was a powwow somewhere, and I had automatically assumed that was our destination. I was suddenly concerned that my presence would cause offense to the other participants. I didn't want to be seen in the same light as the school-bus people.

"Naw, that's fine. I like it when white people come to the powwow. But the wannabe's are different. They try to be Indians."

The man in the ponytail shifted in his seat. He seemed to be ready to stand up. Dan hunched over even further, as if by hiding his eyes he could become invisible.

"How come you're not so bothered?" I said to Grover.

"They don't ever talk to me," he answered.

"But they talk to Dan?"

"Yep."

"Why?"

"'Cause I'm a burr Indian," Grover grinned, running his hand over his crewcut. "They don't want to talk to me."

The old man picked up the conversation.

"They see my ponytail and think I'm their soul brother or something. Grover's old burr cut just makes him look like any other old guy."

"Hmm," I said. "So the long hair gives you trouble?"

"Always has. More trouble than anything else. Long hair was the way of my people before the white man. We grew it long because it is part of nature and because it shows our pride. If something bad happened in our lives, or if we disgraced ourselves, we cut it off. We grew it back when we wanted to show our pride again. A lot of our people still keep to this old way.

"In the beginning the white people wanted us to cut our hair. When they sent us to boarding school, that was the first thing they did to us. A lot of us learned to wear it short, like Grover here, and just kept it that way. But some of us wanted to keep to the old way, so we grew it back."

He leaned over and spoke in a low whisper, as if the gaunt man in the ponytail might overhear. "But, you know, that hippie thing came along with the white people, and all the young people were growing their hair long. They would tie it back or put bandanas in it. I guess they were just trying to show that they had some freedom. We could understand that.

"But it wasn't the same as us, and all the hippies saw us with long hair and figured we were hippies, too. We would have these hippies coming to our reservation and giving us hippie handshakes. Damn, I hate those hippie handshakes. They would talk about peyote and drugs and want to be part of us, like maybe we were the same as they were.

"They were like lost little children to us. We felt sorry for how lost they were in their own country. But we never thought they were like us.

"The trouble was, they thought they were like us. They saw the long hair and the pipes. They started wearing Indian clothes and

Indian jewelry. Then they started reading about Indian religions. Pretty soon they wanted to go to peyote ceremonies and sweat lodges and the Sun Dance.

"Now, that guy over there, he's one of them. I can just see it. If he comes over here he'll give me one of those damn hippie handshakes and want to talk, talk, talk. He won't even give a look to Grover."

"I told you to cut that ponytail," Grover laughed.

"I'm not cutting my hair for any damn hippies," the old man grumbled. "I'll bet you anything he follows the powwows all summer. You should see our powwows, Nerburn. Sometimes some white boy on drugs or some girl in a long dress will jump right out and start dancing right in the middle of a grand entry and not even know what they're doing."

"Sometimes they even wear eagle feathers," Grover cut in. "You're not supposed to wear an eagle feather unless you earned it in battle or a veteran gives it to you. Some of the wannabe's have more eagle feathers than Geronimo."

"Hell," Dan countered, "I even saw a wannabe with a whole stuffed eagle head on his bustle. A whole eagle head!"

"Why doesn't someone tell these people that you don't want them to dance in the powwow?" I asked.

"It's not our way," Dan said. "Everyone is responsible for his own heart. And if a person is doing it with a right heart, then I think it's okay if white people want to dance."

"But then there's the other thing," Grover cut in.

"The other thing?" I said.

"Cherokee grandmother," Grover said, and the two men chuckled together.

Out of the corner of my eye I could see the man with the ponytail get up and go to the register to pay his bill. The woman and children followed. Soon we heard the roar of their bus starting up. Dan relaxed visibly.

"I guess he wasn't that interested in you after all," I said.

"Yeah, I guess I was wrong," the old man said. "He's probably a social worker on his way out to Grover's house."

The twinkle was back in his voice and eyes.

"Now that you got me talking about this, let me finish," he said. "There's that other bunch, too, that I don't like. It's those rich people who come in big campers and foreign cars looking to buy Indian stuff. Like in Santa Fe, they have this market once a year and those rich white people come and spend more money than we've got on our whole reservation. Fill up their trunks with everything. Dream catchers. Shields. Paintings. Anything Indian. The richer they are, the more they want Indian stuff. You should see it. Guys in Mercedes with tons of turquoise jewelry all over them. Women with silver jewelry hanging off everything."

"Ah, it's not that big a thing," Grover cut in. "I don't mind those people coming around and buying dream catchers and God's-eyes. It gives our people a chance to earn some money. And there's power in those images. Maybe it'll do those white people some good."

"Just so long as we don't start giving them sacred things," Dan said.

Grover agreed. "That's the real problem," he said. "Selling the sacred things."

"Tell me about it," I said.

Dan looked away and shook his head. "Not now. It hurts me to talk about it. Let me finish about the hippies and the rich people. What do they call those rich people, Nerburn?"

"What do you mean?"

"You know, rich people that like to still think they're hippies and radicals but really just want to have a lot of money."

"You mean, 'Yuppies'?" I suggested.

"Yeah, yeah. That's it. The yuppies. That's better to talk about while we're eating. Maybe later I'll make a little talk about the Indians who sell our sacred things."

It was obvious that this was not a subject to be pushed. I made a mental note to bring it up when the circumstances were right. But, for now, I would let the conversation go where the two men wanted to lead it.

The waitress arrived and took our order. Grover insisted that we each order a bacon double cheeseburger and fries. "I've been here before," he announced. "They make them good." Not wishing to run the risk of offending him, I agreed to the greasy choice and quickly requested coffee with milk to serve as some vague buffer.

Grover and Dan leaned back in their seats and pulled out their cigarettes. Now that the threat of the innocent man in the ponytail was gone, they seemed to take great delight in discussing the idea of white people buying Indian jewelry and crafts. They found the term "yuppies" especially amusing.

"You wouldn't believe what happens when those yuppies come around, Nerburn," Dan said. "The hippies aren't so bad if I don't have to do that hippie handshake. They mostly have good hearts and really are searching for something. But those yuppie ones, they're something different. They'd buy my teeth if I'd let them."

"If you had any," Grover added.

The two men chortled mightily.

"You know, Nerburn," Dan continued. "If I don't quick find a place to hide, they see my long hair and want their picture taken with me. Or else they want to make a video of me with them. Can you imagine someone coming up to you and wanting their picture taken with you because of the way you look? Do they think that's a compliment?"

He went on without waiting for an answer. "Hell, it's like being an animal in a zoo. I do it, though, when they ask me, if they're nice people. Most Indian people do. It doesn't hurt anything. It's just another thing about white people wanting deep down inside to be like Indians. They've been doing it for years. But it sure is strange.

"Think about it. Suppose Indians came up to you and asked to have their picture taken with you in front of your house? What if they asked you to go inside and put on your most white clothes so you would look more like a white person for the picture?"

"I'd be astounded," I said.

"Well, that's what's happened to us Indians for years. It used to happen to my grandmother all the time. She even made money at it. She would sit on a blanket and people would take pictures of her and give her a nickel. They even made some postcards of her. I've got some at home. She never made any money on those, though.

"It still happens all the time. Just go to any Indian fair or pow-wow where there are white people. Some white person will start talking about how wonderful our culture is and pretty soon they will want their picture taken with us. They don't even give us a nickel anymore.

"Now they're doing it in schools. They call it some kind of culture class or something. But it really is the same thing. They pay an Indian to come in and talk about our culture. Then the kids go home and say there was an Indian in school. It's just like the postcard. It's just a cardboard cutout of an Indian that white people say they've seen."

Grover was nodding knowingly as Dan talked. He smudged out his cigarette in the ashtray in front of me. The fine plume of acrid smoke rose directly toward my face. "I wish one of those rent-a-Indians would go into the school and talk about how their car didn't start or how they are having trouble with their kids," he said. "Everyone would get mad and say, 'We want to hear about Indian culture. We don't want to hear that stuff.'"

"That's right," the old man said. "All they want to hear about is the Great Spirit and the sacred land, that kind of Indian talk. They already know what they want to hear. They just want an Indian to provide it.

"That's why it makes me smile to see white people wearing Indian jewelry. Because to most of America, that's all we are. Just jewelry on the American culture. It's our job to be bright and colorful."

"Exotic?" I volunteered.

"Yeah, exotic. That's a good word. That's what white people really want from us now. We make them exotic, like jewelry. We're supposed to be there for you to pick up whenever you need to feel different and special. Have an Indian into class. Put a Navajo blanket on the wall. Read that book about Black Elk. Makes them think they are part Indian in their heart."

Grover was immersed in the greasy pleasure of his cheeseburger. But he clearly was enjoying Dan's little lecture. He swallowed hard and interjected himself into the conversation.

"I still think it's okay, though," he said. "It makes the little kids happy. It makes our people feel like they are worth something to the white culture. It might even teach the *wasichu* something to put dream catchers over their beds and to have us into their schools."

The old man nodded. "Yeah, I know," he said. "But I just don't want people thinking that taking a picture of us and having us talk to a school class is the same as knowing us. Or that buying a dream catcher or going to a powwow makes someone an Indian. You can't buy a culture by giving it a nickel."

"And you can't become an Indian by growing a ponytail," Grover added.

They grunted their approval of each other's insights, and turned their attention back to their red plastic baskets of burgers and french fries. I tapped a silent rhythm on the rim of my coffee cup and stared out the window. The green school bus was disappearing off into the distance over an amber rise.

Chapter 11

The Selling of the Sacred

The sun had almost set by the time we got back on the road. Dan had saved a corner of his cheeseburger for Fatback, and the dog was making a great ceremony out of licking the ketchup and onions off the greasy bun onto the seat beside me.

We drove without speaking. Only the sound of Fatback's incessant licking punctuated the great peace of the high-plains evening.

I marveled at the sense of well-being that this vast landscape induced in me. There were no jagged edges, no fragments of meaning. All was massive, singular, and soft under the prayerful canopy of the sky.

I thought of an old farmer I had met once in Bismarck. I had asked him if he ever went east. "Nah," he answered. "Trees make me nervous."

In the deep amber peace of this prairie twilight, I could well understand what he meant.

Grover and Dan rode in the front seat in silence. It had been years since I had ridden in a silent car. I generally tried to fill the space with music or talk from the radio or a tape. I counted it a deficiency when I was forced to ride in quiet.

Now, in the enveloping dark of Grover's old Buick, the pleasures of silent travel came back to me from my childhood. I slid down in the back seat and listened to the whining of the tires and the steady, purring throb of the ancient V-8 under the hood. Fatback crawled over and put her head on my lap. The sky outside had changed from golden to orange to a blazing red, and was beginning to deepen to a velvety purple. My truck, my indecisions, and my petty grievances and angers seemed light years away. I was in Indian country, and I was traveling on Indian time.

Grover and Dan must have sensed my improved state of mind, but they said nothing. Instead, they started singing a plaintive, warbling song in Lakota. They sang it like it was part of them, issuing forth from their mouths as naturally as breath. It sent shivers through me to hear these two men, one almost eighty, the other a generation younger, singing together as we passed through the growing high-plains darkness. Their song seemed to come as much from the land as from themselves. I could not imagine another sound more fitting to the spaces through which we were traveling.

Suddenly I was overcome with an almost uncontrollable urge to sob. Feelings that I could not name welled up and begged for release. It was beauty, it was contrition; it was loneliness and it was joy. In a way that I can never explain, it felt like the first time I had ever heard Bach's Mass in B Minor.

The *Sanctus*, the *Agnus Dei*, the *Kyrie* of the American plains was finding its voice in the song of two old Lakota men and the humming purr of a Buick V-8.

I turned my head toward the window so the men would not see me cry. But I think they knew. There were sobs in their voices, too, but they were sobs of the land, far bigger, far greater, far deeper than mine.

Finally, Dan stopped singing and turned in his seat. He never looked at me, but stayed in profile, like a priest giving a penance or a ritual benediction. His voice assumed a formal tone.

"I will make my little talk, now," he said. "And I want you to listen."

I reached into my pocket and clicked on the tape recorder.

"It is hard for me to make this talk, because it makes me talk against my own people. I don't like to do that. You should not talk against your own people. Except in this case, I am talking against some people who are harming us and not respecting what we have been taught.

"I am talking about Indians who sell the things that are sacred."

Dan inhaled deeply. This was a talk he meant to do right.

"These Indians I am talking about go around selling Indian culture to white people. They take some Indian name and say that they will give a ceremony for white people, then they charge money. They give sweats for white people, or pipe ceremonies. I have heard that some give naming ceremonies or peyote ceremonies or tell our stories that are not supposed to be told.

"These people are doing something wrong. They know it. But for some reason they don't care.

"I'm not talking about Indians who are trying to share our culture. I'm talking about Indians who are selling the sacred truths of our ancestors. It is alright to show dances or tell legends that can help people. I think white people need to hear these things to understand us better. What I think is wrong is when an Indian sells his birthright as an Indian by taking money to make other people feel like Indians.

"I have thought about this a great deal. It troubles me. We know that white people have an endless hunger. They want to consume everything and make it part of them. Even if they don't own it physically, they want to own it spiritually. That is what is happening with the Indian, now. The white people want to own us spiritually. You want to swallow us so you can say you are us. This is something new. Before you wanted to make us you. But now you are unhappy with who you are, so you want to make you into us. You want our ceremonies and our ways so you can say you are spiritual. You are trying to become white Indians.

"If this is meant to happen, it will happen in the Creator's time.

We cannot make you us by giving you those things that are ours. All that does is make us lose what we are, because we no longer hold it in value.

"These Indian people who sell the sacred ways, and even the ones who make up the ceremonies and pretend to sell the sacred ways, are killing our people. They are betraying the one thing they should hold most valuable."

He paused and lapsed into silence, as if gathering himself. He sat that way for almost a minute before he spoke again.

"Here is something that is important to understand. When something is sacred, it does not have a price. I don't care if it is white people talking about heaven or Indian people talking about ceremonies. If you can buy it, it isn't sacred. And once you start to sell it, it doesn't matter whether your reasons are good or not. You are taking what is sacred and making it ordinary.

"We Indians can't lose what is sacred to us. We don't have much left. What we have is in our hearts and in our ceremonies. The land is gone. It was sold by false Indians who were made into chiefs by white people. Our sacred objects are gone. They were collected by anthropologists who put them in museums. Now there are Indians who are selling ceremonies in order to make money.

"When they are gone, all we will have is our hearts. And without our ceremonies, our hearts will not speak. We will be like the white man who is afraid to say the word 'God' out loud and goes around trying to buy sacred ceremonies from other people. We will have the same hunger in our hearts and the same silence on our lips.

"I don't want us to be this way. I want us to have something that does not have a price. If we don't, my grandchildren who are not yet born are already dead.

"That is all I have to say."

When he was finished, he turned forward again in his seat, without ever looking at me for approval, or even for assent. The whole talk had been given in a low whisper, and I had been forced to lean forward, like a man listening to a secret or a prayer.

The earth moved by outside, almost black now, a rolling land of silhouettes and silence. A thin band of light outlined the horizon. Above it, the sky was breaking forth into a symphony of stars.

Grover said nothing. Dan said nothing. Even Fatback had ceased her licking and settled into a contented silence. I sat like a child, transfixed by the landscape, lost in a world of unknown thoughts and feelings, like a sailor adrift on an inland sea.

Chapter 12

Welcome to Our Land

Morning came like birdsong, soft and sweet. I did not remember falling asleep. Grover must have driven miles after I had drifted off.

Feathery clouds with orange edges wisped across the sky to the east. We were parked on a rise, somewhere in hill country, ever more westerly than we had been the night before. Craggy rock outcroppings hinted of the mountains, but this was still the high plains, alive with the buzz of insects and the dancing of the winds.

I lifted myself up from my resting place in the back seat of the car. The old man and Grover and Fatback had risen earlier. I had heard the car doors open and close, but had chosen to burrow deeper into my sleep rather than to rise up before the dawn.

Dan was squatting on his haunches on a hilltop in front of the car, watching the sun rise. His back was toward me, and a small ribbon of cigarette smoke rose around his head. I marveled at the way he could sit for hours like that, squatting on the earth, at once vigilant and relaxed.

The leathery taste in my mouth brought me out of my reverie. I craved coffee, and I craved a bath.

Grover had built a small fire near the car and was tending a pot of coffee that was propped up on several rocks. Somehow he had managed to make himself clean and tidy. His white T-shirt looked like it had been laundered and ironed. Each sleeve was rolled up twice to reveal his sinewy biceps. The eagle tattoo on his right arm moved and jiggled as he poked the tiny flame with a stick. He saw me sit up, and motioned me over.

"Coffee, Nerburn," he announced as I opened the door. The rich acrid aroma of cheap, potent coffee cut like a razor through the clear air of the high-plains morning. Grover thrust me a cup and leaned back on the ground.

"It's a good day, Nerburn," he said.

"It is a good day," I answered. And I meant it.

The rise on which we were parked overlooked an endless expanse of grassland. The field that stretched out before us was alive with cars and tents and people walking back and forth in bright, feathered costumes.

I surveyed the scene like a man encamped on an escarpment above a medieval battlefield. All the action below me was purposeful and full of life. Fires were sending plumes of smoke high into the sky. Brightly colored nylon tents stood side by side with teepees and conversion vans.

In the center of the field a large ring had been marked off with weathered posts. Erratic squeaks and squawkings issued forth from a PA system that was being tested or adjusted somewhere, though I could see no signs of an electrical power source anywhere. Here and there a peal of laughter would arise, soon to be drowned out by short bursts of drum beats and singing.

"Powwow," Grover said.

I nodded. I glanced around furtively to see if the green bus was anywhere. It wasn't. I breathed a quiet sigh of relief and took a deep draught of Grover's vile and ferocious coffee.

"Navy brew," he said proudly.

"Serious stuff," I said, hoping to imply no value judgment.

Grover beamed wickedly.

The air of festivity created a sense of anticipation. I had been to powwows before, but they had been larger events, more established. This one seemed personal and private. There were no vendors' stands in sight, no milling group of hangers-on.

"Is this where we're going?" I asked Grover.

"Don't know," he said. "Ask the old man."

I walked over to where Dan was squatting. He had a passive, satisfied air about him.

"Is this where we're going?" I repeated.

He didn't answer. Instead, he gingerly shook his gnarled hand out toward the horizon.

"Look out there, Nerburn," he said. I surveyed the lavender morning sky and the distant rolling foothills. "This is what my people care about. This is our mother, the earth."

"It's a beautiful place," I offered.

He snubbed out his cigarette. "It's not just a place. That's white man's talk. She's alive. We are standing on her. We're part of her."

I kept my silence. He was beginning the morning philosophically. Hills seemed to do that to him.

"Feel her breathe. Stop worrying about where we're going. Forget your white man ideas."

"I'm trying," I said. "I'm just trying to get a handle on things." Too much was just too open-ended. I wanted some sense of direction — what we were doing, how long it would take, if my truck was going to be okay. "I'll be okay."

He turned to face me.

"You're lying again," he said. "Listen to me. I'm trying to teach you some things. You're not listening. You keep worrying about that truck of yours. It's not that big a deal. Either Jumbo will fix it or he won't. If he can't, then you will go home another way. You'll get another truck. They're making trucks every day. Don't worry about that truck. Think about the day. Listen to the earth. The earth is here forever, but it will only be exactly like this on one day. Today."

"I know that," I said. "But it's not just the truck."

"You're not listening to what I said," he cut me off. There was an air of harsh authority in his voice, far different from the quiet ruminations and outbursts of anger I had come to expect from him.

"I'm trying," I said. "I want to enjoy this. This is a beautiful day. Last night was a beautiful night. But I miss my family. I want to put some kind of frame around things. I need a sense of what's going on."

"Yeah," he said sarcastically, "you sure do." Something was on his mind.

He took a deep drag on his cigarette. "Nerburn," he said, "you ever watched water flow across the ground?"

"Sure."

"Where does it go?"

"To the low spots, around obstacles."

"How long does it take?"

"It depends."

He exhaled the smoke into the pure morning air. "That's how long we're going to be gone."

I started to protest. He raised his hand and waved me to silence.

"You think too much about time." He gestured toward my wrist. "I didn't think you were like that when I first met you. You don't wear a watch."

"They feel heavy on my wrist," I answered, feeling stupid as I made the comment.

"They are heavy. They make every minute weigh more than the whole day."

"I still want to know how long we'll be gone. I want to call my family."

The old man rocked forward onto the balls of his feet and stood up. He walked slowly to the edge of the hill. Then he turned back toward me. His one bad eye seemed to stare right at me.

"You still haven't figured it out, have you?" he said.

"I don't know. You tell me," I responded.

His bad eye stayed locked on mine. It was an unnerving stare, at once empty and intense, like the gaze of a blind man. "The world is not an accident, Nerburn," he said. "Nothing is an accident."

I held my silence.

"Everything happens for a reason. You're here for a reason. It's time you stopped worrying about some damn truck and got about figuring out what that reason is." He flapped his hand toward me. "Come over here."

I stood up and walked slowly toward him. He was standing completely still, like an animal. I walked up to him like a child, uncertain of what I should do or what I would find. I wanted to look away, but dared not. His expression was completely flat and without affect, but behind it lurked a silent fury. Though I easily towered over him by a head, I felt small and afraid.

"Listen to me, Nerburn," he whispered, placing his face so close to mine that I could feel his breath. "The Creator has given you a task, just like he gave me a task. This is not a joke. He chose you to do this. You need to do it right."

I felt all my defenses drop away as I stared into his tiny hard eyes.

"I want to," I said. "I just don't know how. I really don't. I don't know if I'm the right person for this."

"That's not for you to decide. You just do it. I need you to help me."

With that sentence, the whole world seemed to swirl inside my head. "Help me," he had said. The one thing I most wanted to do. The one thing I felt least qualified to do. The one thing that I feared most about being a white man working with the Indians — that I would try to help, and like so many before, would do harm and damage I could not repair.

Still, he had said it: "Help me." Suddenly I knew the fury behind those eyes. I heard the echoes of a thousand dead voices — of women, of children, of old men too slow to run when the Hotchkiss guns were turned against them. I saw the legions of drunken Indians who had accosted me over the years, weaving over to me on city sidewalks, stinking of cheap wine and grabbing at my shoulder, asking for money and staring up at me with blood-shot eyes. I saw the defeated chiefs, weary of battle, reaching their hands out to arrogant soldiers, asking for mercy for their people.

"Help me." It must have been the hardest sentence in the world for him to say. Images swirled out of control. The shame of my own blood surged through me. He should not need my help. His people had been whole. His truth had been singular, unassailable, in balance with the land. It was my people, my race, my heritage that had placed him before me like this.

I looked at his hard, expressionless eyes, the one white and cloudy, the other dark and unfathomable. They were strong, wise, deep; full of anger and pride — eyes that flashed, but did not reveal. All of this I could feel, like a wind upon my skin. Yet his expression never changed. He stood before me, still and vigilant, awaiting my response.

My voice came from my mouth with a tentative quaver. "I will help," I said. "I want to. I really do." Then, without thinking, I whispered, "Forgive me." The words passed from me like stones — hard, evil little balls of an illness that had stricken my soul, suddenly flung free, releasing me from years of torment. That was why I was here — not to help, but to earn forgiveness, to earn forgiveness for the shame in my blood.

"Forgive me," I said again, confessing to unknown sins and transgressions, to my desire to leave, to my sense of righteousness and superiority, to my whiteness.

The old man remained expressionless. But something within

him relaxed. He gestured over to Grover, who was slouching against the Buick, fingering the rim of his coffee mug.

"Listen to me more," the old man said, suddenly gentler. "There is more going on here than you know. Indian people have had bad things happen to us. We don't know why. Sometimes good things happen to us. We don't know why. I don't know whether you're good or bad. But you're here. And you try. I think you are good. I think maybe you were sent here to help. But you need to stop worrying about things that aren't important and try to see what the Creator wants you to do."

I wanted to cry. The sense of release was palpable. But the old man would not let go with his eyes. It was not my contrition he wanted, but my strength.

Out of the corner of my vision I could see Grover rummaging in the trunk of his car. Soon he emerged with a large object wrapped in a multi-colored blanket. He carried it over to us and set it on the ground.

"Sit down, Nerburn," Dan said. He pointed to a place about ten feet back from where we were standing.

I walked over and situated myself in the sharp bristly grass.

Dan and Grover began unwrapping the bundle. Inside was a drum, about two feet in diameter. The top and bottom were made from animal hides, and the drum body itself appeared to be made from a piece of hollowed-out tree trunk. Crosslacing of animal hide held the two heads in place.

Grover spread the blanket out beneath the drum. Then he took two two-by-fours that had been wrapped in a separate bundle and placed them on the blanket. They were notched at the middle, so that when he placed them at right angles they locked together into a cross-like frame. Then he took four sticks and fitted them into holes at the end of the two-by-fours, so they stood up like posts.

He slowly reached over and picked up the drum. There was ceremony in his manner. He took one of the rawhide loops hanging from the side of the drum and fastened it over one of the posts. Then he did the same on the opposite side. Finally he attached the drum to the other two posts and stepped back. It sat there, suspended above the ground, humming slightly in the breeze.

Dan stepped forward and took a pack of Prince Albert from his pocket. He took pinches of tobacco between his fingers and placed them on the head of the drum, one in front of each post. Then he placed one in the middle.

Grover handed Dan a leather bag that had been wrapped in the blanket. The old man reached inside and pulled out a long thin stick that had been wrapped with padded leather on both ends, then handed the bag back to Grover. Grover accepted it formally and drew out a stick that had been sewn all around with beads.

The warm morning winds picked up the tobacco and swirled it around, scattering it like seeds.

The two men seated themselves on opposite sides of the drum and began to pound out a low, rhythmic beat. At first it was almost inaudible, lost in the growing keen of the morning winds and the noise from the powwow ground below. But slowly the beat increased in volume and intensity. Then Dan began to sing in a high, warbling wail. Grover joined in, clearly following, but with a voice as strong and clear as the summer air.

I sat silently, outside the small circle they had made, and watched the two men sing. Fatback came rustling through the grass and nudged up against me. The morning sun rose higher behind us, chasing the feathery orange clouds and turning the sky a lapis blue.

The two men drummed and sang for almost five minutes. Then, as quickly as they had begun, they stopped. Dan stood up and walked away down the ridge. Grover gently and meticulously rewrapped the drum and carried it back to the car. I got up and followed him at a distance.

When Grover had placed the drum in the trunk, he walked over to the coffee pot and poured himself another cup. He smiled at me with the corners of his eyes and beckoned me over. It was alright to speak again.

"Have some more coffee, Nerburn," he said softly. "You need it."

I took my cup and filled it with the potent "navy brew." "Can I ask what the song was?" I ventured.

Grover rubbed his hand over his head. "It was a song Dan made up a long time ago. He makes up songs a lot. He calls it one of his 'Grandfather' songs."

"Can I know what it says?"

"I guess so. He made it for you. It goes like this:

> My heart is filled with anger.
> My heart is filled with anger.
> It is like the prairie fire that burns.
> I send my anger like smoke to the heavens.
> The earth is crying now.
> The earth is crying now.
> We need to stop her tears.
> Fire will not stop her tears.
> This song is for my grandfathers.
> I sing this song for my grandfathers.

"It doesn't sound so good in English."

"I think it sounds beautiful," I said. "How do you mean, he made it for me?"

"I made it when I knew you were coming," said a voice behind me. It was Dan. He had come over while Grover and I were talking, and was standing directly behind me.

"When you knew I was coming?" I said.

"I wrote it when I knew I wanted to speak. I went to my hill and spoke to my grandfathers. They gave me that song. They gave it to me in the wind. They said I had too much anger to speak. They told me that anger is only for the one who speaks. It never opens the heart of one who listens. There are good white people, they told me. They want to do right. They are not the enemy anymore. The enemy is blindness to each other's ways. Put away your anger, they said. Our earth is crying now, and we need to remove her tears. That is what they told me. Someone will come, they said. Then they gave me that song."

There was nothing I could say. I sipped at my coffee and stared at the cup. But Dan was not done. He took out a small leather pouch and began dipping his fingers into it as if grabbing for a pinch of snuff. His eyes were closed and he was half humming, half singing, another mournful-sounding song.

He picked the substance from the bag and sprinkled it on the glowing coals of the fire.

I glanced over at Grover. "Sweetgrass," Grover said quietly. "It pleases God."

The strong perfume of the herb filled the air. I put down my coffee cup and sat in silence. Dan continued to feed the sweetgrass onto the fire. He seemed oblivious to my presence. Then, abruptly, he stopped and turned his attention to me.

"I think it is time you should understand why you are here, little brother," he began. "It is time you should know why I am telling you these things."

The phrase "little brother" shocked and exhilarated me.

"The Creator gives us gifts. He did not make me a *wichasha wakan*, a holy man. He only made me a man. But he gave me the gift to see clearly. He gave me the gift to put on white man's eyes.

"My father always said I had this gift. He saw it when I would come home from boarding school and tell him the things I had seen. 'You understand the white man,' he said. 'You make his mind come alive for me. That is a dangerous gift. It could turn you into a white man if you are not careful. But if you stay on the good road, and if you do not hurry, you will find a way to make that gift be of service to your people.'

"I never forgot those words. I have lived with them every day of my life. There were times when I almost spoke. But always when I wanted to speak, I would wait. The time was not right. Instead I read. I wrote. I kept my Indian eyes and I kept my white eyes. But I remained patient. I did not speak.

"Now I see that it is a good time to talk again to your people."

He inched closer to me.

"You see, Nerburn, you white people go in cycles. For a while you hate Indians. Then for a while you love Indians. Right now you love Indians, and that's good.

"Some of my people think this will pass again. They say that you will get angry with us for casinos and wanting to keep our land pure. They say you have always wanted what we have, and that nothing has changed. They say you will turn on us again.

"But others say that this time there is a change, that now it is time for you to really hear. They think you know that you are lost and that you want us to help you find your way.

"That is what I think. That is why I am talking. When I would write my notes over the years, my friends would laugh. They would say I am a crazy old Indian. I told them what my father had told me, and that different times would come, and that those notes would mean something.

"Every day as I wrote I offered those notes to the Creator as my gift. I knew he would use them. When I read your other book, I knew you would help me use them.

"Listen to me. We Indians don't talk to white people much. We never have. There is a reason. White people have never listened to us when we talked. They have only heard what they wanted to hear. Sometimes they pretended to hear and made promises. Then they broke those promises. There was no more reason for us to talk. So we stopped talking. Even now, we tell our children, 'Be careful when talking to the *wasichu*. They will use your words against you.'

"This is a wise teaching. But it is a bad one. It is not good that we do not talk. But we have learned not to trust your people. It was not something we wanted to learn. You forced us to learn it.

"When your white people first came among us, you didn't know what to think of us. You didn't know if we were devils or if we were people who were pure and free. You didn't even know if we were people. We welcomed you to our land. We gave you food and smoked with you. We taught you our ways.

"We trusted the goodness in your hearts. We tried to share with you. But our trust was not returned. No matter what we gave you, there was always something else. For the Spanish, it was gold. For the French, it was furs. For the English, it was land. But always there was something. Always you were looking past us at something else.

"We could see in your eyes that you were not hearing us. Soon we learned to be silent.

"When I look in your eyes, Nerburn, I see that something else is there, too. I want it to go away. It is not something bad. Some of it is your family. That's good. Some of it is your truck. That is not good. That is a waste of your heart. Some of it might be greed. I don't know. But I want it to go away. All of it. For now it has to go away.

"To speak out like I am doing is not easy. I am not a leader. No one has elected me to speak. I am just an old man with clear eyes. Some Indians will be mad at me. But others will understand. They will see what I am doing and they will respect me. They know that I am reaching out for the grandchildren.

"I am reaching out to you, Nerburn. You must help the grandchildren, too. If you are afraid, or if you are too small, it is too late. You are here."

At that point he stopped and turned back to the fire. He reached into his pocket and removed a second pouch, took something from it, and sprinkled it on the coals. A different smell rose into the morning air. "Sage," Grover whispered. "The bad spirits hate sage. It fills them with fear and they go away. He is telling you important things, Nerburn. You'd better listen."

Dan was rocking, almost hypnotically. "Listen to me some

more," he said. "I have a little more to say.

"I have called you to come. In the old days our people did not call your people to come. They waited for you to come, because they did not know what to do with the white man. Some of them wanted to fight you. Some wanted to live with you. No one knew what was right. The white man did terrible things to us. You lied to us and you took our land. You killed our people and you never heard when we tried to speak.

"But now your people are here. We cannot make you go away, even if we want to. There is a reason why the white man came and took our land. Only the Creator knows it. We can only do what we think is best.

"I think that talking to you is best.

"That is why I am welcoming you. Our people tried to welcome your people once before. But you destroyed that welcome. You destroyed it with crosses and diseases and whiskey and guns.

"Now I am trying to welcome you as one person. I have called you to my house and you have come. I reach out my hand to you in welcome. *Wakan Tanka,* the Great Spirit, hears and knows. We will work together."

As he finished, Dan reached over and extended his hand toward me. I stood up and reached my hand toward his. He grasped my hand in his fingers and took hold with a soft firmness that held my fingers like a vice. Though it looked like a handshake, it was more. His whole being was in that grasp. It was a pact, a sealing, a promise.

We stood there, united by that grasp. My hand, so used to perfunctory shakings in greetings and casual introductions, wanted to wriggle and escape. But the old man would not let go. He held my hand until our touch had an understanding.

"I welcome you," he said. "Welcome to our land."

Chapter 13

Tatanka

We did not go to the powwow. Dan and Grover conferred at some length before getting into the car, but finally decided that the "little trip" needed to go in other directions.

"Nerburn needs to call home," he told Grover. "He needs to get his mind straight." It was said without rancor, a concession to my world and my life. We were now working together.

Grover nodded gravely, then turned the car onto a faint path through the wiregrass. "Shortcut," was all the explanation he offered.

The car bucked and clanked over the grassy ridges. The faint tracks in the grasses often seemed to disappear. But Grover drove with confidence. One time he hit a particularly deep rut and his exhaust pipe clunked hard against the dusty ground. He muttered something like, "Easy, junker," and continued without stopping to inspect the damage.

I sat in amazement as we jolted and bumped through the hills and hollows. Grover seemed oblivious to the perils of the terrain. He churned along, his front bumper pushing down grasses like a ship plowing through the sea.

Our pace was not rapid, but it was inexorable. Before long we were out of sight of all indications of roads or houses. The land flowed like a retreating tide toward the horizon. Grover was enjoying himself immensely.

Fatback was not a good rider on these bumpy ruts. She began burping and swallowing and licking her lips. "Shove her head out the window," Grover suggested.

"It was those cheeseburgers," Dan chimed in.

"I think it was the onions," I offered from my vantage point nearer her mouth. Fatback issued a long and doleful "errup" from her throat and stared at me with pained eyes.

"I think you'd better stop, Grover," I said. "Fatback's not going to last."

Grover just laughed and bounced the car into another set of dusty ruts. "It ain't gonna get any easier for a while. She's a good dog. She'll make it."

"That's easy for you to say," I hollered, trying to make myself heard over the creaks of the springs and the clanks from the undercarriage. "You're in the front seat." The old dog gurgled and hung her head out the window. I rolled down the window on my side, half in anticipation of some Vesuvian disaster from Fatback, and half to drink in the sweet warmth of the growing high-plains morning. The buzzing of insects mingled with the clanking and the urping.

"So, you want to call the old lady," Grover shouted over his shoulder.

"I think I'd better," I said. "She's probably expecting me back pretty soon."

"You need an Indian squaw," said Grover. "They never ask any questions."

"Not much for women's rights, are you," I chided.

Grover took both hands off the wheel and held them up like a man supplicating heaven.

"Women's rights. You white guys don't know anything about women's rights," he said. "All your women want to wear pants and do men's stuff. Then they call that equality."

"There's a little more to it than that," I said. "Besides, that is equality of a sort."

"It ain't worth a damn, if you ask me," Grover snorted. The car lurched once in sympathy, as if choreographed to accentuate Grover's comments.

"Stop this damn car," Dan ordered. "I don't have a stallion's bladder."

Grover ground to a halt. Fatback scrambled out the window and rushed off into the weeds. Dan pushed open his door and made his way unsteadily to a stand of trees that were bent over a dry-wash a hundred feet away.

Grover settled back in his seat. "This is the pit stop, Nerburn. Better go with the old man and the dog if you think you need to."

"Bladder of steel," I answered.

Grover opened his door and stepped outside. The silence of the landscape flooded in on us. Actually, it was no silence at all, but a teeming, buzzing, chirping symphony of small sounds that had been masked by the clunking thunder of the forging automobile. But it was all of a piece, with no sharp edges or punctuating sounds. Like the sweet smell of the air, it was an overpowering, intoxicating presence that seemed to come from nowhere and everywhere at the same time.

Once stopped, the breadth and distance of the landscape stunned me. "Do you know where we are?" I asked Grover.

"There's the sun," he pointed. "So that's west."

"That's a start."

"It's good enough. There's a road over here not too far, if I've got my figuring right." He gestured broadly in the direction of the distant hills.

"Are you serious? You're just plowing your way through these backlands, expecting to come to some road in the distance?"

"Sure. Why not?"

I was incredulous. "What about draws? What about holes?

You're not driving a tractor, Grover. You could blow a tire and we'd be sitting out here in the middle of nowhere . . ."

"This ain't nowhere, Nerburn. This is Indian land. Just because you don't see a house or a road doesn't mean that we're in the middle of some goddamn ocean."

I surveyed the land around me. In point of fact it did look like an ocean: the sea that had once covered these plains had left its undulations on the land it had left behind. Gentle swells and rises gave way to dips and hollows. It was a feminine landscape in its shapes if not in its textures — a terrain of graceful movement frozen into a finality of sculptural form. It took no imagination at all to see the figure of a single horseman, or a herd of bison, making their way across this burnished landscape beneath a cobalt sky.

"Maybe it's just the white man in me, Grover, but I kind of associate automobiles with roads. This seems to be more horse kind of country."

"Didn't you hear me calling my car, *'shunka 'kan'*?"

"I thought you were saying something about a junker."

Grover let out a guffaw. " *'Shunka 'kan'* means 'horse'. You white guys buy cars called ponies and colts and mustangs, but you pee in your pants when you treat them like one. Old *Shunka 'kan* is the real thing."

The old man had still not returned from the copse of trees down in the draw. "Speaking of peeing in the pants," I said, "Do you think Dan's alright? He's been gone an awfully long time."

Grover picked up a piece of wiregrass and started filing it between his teeth. "He's okay. He likes to stay places sometimes."

"Like how long?"

"I don't know. You got someplace you have to go?"

"I'm going to go look for him."

Grover gave a noncommittal shrug. I turned toward the draw and began searching for the old man.

I saw no sign of him until I made my way over a rise. Then I saw his familiar form frozen in that vigilant squat next to a small gathering of trees at the edge of the drycreek. He didn't turn around, but obviously was aware of my coming. He reached back with his right hand and made several downward gestures, like a conductor quieting a noisy section in an orchestra. I made my way slowly down toward him. When I arrived he gestured me down.

"Look over there," he said.

The hills on the other side of the draw were turning golden in the early afternoon sun. Shadows moved across them like great winged birds as the clouds overhead obscured the sun for a moment, then moved on.

I saw nothing other than the lyrical folds of the landscape punctuated by an occasional dark bush or gnarled tree.

I squatted beside him and stared toward the horizon.

"See?" he said.

"What?"

"Watch."

The wind blew the grasses like waves on the sea. An occasional tumbleweed bounced and raced its way across our line of vision. Other than that, there was nothing.

"Watch that bush."

I stared intently in the direction he was pointing. A large dark clump clung to the side of one of the hills in the distance. From where we were I could not tell if it was a bush or a small tree, grown low against the incessant winds. I stared for a few more seconds. The bush seemed to move. Then, in the next instant, it shifted. It was not the movement of vegetation responding to the wind. This movement had volition and intention, a kind of muscular certainty.

"*Tatanka*. The buffalo."

I squinted my eyes to see more clearly. Slowly, the large animal moved its head and took on the familiar configuration of a buffalo.

"That's amazing," I said. "I didn't even see it."

"You weren't supposed to see it. *Tatanka* didn't want you to see him."

I absorbed the mysterious possibility without comment.

"*Tatanka* is more powerful than you know, Nerburn."

The buffalo shifted its weight again and moved slowly along the hill.

I thought back to the time near his home when he had "called" Fatback without ever saying a word.

"Dan," I said. "Let me ask you something. I mean this with no disrespect. I really want to know."

"Go ahead."

"Do you really believe that the buffalo can cloud our minds in some mystical fashion like that?"

"What's mystical about it?"

"You say he didn't want me to see him."

"That's not mystical. That's science. If a lizard doesn't want you to see him, what does he do?"

"I don't know. Hides under a rock. Blends in somehow, I suppose."

"Exactly. Now, how does a buffalo blend in?"

"Hides his contour?"

"Tricks your eye. He understands how you see. Knows that you see outline. Knows that you see movement. All big animals know that."

"So they stay still when they sense danger?"

"And when they want to learn about you. Sometimes they are watching you when you think you are watching them."

"Was he watching us?"

"I can't say. He knew we were here, I know that."

"But he wasn't afraid. How did he know he didn't have to fear us?"

"I told you. He's a powerful animal."

"But we might have had a gun."

"I don't mean 'powerful' that way. I mean he has power. He knows things."

I pushed a bit. "You mean he knows whether or not we have a gun?"

Dan was a little irritated. "I didn't say that. I said he knows things. He knew whether or not he had to fear us."

"By smell? By some psychic power?"

"Maybe. I don't know. How do you know whether you like somebody or not?"

I smiled and shrugged. He had me.

"Look, Nerburn. You ever had a dog?"

"Sure," I answered.

"How about a cat?"

"Got one now. A rasty orange thing."

"Were the dog and the cat different?"

"Of course. From each other. From other dogs and cats, too."

"And they each knew different things."

"Right."

"So why is it so hard for you to understand that *Tatanka* is different from other animals?"

"I've never had a lot of dealings with buffalo."

"Well, my people have. The buffalo gave us our food, our clothes, our shelter, almost everything we needed to live. We lived around them like brothers and sisters. We know more about them than you know about your dogs and cats. And I'm telling you that they have power."

In the distance the buffalo continued to graze. Its sense of indifference to us was palpable.

"I didn't mean to sound disrespectful," I began.

Dan waved me off. "I know. You're trying to learn. White people like to learn by asking questions. Come on. Let's go back to the car."

We struggled our way up the rise. The old man walked slowly and unsteadily. He stepped cautiously; his eyes were in his feet. I wanted to reach over and take his arm, but it felt more demeaning than respectful. I almost asked him if he wanted some help. But the words stuck in my throat.

Then it struck me. If he could barely see the ground in front of him, how had he seen the buffalo on that ridgetop almost half a mile away?

"How did you see that buffalo?" I asked him.

He turned his head and nodded several times, as if satisfied with the question. "I didn't see him, Nerburn," he said. "He showed himself to me."

Grover had stretched out on the car hood like a cowboy in some cheap cigarette ad. He had his legs crossed at the ankles and his hands folded behind his head. The cowboy hat was tilted down over his eyes. Sunlight sparkled and glanced off its silver hatband.

"You save him, Nerburn?" he asked from beneath the hat.

"It was close," I answered. "If I hadn't shown up he was going to turn into a buffalo."

"Glad he didn't. Never fit in the car," Grover said, pulling himself up to a sitting position.

Dan choffed a low sound and made his way over to the front passenger door. Fatback was chewing hard at some burr between the pads on her back foot. Dan leaned over in a slow, arthritic bend. "Tsuk, tsuk," he sucked to get her attention. She stopped her gnawing and looked at him. Then, without further command, she rolled on her back and stuck her back foot toward him. With practiced fingers he spread the pads of her foot and reached in and pulled out the burr. Fatback curved up and licked his hand several times, then delved her tongue back into the crevice between the pads and began licking away at the wound. Dan cuffed the scruff of her neck and opened the car door.

It was a small moment, but full of love and understanding. Maybe Grover had meant more than I thought when he had told me to watch Fatback and get my book from her.

Chapter 14

Seeing with Both Eyes

In a manner that seemed almost incredible to me, Grover continued through the trackless hills for almost the entire afternoon. Occasionally he would find an old path and follow it for a bit. Once or twice we had crossed gravel roads, but rather than turn onto one, Grover pushed across them like fording a stream, then plunged back into the grasslands. I had no idea what he was doing or why he was doing it. All he would ever say was, "Shortcut."

Dan assured me that there was a track here. "How the hell else would he know where he was going?" he said. I could not tell if it was a joke or a statement of fact.

I had the distinct sense that there was a purpose behind our journey, but it seemed so random, so serendipitous. Grover tried to get me to eat a steamy baloney sandwich that he had stored under the front seat, but I declined. He shrugged and ate two. Dan did some housekeeping on his with ketchup and mayonnaise packs that he found in the glove compartment, then chewed it down in contented, rhythmic bites. Fatback looked longingly from the back seat. "Bad for the stomach," I consoled her.

As the shadows began to lengthen we came to a gravel road that stretched off over the hills. To my surprise, Grover turned onto it and headed south.

"Annie," he said. The shorthand meant nothing to me, but elicited great nods of approval from Dan.

"Good," he said. "Haven't seen that old squaw for a while."

My spirit lightened considerably now that we were on a recognizable road. My life had been full of too many tiny automotive apocalypses where a tire had blown or a warning light had suddenly come on, and I now unconsciously found solace on well-traveled roads where solutions were close at hand and small problems were less likely to turn into automotive nightmares.

This dusty gravel path was no highway, but at least it spoke of intention and destination in a way that the trackless fields of our day's travel had not.

Dan turned around and looked at me with a cockeyed grin. "Happy now?"

"I was happy before."

"Yeah, but you like roads. I could tell it from that first time we drove up on the hill behind my house. You go where they send you."

"Like I said to Grover, cars and roads sort of go together."

"Not in Indian country," he laughed.

"Besides, they tend to lead to phones," I said, "and I still would like to find one. Does this Annie have one?"

Grover guffawed. "Where the hell do you think you are, Nerburn? America? They don't put phone lines out here. Electric lines, either." His voice was tinged with bitterness.

"And it's a good thing, too, as far as I'm concerned," Dan added. "This is a better way to live. The people are happier. This is the way it was when I was a kid. We all helped each other because we had to. Nobody had anything. We just shared. When someone came to your house it meant they really wanted to see you. You honored them."

Grover leaned back in his seat and sighed. "Yeah, that was the thing when we were young. Honor and respect. We were taught honor. I don't know what the hell happened."

A pickup roared by in the opposite direction. Grover and the other driver exchanged waves.

Dan picked up the conversation. "That's something you should think about, Nerburn."

"Huh?" I blurted. I was thinking about roads and telephones.

"Freedom and honor."

It sounded like a military slogan. "What do you mean?" I said, only vaguely interested.

"This is important," Dan emphasized. "I want you to get it down."

I remembered that his shoe box full of notes had contained many references to freedom and honor. I rummaged in my duffel bag and pulled out the tape recorder.

"Okay," he said. "Ready?"

"Ready." I really wasn't; I wanted to just sit and think. But it was clear that Dan was going to give one of his "little talks." I fiddled with the volume control on the tiny recorder and slipped in a new cassette.

"This is something I've thought about for a long time. It's about white people and why they don't understand us. I think I know why."

"Go ahead, tell me," I said.

"I think it's because the most important thing for white people is freedom. The most important thing for Indian people is honor.

"This is why white people have listened to the black people more than to us Indians," he said. "The black people want freedom, too, just like white people. And since the white people took freedom from the black people, the whites feel guilty about the blacks. You see what I'm saying?"

I nodded absently.

"But the Indian has always been free. We are free today. We have always been freer than the white man, even when he first came here. When you came to our shore your people wore clothes made out of chains. Our people wore nothing at all. Yet you tried to bring us freedom.

"The white world puts all the power at the top, Nerburn. When someone gets to the top, they have the power to take your freedom. When your people first came to our land they were trying to get away from those people at the top. But they still thought the same, and soon there were new people at the top in the new country. It is just the way you were taught to think.

"In your churches there is someone at the top. In your schools, too. In your government. In your business. There is always someone at the top and that person has the right to say whether you are good or bad. They own you.

"No wonder Americans always worry about freedom. You have so damn little of it. If you don't protect it, someone will take it away from you. You have to guard it every second, like a dog guards a bone."

"This is a good talk, Dan," Grover interjected. Dan nodded in acknowledgment.

"When you came among us, you couldn't understand our way. You wanted to find the person at the top. You wanted to find the fences that bound us in — how far our land went, how far our government went. Your world was made of cages and you thought ours was, too. Even though you hated your cages you believed in them. They defined your world and you needed them to define ours.

"Our old people noticed this from the beginning. They said that the white man lived in a world of cages, and that if we didn't look out, they would make us live in a world of cages, too.

"So we started noticing. Everything looked like cages. Your clothes fit like cages. Your houses looked like cages. You put fences around your yards so they looked like cages. Everything was a cage. You turned the land into cages. Little squares.

"Then after you had all these cages you made a government to protect these cages. And that government was all cages. All laws about what you couldn't do. The only freedom you had was inside your own cage. Then you wondered why you weren't happy and didn't feel free. You made all the cages, then you wondered why you didn't feel free.

"We Indians never thought that way. Everyone was free. We didn't make cages of laws or land. We believed in honor. To us the white man looked like a blind man walking. He knew he was on the wrong path when he bumped into the edge of one of the cages. Our guide was inside, not outside. It was honor. It was more important for us to know what was right than to know what was wrong.

"We looked at the animals and saw what was right. We saw how the deer would trick the more powerful animals and how the bear would make her children strong by running them without mercy.

"We saw how the buffalo would stand and watch until it understood. We saw how every animal had wisdom and we tried to learn that wisdom. We would look to them to see how they got along and how they raised their young. Then we would copy them. We did not look for what was wrong. Instead we always reached for what was right.

"It was this search that kept us on a good path, not rules and fences. We wanted honor for ourselves and our families. We wanted others to say, 'He is a good man. He is as brave as the bear' or 'as clean as the fox.' We had freedom so we did not seek it. We sought honor, and honor was duty. The man who sought freedom was just running from duty, so he was weak.

"The only time freedom is important is when others are trying to put you in chains. We had no chains so we needed no freedom."

Dan paused to let me take it all in.

"Does this make any sense to you? The world your people brought saw everything in terms of freedom. We have always had our freedom so you had nothing of value to give us. All you could do is take it away and give it back to us in the form of cages.

"That is what you did when you took our land and tried to give it back to us in allotments. You took all our Indian land and gave it back to us in squares and said, 'You now have the freedom to be farmers and ranchers.' We didn't want to be farmers and ranchers. We had been farmers when we had to. But we didn't want to be told to be farmers.

"When we didn't farm you got angry and couldn't understand. 'We have given you the freedom to have your own land and be farmers,' you said. 'And you aren't doing anything.' To us, all you had done is given us our own cage.

"If you take an animal from the woods or the prairie and give him a house inside a fence, is that giving him freedom? No. All it is doing is taking away his honor, because if he accepts it, he is no longer free.

"Yet that is what you did to us. 'Either accept this cage or be killed' is what you told us. You took our honor and gave us your freedom. And even you know that is no freedom at all. It is just the freedom to live inside your own locked cage.

"Here is what I really think. White people are jealous of us. If it hadn't been for your religion you would have lived just like us from the first minute you got to this land. You knew we were right. You started wearing our clothes. You started eating our food. You learned how to hunt like us. When you fought the English you even fought like us.

"You came to this country because you really wanted to be like us. But when you got here you got scared and tried to build the same cages you had run away from. If you had listened to us instead of trying to convert us and kill us, what a country this would be."

"Hannh, hannh," Grover said in a subdued gesture of approval. "That's damn straight, Dan."

Dan sat erect and facing forward. He knew he had spoken well.

His chin was held high; his arms folded across his chest. There was a pride and a peace in his bearing.

"Thank you, Dan," I said.

"I will speak more if you want me to," he offered. He was like a concert pianist, in full command of his powers, offering to play an encore for an audience that had pleased him with its intelligent attentiveness.

"I would be honored," I said.

"What should I speak of?"

This was a rare opening for me. I was caught up short. I wanted to ask a big question, but none came to mind. "What's important to you?"

"Many things, Nerburn, and I will say them when it is time."

There was a silence.

"I think I should talk about words. Your language. It is another thing that bothers me, and I think I should take away the burdens of the things that bother me. That is what I heard from the old ones."

He had taken on his formal manner again. He was once more the solitary orator, speaking the truths that he had worked out over so many years, with only an old friend, a white man, and a sleeping Labrador to hear him. I said a silent prayer to the gods of technology that my little discount-store tape recorder would catch his words so I could pass them on.

"Do you speak another language, Nerburn?" he asked.

"Not well," I answered. "I can muddle along in German and Italian. But I'm no good."

"So you know how hard it is."

"It's hard for me."

"It's hard for everybody. Can you say what you want in those languages?"

"No. If I'm lucky, I can say things one way. And it's probably wrong."

"Would you like to read contracts in those languages?"

"No." I could see where he was heading.

"Would you like to have someone you didn't trust tell you what those contracts said?"

"No."

"That's what our treaties were. Pieces of paper written in a language we didn't understand and read to us by people we didn't trust. Then they were signed by Indians who were bribed to sign them, or maybe were threatened if they didn't. Then if there was anything in them that actually helped the Indian people, they were changed by lawyers for the government or taken into courts where the judges for the government made them mean whatever the government wanted.

"But you know this, don't you."

"Pretty much," I said. "I think the treaty injustices are something that most Americans are beginning to understand."

"'Understand', maybe. But not 'fix'. But those are not what I want to talk about. They are like a large bear attacking us. Anyone can see them. It is the snakes I want to talk about.

"Here. Let me talk some more. I am going to say some things that you should think about."

He drew in a large breath and began.

"I grew up speaking the language of my people. It wasn't until school I had to learn English. They just marched us into the classroom and started talking in English. We had to learn.

"I remember how funny it sounded when I first heard it. There were so many words. The teacher could talk for an hour and not even stop. She could talk about anything. She didn't need to move her hands, even. She just talked. Some days I would sit and watch her just to see all the words she said. One other boy once told me he thought she said as many words in a day as there were stars in the sky. I never forgot that.

"When I learned English I realized it was a trick. You could use it to say the same thing a hundred ways. What was important to Indian people was saying something the best way. In English you had to learn to say things a hundred ways. I never heard anything like it. I still watch white people talk and I'm surprised at all the words. Sometimes they will say the same thing over and over and over in different ways. They are like a hunter who rushes all over the forest hoping to bump into something instead of sitting quietly until he can capture it.

"I don't mind this, mostly. But I don't like it when it is used to hurt us or other people. Now I'm going to tell you some of those things that hurt because of the way people say them. I wonder if you ever thought of them.

"The first one is about the battles. Whenever the white people won it was a victory. Whenever we won it was a massacre. What was the difference? There were bodies on the ground and children lost their parents, whether the bodies were Indian or white. But the whites used their language to make their killing good and our killing bad. They 'won'; we 'massacred'. I don't even know what a massacre is, but it sounds like dead women and little babies with their throats cut. If that's right, it was the white people who massacred more than we did. But I have hardly ever heard anyone talk about the white massacres. I don't like it when people use that word only about the killing we did. It makes our killing seem uglier than yours, so it makes our people seem worse than yours.

"Here's another one: uprising. You use that word to talk about anytime our people couldn't stand what was happening to them anymore and tried to get our rights. Then you should call your Revolutionary War an uprising. But you don't. Why not? There was a government taking freedom away from you and you stood up against it. But you called it a revolution, like maybe the earth was turning to something better.

"When we did it, it was called an uprising, like everything was peaceful and orderly until we 'rose up'. Well, maybe we should make those words backward and call those 'downkeepings', because to us, we were being kept down all the time. I'd like it a lot better if history books said, 'Then the Indians were kept down again,' rather than, 'Then the Indians rose up again.' It would be more of the truth.

"See, that's how the English language is used on us. It is like a weapon you use against us now that you don't use guns anymore.

"What about 'warpath'? When you came out against us you 'formed an army'. When we came out to defend our families we 'went on the warpath'. I won't even talk about words like 'blood-thirsty' and 'savage'.

"But those are things from the old days, and you probably don't even think they are real any more. Well, they are.

"My little great grandson came home one day and told me they were studying the frontier in American history. I asked him what it was. He told me it was where civilization stopped. I almost told him he couldn't go back to that school anymore.

"Just look at that! They were teaching him that civilization only existed up to where the white men had reached. That means every-thing on the other side of that line was uncivilized. Well, we were on the other side of that line. We had governments and laws, too. Our people were better behaved than the people that came into our lands. We thought we were at least as civilized as the white man. But here is my little great grandson coming home from school talk-ing about the frontier and civilization. It was like we didn't exist.

"Every time you talk about the frontier you are telling us that we don't matter. I looked up the word. It means the edge between the known and the unknown. Whenever you use it you are saying that our people are part of the unknown. You are teaching your children and our children a history that says Indian people were part of a big, dangerous, empty space on the other side of the line where people had laws and culture. It is like there were wildcats and poisonous snakes and Indians, and they all were the same — just something unknown that made the land dangerous.

"See, this is part of the big story you don't even see. You teach about the frontier. You talk about the wilderness and how empty the land was, even though to us the land was always full. You talk about civilization like we didn't have any, just because we didn't try to haul big chairs and wooden chests across the desert in a cart.

"The way you teach it, America started from some ships that came to Massachusetts and Virginia. The people got off and had to push their way through some big empty land that was full of danger. When they got to these plains, they sent the wagon trains across the mountains and the desert, like little streams cutting their way through the earth. Once they got across, then more people followed their paths, and things were built along the way, and it was like these little streams of people became big rivers of people that all flowed across to California and Oregon and Washington. It was like the place was empty and you filled it up, and history is the story of how you filled it up and what happened while you were filling it.

"You can tell me you don't think that way, but you do. I look at the history books of the kids. They start in the east and come west, all of them, like that is the way history happened.

"Just think what that does to our kids. It tells them to see the past like white people. It teaches them to understand this country like they were on those boats and covered wagons. That's not the way it was to us. For us, this was a big land where people lived everywhere. Then some people came and landed on the shores in the east while others came up from the south. They started pushing us. Then some others came down the rivers from the north. All these people were fighting each other. They all wanted something from us — furs, land, gold. They either took it or made us sell it to them. They all had guns. They all killed us if we didn't believe that God was some man named Jesus who had lived in a desert across the sea. They wouldn't leave us alone.

"Pretty soon they set up a government way back somewhere in the east and said this all was their land. Not just where they lived, but everywhere they had been or even where they had heard of. If they could get one man to go to a place and put a flag in the ground, they said they owned everything between where they started and that flag. They started pushing us backward on top of each other. All of us who had lived side by side leaving each other alone had to fight each other for hunting land.

"We had to make deals with the white men or else fight them. There wasn't enough food. Everything started to fall apart. We lost the land our ancestors were buried in. We got pushed into little ponds of land. We were like fish who had been swimming in the sea who were sent into little ponds.

"See, to us, American history is how the big sea became little ponds and whether those are going to be taken from us or not. It doesn't have anything to do with thirteen colonies and some covered wagons going west. Our land was taken from us from every direction. We can look at the same facts as you and it is something completely different. But you build your history on words like 'frontier' and 'civilization', and those words are just your ideas put into little shapes that you can use in sentences. The big ideas behind them are weapons that take our past from us.

"I think that's a lot of where our people went wrong with your people. We didn't see the big ideas behind the words you used. We didn't see that you had to name everything to make it exist, and that the name you gave something made it what it was. You named us savages so that made us savages. You named where we lived the wilderness, so that made it a wild and dangerous place. Without even knowing it, you made us who we are in your minds by the words you used. You are still doing that, and you don't even know it is happening.

"I hope you'll learn to be more careful with your words. Our children don't know the old language so well, so it is your English that is giving them the world. Right now some of the ideas in your words are wrong. They are giving our children and yours the world in a wrong way.

"There was an old man who told me when I was a boy that I

should look at words like beautiful stones. He said I should lift each one and look at it from all sides before I used it. Then I would respect it.

"I think he gave me good advice. You people have so many words that you don't respect them the way you should. There is always another one, so you just throw them out there without thinking.

"I think you need to be careful. Those words are like stones. Even if they are very beautiful, if you throw them out without thinking, they can hurt someone.

"I have spoken now."

I had said nothing during the discourse. Watching Dan had been almost like watching a man go into a trance. He hadn't seemed to form his thoughts, but to catch them and ride them like a hawk rides wind currents. He had kept his eyes closed for the entire time he spoke.

I thought back to some reading I had done on the orations of the Seneca chief Red Jacket, and how he had practiced speaking in his youth, so that he might one day become a great orator to give voice to his people.

This is what Dan had done, and he had done it in private, with no thought of audience, no thought of reward. He was speaking for his ancestors, voicing the feelings of his people, and I was to be his mouthpiece. A shudder went through me as I sensed the honor and responsibility that had been accorded me. This was not a game anymore, nor even a simple literary exercise. This was for real, for keeps, for all the voices that had been silenced and all the voices that did not know how to speak.

Grover was nodding his approval as he steered the car down the dusty road. "You spoke well, *Tunkashila*," he said, using the word of highest respect for a grandfather, the words used to refer to the old ones. Then, to me he added, "I hope you are learning something, Nerburn." Fatback wheezed and shifted in her seat.

I had this momentary image of us being adrift on an inland sea, a kind of Great Plains *Odyssey*, the old seer, the navigator, and the scribe, with a surreal canine chorus making commentary in the background.

"You're lucky to hear these things," Grover continued. "The old man has kept silent for a long time."

"Lucky to hear these things." It was the same sentiment Wenonah had expressed while berating me from her front porch. Though they never said it in words, they revered this old man and his knowledge. They expected me to do the same.

"I will make your words heard, Dan," I said. The formality in my own voice surprised me, but it felt appropriate and natural. Dan just nodded. I ventured further: "How did you come to speak of these things, Dan?"

The old man spoke slowly. "I will tell you now.

"When I was a boy, an old man who was *wakan* looked at my eye and said I had a special way of seeing. He said I had one Indian eye and one white eye. He told my father I must learn to see with both these eyes. 'You must use your gift,' he told me.

"My father was a smart man. He knew I must listen to the old one. So he told me I must learn to watch, and even if others laughed at me, I must always watch. Then I would learn to see with two eyes.

"When I went to white school I was unhappy. I cried every night beneath my covers. A boy was not supposed to cry, and I was ashamed. When I came home for the summer I told my grandmother that I cried all the time and that I didn't know why. I told her I was not brave like the other boys. She told me I was wrong. That there were special ones who felt the pain for all their people so the rest could be brave. 'Maybe you are one of the special ones,' she said. 'You are a smart boy. Learn to speak. It will be good for you.'

"So I tried to learn to speak. Most of the kids were afraid to speak. The teachers hit them when they said the wrong words.

They thought it was better to be silent. But I remembered what my grandmother had said.

"I told the teacher I wanted to learn to speak. She gave me one book of President Abraham Lincoln and another about Rome. They were full of speeches. She told me to learn one every week and say it to her after school.

"When I looked at them there were so many words I wanted to run away. But I didn't. I tried to learn those speeches. I didn't know most of the words, so I just learned the sounds. The teacher said that was good. I would have my own words, she said, but the sounds were like music. They were there for everybody.

"I learned those speeches. I still know them today.

"I thought they were the greatest speeches in the world. I never even knew there were Indians who gave speeches until one of the elders heard me saying my speech. He told me there had been great Indian speakers, too. He told me about Big Elk and Sitting Bull. He told me some Indian speeches in my own language. 'That is a good gift,' he said, 'to be able to speak.'

"Then I knew how to see with both eyes. I heard the same sounds in the Indian speeches as in the white speeches. I heard the footsteps of men walking. I heard birds and animals. I heard the songs of all the earth in the words and in the spaces between the words. I knew I could learn to speak by listening to the animals just like I could learn to speak from reading speeches in books.

"Since then I have not been afraid to speak. I have studied and learned words. I have watched, with my Indian eye and with my white eye. I have spoken in Indian and in English. I have honored my gift."

Abruptly, he stopped. "What is your gift, Nerburn?"

I was unprepared for the question. "I don't exactly know," I stammered.

"Then I will tell you. You are honest. You are not living a large lie. You do not need to sit in the center of a house. You hear others."

I was taken aback by the strange construction Dan had put on my personality.

"But you're a coward."

The words hit hard. "You're afraid of other people's anger. Wenonah told me that. She told me I could make you do anything by getting angry."

I let out a nervous involuntary laugh. The accuracy of the insight was frightening.

"Do you see everything so clearly?" I asked.

"There's a reason why my people have survived," he said. "Now, I want you to understand this. People are going to get angry with what you write. They are going to be angry at you and they are going to be angry at me. I don't care. I am not a coward."

I made a mild protest. "That's an awfully harsh word."

"Let me finish. You cannot be afraid. There is good anger, too, and you have that. It is the anger from seeing clearly. It's the same anger I have. It's the anger the Old Ones warned me about. You must learn to control that anger, then it can be of use. But there is bad anger, too. It is the anger of people who only want their own way. That anger is selfish. It is a child's anger, and you must not back down from that anger. If you back down from it you are being a coward. Do you understand me?"

"I think so," I said.

"Good," he answered with a finality. "You will use your gift well if you stop being afraid of other people's bad anger."

Grover wanted to emphasize the point. He was ever the watchful guardian, making sure I understood the dimensions of my task. "He's saying you write what you see and you write what you hear. You are a keeper of the fire."

Dan nodded his approval. "Keepers of the fire cannot be cowards. They are carrying light."

Chapter 15

Shiny Soup

Soon signs of human habitation began to appear. A small dot in the distance proved to be a mailbox on a post, set next to a rutted dirt roadway that curved off over the hills. About a mile further down two white men in cowboy hats were herding several dozen cattle along the side of the road. The man in the lead was driving a tractor, while the man in the rear rode a large brown horse. They waved and smiled as Grover slowed to pass them.

"Good town for you up here," Grover said.

"How do you mean?" I asked.

"White town. Homestead town. You'll feel at home. We'll stop for something to eat. You can make your phone call."

I puzzled at his characterization of the town, but as it appeared in the distance, I understood. This was not a "reservation" town of trailers, random pockets of gone-to-seed tract housing, junk cars in yards, and the occasional commercial enterprise sitting back from a dusty, rutted, dirt parking area. Instead, it loomed in the distance like any of a thousand rural enclaves that dot the plains and prairies of the central U.S. — a tiny huddling of buildings standing proud against the horizontal landscape, capped by those two proud monuments to civic and spiritual accomplishment — the water tower and the church steeple.

Though it was in the middle of a reservation, this was a white town; a product of the Dawes Act of 1887 that had chopped up reservations into 160-acre parcels and allotted them to individual Indians in an attempt to convert them to the ways of farming and private ownership. Few Indians had ever taken to farming, and even fewer had understood the subtleties of private land ownership. Before long, through legal maneuvers, swindles, and sales agreements of varying legitimacy, white settlers had obtained the best land on almost all the reservations in the country. In addition, land that had been left over after all eligible Indians had received the 160 acres had then been opened up for white homesteaders. Though the land technically remained within the boundaries of the reservations, it was settled and developed like white towns all over the prairies and plains. A traveler who was paying no attention to maps or road signs might drive into one of these towns and never know he or she was on a reservation, except for the unusual number of Indians conducting their business there.

Even from a mile away I marveled at how completely different this little town seemed from the world in which I had spent the last week. There was an implied sense of order here. The road was tarred. The approach of the town was heralded by the gradual and orderly increase in human habitation. The commercial and the residential areas were distinct and demarcated. The signage, though intrusive, was professional and of a piece. In concept and in layout, there was an underlying mathematics to the experience.

Grover switched on his turn signal as we passed the black and white highway sign that announced, "Business District." The powerful metronomic "click" and the heavy green flash from the dashboard seemed a perfect herald for the world we were entering. At the sound of the turn signal, Fatback popped up from her lethargy and scrambled upright in the seat next to me.

We pulled off the highway onto the main street. The business section was short, only two blocks long, with side streets that trailed off into dead ends after a block or so. At the far end of town, you could see the beginnings of a small residential area of right-angle streets canopied by shade trees.

I looked at the small storefronts. A Coast-to-Coast, a Cenex feed station, an empty two-story brick building that might once have been a hotel. This was a farm country town, once proud of its self-sufficiency, now populated by old men in pickup trucks who swapped stories at the local cafe.

There was a peace and an order here that was comforting. But the edge of decay was everywhere. It was different from the "Indian towns," where poverty had kept anything from rising to a level of refinement. Here there was a memory of proper days and roadsters and men in blocky suits leading well-scrubbed families up church steps on Easter morning.

Now, however, there was no activity anywhere. With the exception of a low cinder-block bank and a convenience store at the junction with the highway, there appeared to have been no new construction here for at least fifty years.

"Like it, Nerburn?" Grover asked.

"It feels like a perpetual Sunday afternoon," I said.

"It's got a phone, though."

Grover made his way slowly down the wide, empty main street and pulled in on a diagonal in front of a run-down corner building. At first I thought it might have been abandoned, despite the three or four vehicles parked outside. But then an old man in a cowboy hat pushed open the metal storm door and stepped out. He squinted toward the sky, like a man emerging from darkness, and made his way down the street.

"Nice place, Grover," I said.

"Got a phone," he answered.

The building at which we had stopped had almost no identifying marks. The original display windows had been covered over with whitewashed plywood, leaving only two small apertures the size of bathroom windows to face the main street. A yellow plastic mold-injected sign with raised black letters hung over the metal storm door. It read, simply, "Cafe. Homemade pies." I wondered if someone had thought long about that description, or had just ordered a generic sign from some restaurant supply company hundreds of miles away.

I looked again at the characterless block lettering. The lack of any personal touch just added to the sense of decay. Surely someone could have come up with a name like "Ma's" or "Emma's" or anything else. It was as if there had not been enough energy or hope to strive for any personal expression. Even the sign over Jumbo's garage, with its dripping letters and indecipherable message, spoke of more personal interest and initiative.

Grover got out and headed for the door. Now that we were traveling, he had assumed the role of leader. Dan walked slowly behind, craning his neck in an idle curiosity that was quite different from the attentive vigilance he lavished on the draws and hillsides. It was as if he were a tourist here, taking in the unfamiliar with an unabashed awe, while on the hills he was a silent observer, aware of everything around him, picking and choosing from the sights and sounds and smells until he could establish a pattern of meaning.

I consoled Fatback, who had slumped morosely back into her seat, and promised her a bounty of leftovers if she would wait patiently while we ate our people meal. She made a flubbering sound and closed her eyes.

The exiting cowboy had been squinting for a reason. The inside of the restaurant was as dark as a cheap bar. Directly inside the door three pedestal tables had been pushed together to form a long banquet-style seating area. Six old white men sat along it, wearing feed caps and smoking cigarettes. On the wall above them was a xeroxed sheet of white paper that read, "Cows may come and cows may go, but the bull in this place goes on forever."

The waitress was somewhere in her late twenties, white, disinterested. She sat on a bar stool near the kitchen door listening to country-western songs on a small boom box. She was absently twirling a strand of her bleach-blond hair while blowing streams of cigarette smoke out through her nostrils.

Grover gestured us to the opposite side of the restaurant. We took a place at a square brown table with four yellow vinyl chairs.

The woman put down her cigarette and came over to us. She had that trailer-court look of someone who had had too many beers, too many kids, and too many men; who had missed her chance to get in the car with that one stranger years ago, and now accepted her life with a world-weary cynicism that contained no trace of self-pity. She stood above us with one hand on her hip, chewing gum in time to the music. "Coffee?" she asked.

"Black," said Grover.

Dan nodded.

"Me too," I added. "But I'd like mine with milk."

"Cream?" she corrected.

"No, I'd rather have milk," I said. She gave an indifferent shrug and stabbed something on her notepad, turned, and walked over to a hotplate containing two glass pots. She grabbed one, then whisked up three white restaurant cups from a phalanx that were sitting upside down on a dishtowel.

She banged the cups down on our table and poured uneven amounts of coffee into each. Drips tracked along the table as she moved from one cup to the next.

"Milk?" I reminded.

She turned away without answering.

"You better turn on the charm, Nerburn," Dan said.

"If she comes out with a rolling pin, I'm taking off," Grover said.

"Why don't you try some of those hot lines you use on Wenonah?" I suggested to Grover.

"Nope. This is a frying-pan woman. Whack you on the side of the head."

"Wouldn't be the first time for you," Dan said. The two men chuckled and sipped at their coffee.

"Damn, this is bad!" I choked. There was a greasy film floating on the top of the brown liquid.

"Suppose you drink that yuppie Capustrino stuff?" Grover said.

"Used to be my favorite," I said. "Then I tasted yours." The thought of Grover's coffee reminded me of how far we had come in a single day. I had no sense of the miles we had traveled, but the cross-country bumping and lack of any traceable route made it seem as if we were in a different country.

The waitress slammed a half-filled plastic cup of milk down on the table beside me. "Ready to order?" she asked.

Dan and Grover both ordered pie. I opted for soup. Then I remembered Fatback.

"You don't have any bones back there, do you?" I asked.

"Bones?" she repeated, as if it were the stupidest question she had ever heard.

"Bones, like from the soup. We've got a hungry dog out in the car."

"Comes from a can," was all she answered.

"You're striking out, Nerburn," Grover laughed.

The door creaked behind us and a long shaft of sunlight cut into the room. A loud laugh broke the quiet gloom of the cafe, followed by the heavy thumping of feet and the slam of the storm door. More clumping, and an Indian couple stood in the door. The man was in his early thirties. He had a long mane of shiny black hair that reached below his shoulders. He was lurching and stumbling. The woman was as skinny as a reed and wore skin-tight jeans that seemed ready to burst. They were both drunk.

Grover and Dan paid them no mind. Their thoughts were on pie, and this was not an unfamiliar scene to them.

The couple continued their loud conversation; it made no difference that they were in a dark, quiet cafe. The man dragged a chair across the floor in front of Dan.

"Hey, brother," he oozed.

Dan nodded. The waitress was standing in the entryway to the kitchen with her hands on her hips. The six men hunched over the long table began murmuring.

The woman flopped down in the chair and hollered out to her partner, "Get me some goddamn coffee." The man had already made his way over to a cigarette machine and was reading loudly, "Minors are forbidden by law . . ."

"I want a cup of coffee."

He punched his hand down in irritation on top of the machine. "Just a goddamn minute. I'm getting some goddamn cigarettes."

He fumbled violently in his pockets.

"Hey, bro," he said to me, bypassing Grover and Dan, "You got any quarters?"

I looked quickly from Dan to Grover. For some reason it seemed to be their decision. Grover shook his head slightly.

"No, man, sorry."

"Oh," he said, and stumbled back to his table as if he had forgotten why he was there.

The waitress had decided to intervene. She snuffed her cigarette out with authority and stalked over to the table where the couple was sprawled on their seats.

She minced no words. "You got any money?"

"Yeah, we got money," said the man.

"Let's see it."

"He said we got money," the woman cut in. "Get us some goddamn coffee."

The waitress turned on her with an angry eye. "Listen, honey. If you got money, you get coffee. But until I see it, I don't think you got it."

"Aw, the hell with her," the man muttered. He swung his arm clumsily across the table, sending a plastic squeeze bottle of ketchup tumbling onto the floor. "Let's get out of here."

The two of them stood up and lurched their way toward the door. The shaft of daylight appeared, followed by a slam, and the noisy conversation disappeared into the street.

I sat glumly looking into my cup. I was embarrassed, but I wasn't sure for whom. I felt like I had witnessed a racial flaw that I had wanted to avoid. Though it made no logical sense, it was as if Dan and Grover were darkened by the same stain that had reduced that couple to a slobbering caricature, and I was witness to their common weakness.

The table of white men obviously felt the same. They had turned their collective attention to our table, and here and there a snippet of conversation about drunks or Indians rose up loud enough for us to hear. At one time I distinctly heard the phrase "prairie niggers." I looked at Dan for his response. He seemed oblivious.

"Alcohol has been bad for us," Dan said at last. "I think it was the worst thing the white man brought. It made our people crazy."

"It made those two crazy, anyway," I offered, trying to make the flaw specific to those two.

"It does that to all of us," he said.

"Why do you think that is?" I asked.

"I don't know. It was a test the Creator gave us."

"Did you ever drink?"

"Many years ago. Then a pipe carrier brought me back to the sacred circle. Now I don't drink anymore."

"I drank a lot in the Navy," Grover said. "I still go to AA."

The old white men at the other table seemed to have calmed down a bit. The disruption in their day had settled into a story they could tell their cronies, and the two old Indians and the white man at the table across the room no longer held their interest.

"Do drunks like that embarrass you?" I asked.

"It shames me," Dan said.

"It only bothers me around white people," Grover added. "I don't like them to see our brothers like that. It makes us look weak."

"We are weak," Dan said. "We are weak for alcohol. Just like white people are weak for owning things." He turned to me. "But those weaknesses are gifts, Nerburn. They are gifts, just like our strengths are gifts. Weaknesses make us strong, because they make us stand up to ourselves."

The waitress returned with the pie and soup. She slung them on the table like a dealer distributing cards.

Grover tasted his pie gingerly, grunted his approval, and began sawing into it with the edge of his fork. My soup had an ominous petroleum-like sheen on it that turned blue and green and red depending on the angle from which it was viewed.

"The trouble is not the alcohol," Dan continued. "The alcohol is a challenge to make us strong. The trouble is the way we have let it make us into victims."

"Everyone's a victim in America these days," I said. "It's our new national pastime."

"It's a bunch of shit," said Dan with uncharacteristic vehemence. "That's the white man's way. When your life isn't going right, you blame your parents or your work or something else. You talk about being burned out. You spend all kinds of money to have psychiatrists tell you why you aren't responsible for your life.

"We don't need that. It's not our way. We don't need some social worker or government professor to tell us what's wrong. We need to look to the Great Spirit for strength."

"Great Spirit needs help, sometimes," Grover said.

"Not by a bunch of damn social workers and counselors. Hell, if it wasn't for us, social workers would be out of business. The whole reservation economy is based on weakness."

He glanced over at the table of white men. Dan's volume and vehemence had piqued their interest again. They feigned concern with their sweet rolls and coffee, but you could see the bills of their caps turning toward us when Dan's voice rose.

"It really makes me angry when I see how white people have turned us into victims. I see hundreds of my people getting in line every day to be victims, blaming society or the white man for all their troubles."

"Well, there's some truth in that, isn't there?" I asked.

"Sure there is. But it's a bad truth. Being a victim is weak. I don't want to be weak. I want to be strong, like my grandfathers. My own father used to walk to the river every morning in the winter and cut a hole in the ice to get water. It didn't matter that it was forty below zero. He just did what he had to. It made him strong.

"Now our people are being taught that we were victims of society because at the same time white people had running water. So what? Before you came here we didn't have running water. We still went to the river at forty below and got water. We never thought of ourselves as victims.

"But then the social workers came and told us if we didn't have everything you did, we were all victims. A lot of Indians believe that now."

Grover had made his way through the pie in about five bites and was eyeing Dan's untouched piece.

"You can have my soup," I offered.

"He wants my pie," Dan said.

Grover reached across toward the old man's plate. "You can't talk and eat," he said, "and you sure as hell aren't going to stop talking." Dan seemed unfazed.

"The white man's way is not the Indian way. We don't need to want the same things you do. We have our way. It was given to us by our ancestors. All we have to do is follow that way. To follow your way is to say you are stronger. I don't think you are stronger. I think you are weaker.

"If there are things we can learn from you that will help us follow the way of our ancestors better, then we should learn them. If there are things we can get from you that will help us give our people a better life, we should get them. But we don't need to look at you and say that if we don't have everything that you have, then we are victims. That is giving your way too much power over our way. We should both live the way we think is right and try to help each other as best we can."

"That's a fine sentiment . . ." I began. Dan cut in before I could say more.

"It's more than a sentiment. It's the way it should be. That's the way Indian people thought it was going to be when you first came to our land. We were going to share with you. Trade ideas, knowledge. The gifts of our people for the gifts of yours.

"We listened to you. But you never listened to us. All you did is steal from us."

The old men at the other table had dropped their pretense of disinterest. Dan's voice had risen to the point where you could hear him throughout the whole cafe.

"Hey, old man, calm down," Grover whispered. "You're as loud as those drunks."

"The hell with them. I'm old. Let them think I'm crazy."

"They might be right," Grover said.

Dan forged ahead. "If we never would have listened, we wouldn't have had drunks. We wouldn't have had alcohol or half the problems we have now. We didn't have those before the white man came. Made us a bunch of damn blanket Indians hanging around the trading post looking for a handout. That's when it all started. Now we're hanging around government offices looking for food stamps."

The waitress had turned on her stool and was leaning against the wall with a bemused smirk on her face. The men at the other table had set down their coffee cups and were staring at Dan with undisguised interest. Two dramas in one day were too much to hope for. This would give them almost a whole winter's worth of conversation.

Dan was not to be deterred. His mind was racing and his tongue was not far behind. "Do you know why we listened to the early missionaries? Because they were strong. They slept on the ground with us. They didn't make beds off the floor and try to shut out the world. You may not believe it, but they understood our life and they liked it. They knew we were living close to the earth. From our standpoint the best of them just made their religion to fit with ours, like a hand fits into a glove.

"It was when the other ones came that the real trouble began. The ones who were drunk with their own vision of truth and couldn't see ours. The ones who needed houses with floors and then lifted their beds off the floors and then put a mattress on the bed so they could be as far away from the earth as possible. These people never knew who we were.

"Now a hundred years later you've got us to lift our floors off the ground and our beds off the floors and to shut out nature and to get our food in cellophane wrappings. You tell us that we are victims if we don't have all of those things. Then you go out and go camping and sleep on the ground and say you are living like the Indians did. It is just another way of taking our culture from us. You try to make us feel sad about what we don't have while you try to claim what we do have for yourselves."

"Eat your damn pie or I will," Grover said. There was a humorous gleam in his eye, but his voice betrayed a strained nervousness. He did not like to let things out around white people. Dan would have none of it. He brushed the comment away like a gnat.

"Think of that Thoreau fellow. I've read some of his books. He went out and lived in a shack and looked at a pond. Now he's one of your heroes. If I go out and live in a shack and look at a pond, pretty soon I'll have so many damn social workers beating on my door that I won't be able to sleep.

"They'll start scribbling in some damn notebook: 'No initiative. No self-esteem.' They'll write reports, get grants, start some government program with a bunch of forms. Say it's to help us.

"That's what happened with allotment. They said they were trying to help us. They cut up our reservations into chunks and told us we had to be farmers. When we didn't farm, they said we were lazy. I don't remember anything about Thoreau being a farmer. He mostly talked about how great it was to do nothing, then he went and ate dinner at his friend's house. He didn't want to farm and he's a hero. We don't want to farm and we're lazy. Send us to a social worker."

The waitress was tiring of the scene. Two bellowing Indians in one day were quite enough. She ripped the check off her order pad and walked over to the table. "Anything else?"

"Yeah. I want some more coffee," Dan said.

Grover's eyes widened in shock. "Let's just get the hell out of here."

"I need some coffee to wash down my pie," Dan commented. It was no longer possible to tell whether he was serious or joking. The waitress made an odd face to no one in particular and went to get the coffee pot.

Dan turned his attention directly to me. "See, Nerburn, I want you to understand this. White people don't know what they want. They want these big houses and all kinds of things, then they want to be close to the earth, too. They get cabins, they go hunting, they go camping, they say it makes them close to the earth. But they really think it's okay only because they have all these other things. We Indians, we live in cabins and hunt, but it's not okay because we don't turn around and go back to big houses and big jobs. We don't need two lives like white people. The only reason that Thoreau fellow is a hero is because he lived two lives. Otherwise he just would have been a bum. They would have sent social workers to his house."

Dan's logic had reached a Byzantine state. I no longer knew whether or not he was making sense. I just nodded and stared at the iridescent sheen on my soup. Grover was hunching his head into his shoulders and the old men across the way were conferring amongst themselves about the wisdom of what the crazy Indian was saying. The waitress stood at a distance holding the coffee pot while Tammy Wynette was belting out some big-lunged song from the boom box.

Suddenly Dan's voice got very quiet, like a man sharing a secret. "This is what you've got to remember." I could see the men at the table craning their necks to hear his words over Tammy's sorrowful wails. "For white people there are only two types of Indians. Drunken bums and noble Indians. In the old days, we used to be savages, but that's gone. Now it's drunks and noble Indians. I like the white men better who think we are all drunks. At least they're looking at us as people. They're saying what they see, not what they want to see. Then when they meet one of us who's not a drunk, they have to deal with us.

"The ones who see us all as wise men don't care about Indians at all. They just care about the idea of Indians. It's just another way of stealing our humanity and making us into a fantasy that fits the needs of white people.

"You want to know how to be like Indians? Live close to the earth. Get rid of some of your things. Help each other. Talk to the Creator. Be quiet more. Listen to the earth instead of building things on it all the time.

"Don't blame other people for your troubles and don't try to make people into something they're not."

He sat back in his chair with an air of finality. "There. I'm done," he said.

"About time," Grover grumbled.

I just nodded in a half-hearted gesture of assent. The internal logic, or lack of it, in Dan's rant had left me reeling. The table of men, aware that their interest might be noticed, made a great show of being involved in a private conversation.

"Like the soup?" the waitress asked caustically as she whisked away my untouched bowl.

"Shiny," I answered. For the first time, she cracked a tiny smile. She took the bills I had laid out and went off to the cash register. She returned shortly and dropped a big brown bag on the table.

I looked quizzically at her. "For the dog," she said. Then she winked and walked back to her stool without ever looking at us again.

Chapter 16

The Stranger

I made Grover stop at the convenience store so I could make my call; the phone in the cafe had hung on the wall only about two feet away from where the six men in feed caps were sitting. I figured they had enough stories without hearing me try to explain to my wife how I wasn't coming home because my truck was being dismantled by a giant while I drove across fields in an old Buick with two Indians and an arthritic dog.

When I returned to the car, Grover and Dan were engaged in an animated conversation that had Dan laughing in his old good-hearted cackle.

"You talked more than a white man," Grover was saying.

"Gives those old bastards something to talk about."

"Yeah, it gave them another old bastard to talk about."

Dan cackled his approval.

"Straighten things out?" Grover said as I pulled the door shut behind me.

"I guess so," I answered. It had been a sad conversation, full of unspoken angers and longings and sadnesses. My boy had gotten on the line and begun pouring out stories of his little friends and toys he had gotten and birthday parties he was going to attend. My wife had tried to be supportive, but there was a hard distance in her voice. She was carrying too much on her own. She needed me home.

"You've got to just let it go, Nerburn," Grover said.

His flip attitude angered me. I wanted to recede into my own private hurt. Dan said nothing.

We wheeled back onto the main highway. For reasons that I did not understand, Grover headed east again. The route seemed completely haphazard and without purpose. But I didn't care. My cares were in my mind; what Grover chose to do did not interest me. The Buick settled into its eight-cylinder throb and the three of us lapsed into silence. Fatback was gnawing furiously on one of the bones that the waitress had given us.

We rode without speaking for almost an hour. I gave myself over once more to the rising hills and distant vistas. My child's voice haunted me.

The "little trip" had developed into a routine. Grover determined the route. Dan determined when we would stop and for how long. I rode along in the back with my canine companion, taking notes, observing, and staring out at the plains.

Gradually the pain of my distant family eased. The subtle power of the landscape washed over me once more. The ebbs and swells of the land, and the lure of the distant horizon had a soporific effect on me. I nestled down into my corner of Grover's commodious back seat and let the great sweep of the land hypnotize me.

The waning afternoon passed in this fashion, with no discernible rhythm or moments of individual consequence. Perhaps I had dozed, or merely drifted into deep reverie. But when Dan blurted out, "Go in there," I jumped in my seat like a man jolted from sleep.

Grover slowed the car so quickly that my stomach churned. We had been descending a long, gradual hill, and the car had to fight to come to a halt. We were on a winding drop into a river valley. Far ahead I could see the landscape on the other side of the river stretching out in unrelenting flatness.

The cause of Dan's outburst was a buff-colored, handpainted billboard with a geometric border of blue, yellow, green, and white diamonds. On it was written, "Sitting Bull Burial Site Monument."

"Go in there," Dan repeated.

Grover obliged, and the old Buick dipped and heaved as it made the right angle turn into a winding roadway that snaked back into the hills.

"I want you to see this," Dan said with authority. He stiffened in his seat like a man coming to attention. "Sitting Bull was the Great One, Nerburn. He only gave up because his people were hungry. He was the greatest one, along with Crazy Horse."

I didn't know much about Sitting Bull. In my white education he had been but another of a parade of chiefs with noble visages and exotic names who had appeared as a test question in some historical gallop through the American frontier period. I did remember that he had somehow been involved in Buffalo Bill's Wild West Show, and that had seemed to me a demeaning experience for a man who had once been a leader of a free people.

"He was a great leader," I said vaguely.

"The treaties were a bunch of crap," Dan spat, as if that were a logical response to my comment.

"They were supposed to give us land. But how can you give someone something they already own? All the treaties did was bind the Indian people to the white man's laws. Sitting Bull figured that out. He wasn't going to sign anything that claimed to give him something he already owned. He knew that all he was signing was a paper that made him give up something. So he wouldn't sign them."

In the distance a solitary figure was walking along the road.

"Looks like an Indian," Grover observed.

"Should pick him up," Dan said.

As we got closer the man came into sharper focus. He was young and angular; a full-blood, maybe thirty, with the sharp, chiseled features of an athlete. He was wearing jeans and a T-shirt and had a black vinyl or leather jacket slung over his right shoulder. He walked with the agile lope of one who covered great distances on foot as a matter of course.

Grover slowed down as we drove up beside him. Dan gestured him toward the back seat. The man bent down and looked in the car, then grabbed the door handle in an easy, practiced swing.

He got in the car and gave Dan a nod. Other than that he didn't say a word. His crisp white T-shirt clung tight against his sinewy torso. His jeans were held up by a tooled leather belt with a huge oval turquoise and silver buckle.

He looked over at me, then reached in the pocket of the jacket he had been carrying over his shoulder. He pulled out a pack of Lucky Strikes and wordlessly offered one to me.

I was in a momentary panic. I didn't want a cigarette, but was unsure if perhaps this was not a gesture of thanks and respect.

I declined.

He reached the pack over the front seat. Dan extracted two cigarettes and handed one to Grover. Grover nodded and slipped the cigarette into the corner of his mouth. Still, nobody uttered a word.

The silence was disconcerting to me. Moments before Dan had been warming to the subject of Sitting Bull and had given every indication of launching into a lengthy discourse on the matter. Now, with the arrival of the stranger, all conversation had ceased. We were riding in Indian silence — unselfconscious, wordless, and without pretense. I felt like a complete outsider.

I studied the new passenger out of the corner of my eye. He had the handsomeness of the land. He was burnished brown, almost mahogany, with gigantic, knobbed hands that hung like axheads from his sinewy forearms. Though he was skinny, every muscle on his body stood out, as if the hot sun and endless hard labor had pared every ounce of extraneous fat from his body. But despite his raw physicality, there was something refined, even feminine about his manner. He had the physical presence and readiness of a large cat.

He pulled a comb out of his front pocket and ran it meticulously through his shiny, black 1950s hairdo. Then, in a practiced automatic gesture, he squared his massive hands over his head and boxed and shaped the hair above his forehead into a blocky, protruding wave.

His face was taut but lined. Smile or squint crinkles had worn their way in around his eyes, though sitting in the car he showed no expression. He reached over and scratched Fatback's head without bothering to let her smell his hand. He had obviously spent his life around animals and had no fear of the unexpected.

Grover negotiated the serpentine road with obvious relish. These easy, rolling curves of backroads America were the stuff for which his huge Buick was made.

"Going up to the grave site?" I asked. I was hoping that some minor conversation might compensate for any perceived snub that was contained in my refusal of the cigarette. Dan stiffened in his seat.

"Getting out up here," the man answered laconically. Dan was rigid.

I had backed myself into a corner. Dan was clearly uncomfortable about something, and the man's clipped answer indicated that either by choice or by nature he was not a talker. Grover just wheeled the car around the looping curves. He was not going to help me out.

I wedged myself into the corner of the seat and stared out the window. My simple sentence hung like a dark spider in the middle of the car. What had I said and what had I done? And how could it be so pregnant with significance when it had had so little content?

"Here's good," the man said. Grover pulled to a stop and the man stepped out as lithely as he had gotten in. There were no "thank-yous" or "goodbyes" or ritual pleasantries of any sort. Yet there had been no threat, no danger, no animosity anywhere.

"White man's disease," Dan snapped to me as the Buick got underway.

"We call it politeness," I said testily. "I asked him where he was going."

"No you didn't. You asked him if he was going to the grave site. Some things run deep, Nerburn."

"Like what?" I said, nonplussed.

Dan spoke in a dark anger. "You know what happened to Sitting Bull?"

"No," I admitted, though I saw no connection between the question and my apparent *faux pas*.

"He was killed by the damn reservation police. Bunch of blanket Indians afraid of losing their food rations."

"Called them 'coffee coolers' in those days," Grover interjected, the unlit cigarette still dangling from his mouth. "Good name for you, Nerburn."

Dan was not amused. "Sitting Bull wouldn't sign the treaties. He knew they'd make blanket Indians out of all of us. If it hadn't been for the damn blanket Indians . . ." He snorted angrily through his teeth. "If they would have listened to Sitting Bull and stayed with him, we never would have signed away the Black Hills."

I wanted to say that it was likely that the Black Hills would have been taken some other way, but I didn't feel like contradicting Dan's thinking, wherever it was leading. He was far too angry.

"He was a real chief, Nerburn. He didn't hate the white man. He just loved the Indian people. He knew if we had anything to do with the *wasichus*, we'd turn white ourselves.

"Do you know what he said about the Indians who lived in the white agencies?"

"No."

"I remember the speech. It was one of those I learned when I was young. I learned it in English, too. It went like this. 'I do not wish to be shut up in a corral. All agency Indians I have seen were worthless. They are neither red warriors nor white farmers. They are neither wolf nor dog.'"

He turned in his seat to face me. "Do you see what I mean, Nerburn?"

"No," I answered. I was still peeved at being berated for a simple act of civility.

"That's what happened to us. We listened to the white man. Now we're neither wolf nor dog. Sitting Bull was right."

"So what does this have to do with the guy we picked up?" I ventured.

"Lot of people up in Fort Yates are related to those policemen who tried to arrest Sitting Bull," Dan said. "It was right around here he was camped. The agent sent Indian police to get Sitting Bull. Sitting Bull's people were just trying to go down to see what the Ghost Dance was all about. But the agent didn't want him to see. He thought he'd make trouble. They didn't want Sitting Bull to do anything except be a damn farmer, so they sent Indian police to arrest him. The police shot Sitting Bull in the head. Bunch of cowards. So some of Sitting Bull's band shot the Indian policemen. Killed a bunch of them. You just don't talk about it too much unless you know who you're talking to."

"After a hundred years?" I exclaimed.

"Same thing as the Civil War for white people in the South. Sometimes in towns where things happened there are things you just don't bring up."

I shook my head. "You pick the guy up and then you don't talk to him because he might be related to a policeman who's been dead for a hundred years?"

"That's right," he said harshly. "I don't care if you understand it. For Indian people the family matters. So does the clan. It doesn't stop mattering just because someone dies. It doesn't hurt to have respect for the past. Things aren't dead just because they're over.

"Besides, we're not like white people who have to fill up every damn second of silence with a bunch of talk."

"Okay. Point taken," I said. I didn't want to engage him in any further argument. I turned my attention to Grover. "Tell me really, Grover. Is Dan overreacting?"

Grover looked at me through the rearview mirror. "The old man knows things. I don't know. Only time I've ever gone into Fort Yates is to get a taco. They've got one of those Taco John places there. It doesn't hurt to keep your mouth shut, though."

A momentary image passed through my mind of people standing in sullen silence at Taco John's, eyeing their linemates suspiciously and brooding over past hurts. I was tempted to say that maybe they should have two windows — one for Sitting Bull's relatives and one for the relatives of the policemen — but it seemed way beyond the bounds of good taste.

"You don't understand, Nerburn," Dan said. He was still on a roll. "That's why I'm trying to teach you things. Everyone acts like they're proud of Sitting Bull. 'He was a great chief. He finished off Custer.' All the Indians will tell you that. But that's for white men. Underneath people still remember, especially the old ones. And if the young ones don't remember, they ought to. It's a hell of a lot more important than the kind of tennis shoes you wear."

I said nothing, but Dan wouldn't drop it.

"How'd your grandfather die?" he said.

"I don't know," I answered. "He just died. Lived a hard life. Drank too much."

"Well, what if he'd been shot in the head for wanting to go to church, and the guy who shot him had been given a medal?"

"I'd think it was wrong."

"Would you be angry?"

"At what happened, yes. But probably not at the grandchildren of the shooter."

"Well, Indian people don't forget."

"Or forgive," I muttered.

Dan heard. "It doesn't have to do with forgiveness. It has to do with honor. I tried to tell you that. Forgiveness just sets you free. Lets you think only about yourself. Honor makes you strong. It binds you to your past. Sitting Bull is alive in the hearts of his people. That is how they honor him. They don't honor people who dragged him out of his bed naked and shot him in the head so the *wasichu* agent would give them a medal.

"But his people had to run away to Pine Ridge after the shooting. It's the policemen Indians up here. The ones who shot him. That's what I mean about blanket Indians. Now they get all misty and talk about how great Sitting Bull was, but they were willing to shoot him in the head so they would get their rations."

I marveled at Dan's ferocity, and the way the past and present wove themselves together into a seamless experience in his imagination. He was right; it was like the South and the Civil War, or the Vichy French and the Resistance. There were currents that ran too deep, bones that should not be dug up. Even if his caution were a paranoid delusion, at least it made sense by his own terms.

I turned back to look one more time at the stranger. He was just a tiny figure in the distance disappearing from view as we made a final turn. He was still walking on the road in that rhythmic, loping gate, heading exactly in the direction we were driving.

Chapter 17

Leaders and Rulers

Sitting Bull's monument was an obelisk on a promontory overlooking the Missouri River valley. It stood against the cloudless blue sky with a proud singularity. Though bizarrely classical in its concept, it had a solitary nobility that seemed strangely appropriate for a man who stood alone against a conquering nation.

In front of it was a square stone pillar topped by a garish, ill-carved bust that looked like the work of a junior-high student. I assumed it was a labor of love by some self-trained Indian artist who had wanted to commemorate Sitting Bull in his own humble way.

Since unsolicited comments were not standing me in good stead at that particular moment, I kept my counsel. I kept reminding myself of the advice one of my dear friends had given to his jabbering ten-year-old daughter: "Just because it comes into your mind doesn't mean you have to say it."

Grover and I stood silently in front of the monuments while Dan wandered off on his own. "This one's by that guy who's carving the Crazy Horse sculpture," Grover said as he pointed to the bust.

"You mean the mountain?" I asked, incredulous.

"Yeah. Same guy."

Grover was referring to a Polish immigrant named Ziolkowski who had wanted to help the Indian people memorialize one of their own great leaders in the same way that four white presidents had been commemorated on the side of Mount Rushmore. Self-trained, intensely proud, and with a will of steel, he had begun blocking a mountain in the northern Black Hills into a likeness of a mounted Crazy Horse pointing toward the sacred lands. He was now dead, but his sons were carrying on the task. The sentiment was noble and the task gigantic. But the thought of a sculpture of the quality of this bust as big as a mountain made me shudder.

I didn't have long to contemplate. Dan returned and stood beside us.

"You know why this is here?" he asked.

"What? The carving?"

"No. The whole thing."

I admitted I didn't.

"After Sitting Bull was killed the blanket Indians were so damn scared that they didn't even dare demand a decent burial for him. The soldiers put him in a pine box and threw him in a hole. Left him wrapped in a bloody blanket. I heard they even threw some chemical stuff on his body so he'd decompose faster. This was a man who should have been honored by his people and they were throwing chemicals on him so he would rot fast.

"They gave the policemen who had been killed this big military funeral with all the blanket Indians crying and mourning. Buried them in the Catholic cemetery. Then they stole everything Sitting Bull's people had. This was all up at Fort Yates.

"Sitting Bull's people didn't want to leave him up there. They wanted to take him down here where he was born. I remember hearing about it when I was a boy. Then a few years ago they decided to flood the whole place where Fort Yates is. Make a dam and flood it. Sitting Bull's relatives weren't going to let them flood his grave. They stole his bones and brought them up here. Buried him in his own land. Set his spirit free."

Dan reached in his pocket and took out the cigarette that the stranger had given him. He rolled it between his fingers until the tobacco came out. He walked up to the obelisk and began placing little piles of it on all four sides. Grover did the same. Then they held some up to the sky. The wind scattered it as they let it loose. Finally, they dropped some to the ground.

We walked back to the car in silence. Fatback was lying in the long shadows near the back tire with her head on her paws. We all got in and headed back down the winding road. The stranger we had given the ride was nowhere to be seen.

Dan was thinking hard. I could see him mouthing words low under his breath. Then he spoke.

"I want you to understand this, Nerburn. I don't think you've got it figured out. Sitting Bull was a leader. He was a real chief. People followed him because he was great. He never won any election or was appointed by any government official. That's not how you get to be a leader."

"You're saying the policemen didn't have any real authority."

"That's right. They were policemen because the government told them they were. Gave them uniforms and a job. It didn't have anything to do with the old way, where it was an honor you earned."

"Unfortunately, that's the way the white system works," I said, though not with conviction.

"It doesn't work too damn well," he responded. "At least for Indian people. We had a system that worked, then the white man came along with his elections and laws and now we've got one that doesn't. They should have left us alone."

"So why doesn't it work?" I asked. I was curious to hear Dan's ideas on government.

"Aw, it's too complicated to explain," he said. "You've got to know too much about the old days."

"No. Try me," I said. "I'm interested."

He heaved a weary sigh and held his two hands up like a man comparing the weights of two different objects.

"There are leaders and there are rulers. We Indians are used to leaders. When our leaders don't lead, we walk away from them. When they lead well, we stay with them.

"White people never understood this. Your system makes people rulers by law, even if they are not leaders. We have had to accept your way, because you made us Indians make constitutions and form governments. But we don't like it and we don't think it is right.

"How can a calendar tell us how long a person is a leader? That's crazy. A leader is a leader as long as the people believe in him and as long as he is the best person to lead us. You can only lead as long as the people will follow.

"In the past when we needed a warrior we made a warrior our leader. But when the war was over and we needed a healer to lead us, he became our leader. Or maybe we needed a great speaker or a deep thinker.

"The warrior knew his time had passed and he didn't pretend to be our leader beyond the time he was needed. He was proud to serve his people and he knew when it was time to step aside. If he won't step aside, people will just walk away from him. He cannot make himself a leader except by leading people in the way they want to be lead.

"That's why Sitting Bull was a leader. He was needed by the people and the people followed him. He was brave. He was smart. He knew how to fight when he had to. And he understood what the white man was all about. People saw that he could not be tricked by the white man, so they followed.

"That's why the U.S. government hated him so much. It wasn't just that he set a trap for Custer. Anyone could have done that. It was because he was a leader and people listened to him, and he wouldn't listen to the U.S. government. He listened to the needs of his people."

I nodded my assent.

Dan continued. "If people didn't want to follow his way, that was fine. They could follow another way. That's what happened with Gall. He'd fought with Sitting Bull and Crazy Horse against Custer. But he decided he had to work with the white people if he didn't want all the Indians to be killed. So he left and went his own way. I think he was wrong, but that was his choice. If enough people had decided not to follow Sitting Bull, then he wouldn't have been a leader anymore. But people still followed him, so he stayed a leader."

"It sounds utopian," I said.

Dan looked perplexed. "Perfect," I amended.

"It wasn't perfect. But it sure as hell worked," he went on. "That was the Indian way. A person wasn't a leader because they got votes. They were a leader because the people would follow them. "The same with teachers."

The example seemed pointed. I imagined he was thinking about me teaching Indian children at Red Lake while I was too obtuse to understand why a hundred-year-old grievance should determine the way you greet a stranger. "A person wasn't a teacher because they had been elected or got a certificate. They were a teacher because they knew something and were respected. If they didn't know enough, they weren't teachers. Or if we didn't need to know what they knew, we didn't go to them. Now you send us teachers and you tell us to send our children, when we aren't even sure what the teachers know. We don't even know if they are good people who will build up the hearts of our children. All we know is that they are teachers because someone gave them a piece of paper saying they had taken courses about teaching. Do you follow me?"

"Yes," I said, almost adding, "more than you know."

"What we want to know is what kind of person they are and what they have in their hearts to share. Telling us they have a paper that lets them teach is like putting a fancy wrapping on a box. We want to know what's in that box. An empty box with a fancy wrapper is still an empty box.

"We just don't like people standing in front of us and telling us what to do. Teachers, governments, anything else. We will say who our leaders are. They can't make themselves leaders and laws can't make them leaders for us.

"Those police who shot Sitting Bull, they got scared. They were like little children who were afraid they would be punished if they didn't do what the false leaders said. They thought they wouldn't get food. So they did what the false leaders — the law leaders — said, even though they knew it was wrong.

"There are all these stories about how the police were crying when they shot Sitting Bull. If they thought it was wrong, they shouldn't have shot him. They should have listened to their real leaders, not to their law leaders. They didn't understand the difference between leaders and rulers."

As usual, Dan had wound his way through the hills and valleys of his own logic to arrive at a destination.

"I understand why people followed Sitting Bull," I said. "But he was a chief. Didn't people have to follow a chief?"

"The chiefs weren't like that," Dan answered. "They had to earn their respect. At least with our people. You might be a chief because your father was a chief, but if you were a coward or not a good man, people would just move away from you. You would be a chief only to yourself. To be a chief you had to be a leader.

"You know, this was a lot of the problem with the treaties. Lots of times our real leaders didn't want to sign the treaties. But your government needed to have a piece of paper, so they found an Indian who would sign a piece of paper and they told him he was a leader. Maybe he was from our tribe, but he wasn't a leader unless we all said he was. He couldn't sign that piece of paper any more than someone down the street can sign a piece of paper giving away your house. These men were false chiefs. They were law chiefs, made up by white people who needed one Indian to speak for everybody.

"But no real Indian leader would try to speak for everybody before hearing from everybody. He might get the elders together, or the council of chiefs. It depended on the tribe.

"Then they listened to everyone. Everyone could speak. If someone didn't like the decision that was made, they could leave. If the chief made a decision enough people disagreed with, they could make another chief. All they did was move their tepees near to the new man's, and he was their leader.

"I would rather we had this old way, where the wisest people got together and discussed. If there was one person in the tribe who knew more than any other, he was raised up.

"But now you make us do it differently. You tell us we have to elect a leader to represent us, and he has to represent us in everything. He is supposed to be wise about everything because he is responsible for everything. Even if we don't want him to speak for us on some matter, he gets to because it says so in the constitution you made us write.

"That is not the way it should be. Good leaders wait to be called and they give up their power when they are no longer needed. Selfish men and fools put themselves first and keep their power until someone throws them out. It is no good to have a way where selfish men and fools fight with each other to be leaders, while the good ones watch.

"You made us follow this way, so now we have no government worth the name. Our leaders have no power; our rulers are not leaders.

"That is why Sitting Bull was great. He did not rule. He led."

Chapter 18

Drunk on Jesus

Dan seemed to have finished. Grover grunted his approval. He reached across and dug into the glove compartment. "Got any matches?" he asked.

"I don't have any," I said.

"I need a smoke."

Dan rummaged in his pockets. "Fresh out," he announced.

"Damn!" Grover cursed. "That Indian made me want a cigarette. Got to go into Mobridge to get some fire and smokes."

I could see that Dan wasn't thrilled with the idea. I was gradually realizing that he didn't get to white towns often, and that they made him uncomfortable.

The sun was a flaming orange ball behind us as we descended to the Missouri River basin. The hills were darkening from brown to gold, and the long fingers of evening shadows were creeping down the draws. On the far side of the river you could see Mobridge huddled like an outpost against the banks of the river. Behind it in the distance the rich alluvial farmlands shimmered in the late afternoon sun.

The difference between the two sides of the Missouri was astonishing. It was a difference of spirit as much as of geology. The land to the east had been formed by the glacier. It had been scraped inch by inch into a land of endurance. If you worked it, tilled it, struggled with it, if you gave it your life, inch by inch, it would yield. It was a land for farmers and workers, not for dreamers.

To the west of the river the golden hills of the Missouri Breaks rose into the lyrical swells and undulations of a great dried seabed. It was at this river that the glacier had stopped, and meaning had been washed across the land rather than ground into it. It was a land of surprises and guile, of hiding places and rolling distances that beckoned the eye ever onward with the coursing of the sun. It was a land of freedom more than labor, of hope more than perseverance.

In a word, it was the West.

This fact had not been lost on Grover and Dan. "Sure is different on the other side," Grover observed as we approached the erector-set bridge that spanned the Missouri. I told them about the glacier and how it was at the Missouri that the great ice sheet had stopped.

"Now, that's interesting," Grover said with obvious sincerity. "I guess you're good for something after all."

I smiled weakly. Since the start of the visit everything I thought or knew had been devalued to almost nothing. Who I was, where I came from, and how I saw the world had been of no interest to anybody. I felt like I had no self. With the exception of prodding Dan for information and making rough attempts at humor, I had essentially tried to disappear. Grover's simple acknowledgment, barbed though it was, made me swell with a tiny pride.

It occurred to me that this sense of irrelevance and worthlessness was what most Indians probably experienced constantly around white people. To be agreeable or invisible was the best one could hope for. What one knew mattered little, because it was irrelevant. All that mattered about Indians in our current climate was earth-sated pronouncements of wisdom. I could see why Dan was more willing to be seen as a drunk than as a wise man. To be seen as a drunk was at least to be seen; to be seen as a wise man was to be reduced to a projection of a white fantasy.

Dan's face had frozen into a scowl as we approached Mobridge. He jerked his head from side to side in irritable little movements. Billboards had begun sprouting up along the road, announcing various goods and services. Their ungainly presence seemed an affront to the windswept landscape.

A highway sign declared that we were approaching the Mobridge Indian Bible College. "Look at that," Dan pointed.

"What is it?" I asked.

"One of those places where they turn Indians into missionaries. As bad as the old boarding schools."

"Don't like Christianity much, do you?" I said.

"That's not true," he retorted. "I like Jesus. Ever since I was a little boy and I learned about him I liked him. He was *wakan*. He should have been an Indian."

It was a sentiment I had heard before.

"He didn't own anything," Dan continued. "He slept outside on the earth. He moved around all the time. He shared everything he got. He even talked to the Great Spirit as his Father. He was just like an Indian.

"I loved him, Nerburn. I still love him. I still talk to him. Those were things I learned from the priests and the sisters. They were good.

"But I don't like what the churches did to my people. When I see Indians standing in front of crosses it makes me sad. It is like they are such good people and their belief is so strong. Why can't it still be our old belief? Why was that taken away from us? The old ones shouldn't have to be begging Jesus to listen to them."

He shifted slightly in his seat so he could see my reaction. I gave none.

"I guess it's a good thing Jesus wasn't an Indian," he continued.

"The U.S. government would have hunted him down and killed him. They would have killed him like they killed Crazy Horse and Sitting Bull. Just another dead Indian troublemaker."

Dan stared out at the wide, sluggish expanse of the Missouri. I could see his reflection in the glass of the window. There was a pain in his placid expression.

"You know why Sitting Bull was camped in the hills up there?"

"No," I answered.

"He was going to find out if the Messiah was coming. You've heard of the Ghost Dance?"

"Yes."

"The Ghost Dance was what Sitting Bull wanted to know about. That's why he was down here, why he had left the agency up in Fort Yates. He said he wanted to 'know that pray.' He wanted to see if it was good for his people.

"You know, the Ghost Dance was a dance about Jesus. I don't care what any white book tells you. There was a man out west — a Paiute, name of Wovoka — who said he had died and met the *Wanekia*."

"*Wanekia*?" I said.

"Messiah," Dan explained. "I don't know. I've heard it a couple of ways, that maybe this Wovoka said he was the *Wanekia*, or maybe he was just a messenger to tell that the Messiah was coming. It doesn't matter. What matters is that all the people believed that the Messiah was coming again, just like the missionaries and priests had taught. Only, he was coming to the Indians this time because the white people had killed him the last time he came.

"The white books say that this Wovoka was a crazy man and that all the Indians who followed him were crazy. But let me tell you. The Indian people weren't looking for a man named Wovoka. They didn't care what his name was. They were looking for a man who they would know because of the nail holes in his hands and the spear wound in his side. Who does that sound like?"

"It sounds like Jesus," I said, stating the obvious.

"That's right. The Indian people were looking for Jesus. Maybe he had a new name, but it was still Jesus. The people got excited because they loved Jesus and they wanted to welcome him better than when he had come to the white people."

His voice got soft and distant. "They weren't going to kill him on a cross. They were going to give him feasts. They believed in him. They were going to honor him. That's why they were dancing. Wovoka had said that they had to dance, then they would be saved.

"Sitting Bull just wanted to know about this Messiah for himself, to find out if this dance was *wakan*.

"The people were so excited. They never believed the Great Spirit had abandoned them to be starved and killed by the white people who were coming into the land. They wanted Jesus to come to help them. They were just believing like the white people had taught them."

Dan was almost completely inside his mind by now. He stared emptily out the window.

"But the government got angry. They had killed us because we wouldn't believe in Jesus. Now they were going to kill us because we did. All the women. All the people. So full of hope. Believing what the white man said even more than the white man believed it."

If it had been within his character to shed tears, he would have been crying.

"But it made the government angry. The Indians had hope. If you have hope you come alive again. We had all become dead in our hearts. When the government saw us coming alive again, it had to kill us. We could not have hope. If we had hope we might have dreams. We could not be allowed to have dreams.

"They called it a craze or a frenzy. That was what the papers said. But you know what? You know what is never said? A lot of the white people were scared. They thought we might be right.

They believed in Jesus, too. They thought maybe Jesus was coming back and he was coming to the Indian people.

"The white people knew they were trying to get rich and weren't living like Jesus had told them. They made up excuses. When they looked at us they saw the way Jesus had said to live. We made their excuses look false.

"They were killing us and chasing us from our land just so they could get rich. In their hearts they knew what they were doing was bad. They were afraid we were right! They were afraid Jesus was coming to help us!"

Watching him was like watching a night sea swirl and change. His deep anger would rise, then subside, then emerge again somewhere else, only to be washed over by a great sorrow.

"That was our crime. We believed too much. We believed so much that the white man got scared of our belief. All we were doing was dancing. We were told that if we danced the Ghost Dance and believed, the buffalo would come back. We would see our ancestors. We would get to have our old way of life.

"Our people kept dancing. They wouldn't stop. They just got in a circle and danced until they couldn't stand. Sometimes they had visions. It was *wakan*. The spirit was very close.

"The white people were going crazy. Everything was wrong. The Indians had been broken, now our spirits were rising. We had been cut apart and put on separate lands, now we were together again in the dance. Some of the young men were getting braver. They said the Messiah would help us get back our lands. They were ready to fight.

"We were drunk this time. But it was good drunk. We were drunk on Jesus."

He paused and inhaled deeply — a man trying to take charge of his own thoughts.

"We were making Jesus our own. We were bringing him into our hearts. What was so wrong with that? The only thing you ever gave us was Jesus, and then when we took him and made him one of us you said we couldn't have him."

He lapsed into silence. This time it was not a quiet peaceful silence, but a dark, slow-running silence like the turgid Missouri flowing by outside. The whole car seemed bleak. Fatback looked up with guilty eyes. Grover stared willfully at the road ahead of him.

"You won't even let us have hope," he said finally. "There are no armies to free us. No governments to help us. We cry out and nobody hears us. We starve and nobody cares. All we have left is hope. But if you see hope you kill that, too."

The Bible College stood off to our left. It was made up of long brick dormitory-like buildings set among stands of towering oaks and cottonwoods. It looked like an old military post. I wondered what the students inside those rooms thought about the Ghost Dance.

Dan's words were fading like the last rays of daylight. "We believed too much. We loved Jesus too much. We made him our leader. You didn't want him to be our leader. When we went to see if he was coming back, you killed us. All the women. All the little children. So much hope. Dead. All dead."

The brittle neon of bottle shops and restaurants greeted us as we made the wide turn onto the main thoroughfare through Mobridge. Twilight had overtaken the streets. Dan was morose and silent.

Grover stopped at a supermarket and disappeared into its harsh white glare. His step was stiff. He looked small and out of place — an old Indian in a cowboy shirt and cowboy boots limping his way into the packaged abundance of American culture.

"I'm going to let Fatback out," I told Dan. He waved me off halfheartedly. His chin rested heavy on his right hand. His eyes were silent and distant.

Fatback rushed off toward the edge of the parking lot. After a few steps she squatted and urinated against the tire of a pickup truck. Two old women who were walking across the lot slowed and glowered at me.

"My mother's dog," I said. They smiled and proceeded. Fatback stuck her nose to the ground and charged off toward some unknown destination. Out of the corner of my eye I could see Dan staring blankly into the purple twilight.

I walked in the direction where Fatback had disappeared. The heavy smell of river filled my nostrils. It was fetid, rich, indolent.

Waves of longing broke over me. Crossing back over the Missouri had turned me toward home. Dan's jocularity and anger had given way to a deep weariness of spirit. Sitting there in the car with his long, stringy hair, he looked every bit the old man, stubborn but broken, empty of dreams, devoid of hope. He was tired. We were all tired. It had been a long day.

Fatback reemerged dragging a greasy white fast food bag. "Give it up, Fatback," I said. She skulked off with her booty and crawled under a bush at the edge of the parking lot. Through the supermarket window I could see Grover wheeling a shopping cart toward the checkout counter.

I didn't think I could go much further.

Chapter 19

Pushing

The hills were paper cutouts against the darkening sky as we drove back across the bridge into the growing western night. Within minutes Mobridge was just a memory. The round moon bathed the hills in silver and left the draws in purple dark. It was a landscape painted by giants.

"Got a ways to go," Grover announced. Dan just sat in his seat and smoked.

"How far?" I asked.

"Hour or so. Maybe two."

"Mostly roads?"

Grover laughed. "All but the last part."

Powerpoles stood like silent crucifixes along the side of the highway. The only movement inside the car was the needle of the speedometer making its steady arc against the ghostly numbers on the dashboard.

Dan's mood had not improved. I could see that his spirit had never returned from the bleak landscape into which it had been thrust when he talked about Sitting Bull and the Ghost Dance. I wanted to reach him in some fashion. Yet, at every turn, something stopped me. Words seemed too white; a touch seemed too familiar.

Joking was not called for, and idle conversation was out of the question.

A cat's eyes glinted from the side of the road and disappeared.

I decided to approach straight on, but softly, in the only way I knew how.

"Dan?" I said.

He turned ever so slightly.

"May I talk?"

"Why not?" he answered flatly.

"I don't even know how to say this. It seems so stupid." I was groping for words. "I hate what's happened to your people. I just hate it. I feel like we've committed a crime that can never be undone."

"You have," he said.

"I know. But I didn't do it. Even if my grandparents did it — if blood is on their hands — I can't undo it."

"I know."

"So what's the answer?"

"There isn't one," he said simply.

"Then what's to be done?"

The smoke lingered around his head like a halo. I could hear him sucking on his cigarette as we moved through the darkness.

"I wish I knew," he answered. "Do you see what has happened to my people? We've been torn apart. Sitting Bull fighting with Gall over whether or not to give in to the white man. Young people joining AIM trying to become warriors again. Tribal bigwigs acting just like white bosses. Nobody knows what to do.

"Some of our people trying to be white. Some hating everything about the white man. Some Indians trying to be both. Some even trying to go back to the old ways, like none of this ever happened.

"We are all struggling, and there are never any answers. Every generation has to struggle. Maybe we just have to leave it in the hands of the Great Spirit."

"But that's what's been done," I said. "And look where it's gotten you."

"The Great Spirit's time is not our time," he said. "The well is poisoned now. It is poisoned with anger and despair. Maybe we have to wait until the water is fresh again."

I tried to interrupt. But he stopped me.

"Hell, Nerburn, I don't know," he said sharply. "I'm old. I only know what I see. The young ones have to decide how to fight. If they want to fight."

I didn't want to leave it like this. "This is what we're writing for, though," I persisted. "I thought you wanted to say what you knew."

"I'm tired right now. My spirit is bad. They should learn the language and respect the elders. Try to be Indians. That's all. I have said enough."

He returned to his cigarette. His exhalations rattled from his chest like the sound of death.

A dark form hared across the road in front of us.

"What was that?" I said to Grover.

"Rabbit," he answered. "Or fox. Didn't notice."

Dan spoke up again. "*Wasichu* should listen to the rabbit. He knows how to be quiet. He is humble. *Wasichu* never learned how to be humble."

I was becoming more and more uncomfortable. Dan's dark mood filled the car. The silver land outside was preternatural. I was willing to listen to anything. I just didn't want to ride in silence.

"Talk to me, Dan," I said.

"Unnh," he responded. His mind was full of demons.

"You never stop pushing," he said. "You don't know how much you push." The distant tone in his voice made me unsure if he was talking to me or pursuing some abstract idea. His words were absent, hollow, without emotion.

"Before the white man, we were free in our hearts and our bodies. We went where we wanted. We thought what we wanted. The land was ours to use. But from the moment you set foot upon our shores, we were being pushed. We have been pushed ever since."

I approached carefully. I wanted him to keep talking. "I know," I said. "I want to hear."

"I don't know," he sighed. "It has made us cautious and wary. We don't have the force to resist you. We never did. Our wise men knew this from the beginning and our young men soon found this out. We could not stand up against your force. We needed to find another way to survive."

His voice trailed off into Lakota, then reemerged in English.

"The way we found was cleverness. Cleverness wrapped in silence. We would watch you and listen to you until we knew what you really wanted. Then we would back up even further. If we could see a way to strike back, we would do so. If we couldn't, we would just back up again and again."

He stared out into the night. "Trouble is, when it came to land, there wasn't far enough to back up. Wherever we went, you chased us. We heard you coming and we smelled you coming. Even before you even knew we were there, we knew you were coming. The animals told us. We saw it in their eyes and heard it in their voices. We knew it by their change in numbers, their change in habits."

Again, he fell to silence. He took another cigarette from the pack on the dashboard and tamped it against the back of his hand.

"You see, we could always read the signs. We still can today. You may not be coming with guns and diseases, but you are coming. Instead of alcohol and tobacco, you are bringing money. You don't want our land. You want what is under our land and on our land. You want our minerals. You want our forests. You want to bury nuclear waste and chemicals.

"Ha!" he burst out suddenly, as if his words were only the tip of his thoughts. "But we have learned to be clever. We know that the only thing you really fear is lawyers, because lawyers are the ones who can twist your law. Once, long ago, we believed in the power of your law. But then we saw that you didn't believe in it. It was only for you and it really was only to help you get what you want or to keep others from getting what you have. It never applied to people like us.

"We signed treaty after treaty. We got promises after promises. What did it get us? Nothing. It just lulled us to sleep because it made us trust you. And while we were sleeping you were finding ways to twist that law to get what you wanted.

"Now we don't trust your laws, but we use your lawyers. For money they will twist your laws to work for us, just like they have twisted them to work for you. We have money. So we will use them."

His momentary optimism dropped back to brooding darkness. He was carrying on an argument with himself.

"But if we get too good at what we do, you will find a way to stop us. You always do. You are always pushing."

His voice rose again. He spoke as if he were addressing me; as if, somehow, by understanding, I could do something.

"I wish your people would stop pushing for a while and see what you are doing. You don't even know why you push. You just do.

"You push to be richer. You push to own more things. Columbus pushed against the whole world just to see what would happen.

"I used to think you did it because you are greedy. I don't think that anymore. Now I think it is just part of who you are and what you do, like listening to the land is part of what we are and what we do.

"I feel sorry for your people. You can't be very happy. But I can't trust you, because you will always push on us."

He turned toward me. "My people have done well. You have tried to take everything away from us, but we have survived. We have lived with you pushing against us for five hundred years. We will live with you pushing against us for five hundred more.

"We will do what we have to. But it will hurt us. You have made us careful and suspicious and we never wanted to be this way. Maybe someday things will change. But I don't think so.

"No," he repeated, as if examining his conclusion, "I don't think so."

My discomfort had become acute. He had made the identification I had most feared — me as all white people; him as all Indian people. The brush was too broad, and I knew that he knew it. But his mind was clouded by exhaustion, anger, and hurt. His thoughts had become dangerous — to himself and to me. I wanted to escape from this trap. We needed light.

Grover, ever watchful, had sensed the problem. He pulled to the side of the road and shut off the engine. The darkness swooped in. Dan was now intoning something in Lakota. He stepped out and walked a few feet from the road. He chanted louder.

"What's he saying?" I asked Grover.

"He does this sometimes, when he feels the Old Ones nearby. It's something he learned when he was young. Something Red Cloud said. It's kind of like this: 'The shadows are long and dark before me. Soon I will lie down and not rise up again.' Now he's talking about the sun and how he will always be faithful to the sun."

Dan was walking away from us on unsteady legs. I tried to sound nonchalant. "Why's he doing it? Is it something I did?" My voice came out high and whiny.

"Nothing to worry about. He's old. He's close to the other side. Sometimes he sees across. It's okay." Grover reached into the bag of groceries on the seat beside him and pulled out a tiny pie. "You want some?"

Dan had stopped on a rise and was standing with his arms out-stretched. The moonlight framed him like a ghost.

"No!" I answered. My voice was almost a shout.

Grover shrugged and ripped the edge of the wrapper. "It's apple." At the sound of tearing paper Fatback rose up like a sphinx.

"Here, you old dog," Grover said. He tore off a chunk of crust and held it over the seat. Fatback snapped it desperately out of his hand and smacked it around in her mouth.

"See those big hollows out there?" Grover asked. "The Old Ones said they were made by the buffalo dancing."

Dan was walking farther into the hills.

Fatback started mewling for more pie. Grover flipped a chunk over his shoulder. The old dog grabbed at it but missed. It fell on the floor and bounced under the seat. She lunged after it, scratch-ing me with her hind paws as she scrabbled headfirst onto the floor.

"You know, Nerburn," Grover said, apropos nothing, "The old man really likes you."

"Hnn," I said.

"He's showing you things and telling you things."

There was no reasonable response. "I know," I said.

He rubbed his crewcut with the palm of his hand. "Do you think you'll be able to write a book?"

Fatback's head was lodged under the seat.

"Huh? Yes. Uh, I don't know. Yeah, sure."

"How many pages do you think it will be?"

I was beyond answering. Dan was gone over the hills. Fatback was tearing frantically at the carpet trying to dislodge her head. The sky was ablaze with a fury of stars.

"You know what else the Old Ones said?" Grover asked. "They said there was one star that never moved. All the other stars move around it in a circle. They dance around it. You have to be careful, though. You can't trust the stars because they fear the sun."

The buffalo hollows were filled with ghost light. Fatback had retrieved the pie chunk and was making her way back onto the seat.

I scanned the landscape wildly. We were alone on an empty sea.

"You don't smoke, do you?" Grover said.

"Me? No."

"I noticed you didn't take that cigarette from that Indian."

"No. No, I just never started. Don't like the taste."

Grover lit a match and held it in the air. "I wish the lighter in this car worked. It broke years ago." He lit the end of a new cigarette and leaned back. "Only thing wrong with Buicks. I had a Roadmaster after the service — '55, I think. Nothing stopped it. Once I even made a gasket for the carburetor out of a cardboard box. Drove it for years that way. But the lighter never worked. You ever have a Buick, Nerburn?"

A shooting star coursed across horizon. The shadows pooled and shifted. "Shit, Grover," I blurted. "Why are you talking about Buicks? He's eighty years old. He's almost blind!"

"There are many ways to see," Grover answered lazily. He shifted sideways in his seat and leaned his back against the door. "The old man does what he does. Night's the same as day to him. Let him be." He drew heavily on his cigarette and blew the smoke toward the ceiling.

Over the hills I could hear the roar of another car. Soon the glow of its headlights appeared in the distance. It bore down on us with uncanny speed, then shot past without so much as a wave or a glance. Its dull drone cut the night like a knife.

"What's he doing out there?" I asked.

"Talking to the Ancient Ones," Grover answered. He was rummaging in the bag for something to drink. "He'll be back soon."

"What if something happens to him?"

"Something will happen to him."

"I mean, if he falls or gets hurt."

"Better here than some hospital. He's not going to fall, though. That's not why he's out there."

Something swooped from the sky in the darkness.

"Hawk," Grover said. "Watching the old man. For *Yanpa* — the east wind." He twisted the top off a bottle of iced tea. A hot gust of wind shuddered the car.

"See, I told you," Grover said. Far out on a hillside I could see the tiny movement of a figure. Grover took a deep slug of the iced tea before shifting back upright in his seat. Step by step the small form advanced toward the car, never wavering, never stopping. "Tough old bugger," Grover observed.

Dan made his way through the short, dry grasses. He walked with his arms out, palms down, like someone balancing on rocks while crossing a stream. When he was about twenty feet from the car, he stopped and looked up. His one white eye glinted in the moonlight.

Grover started the engine. The door opened and Dan slid in. Grover shifted into gear and started down the road. No one said a word, but the silence was calm.

Chapter 20

Revelations

"Here," Grover said with authority. A pair of ruts took off from the highway and arched over the moonlit hills. "This is it."

There was no mailbox, no sign, no marking. We had been driving for hours in the shapeless terrain. There had been no roadsigns or markers for miles.

He turned onto the ruts and began bouncing toward the hills. The lights shot crazily skyward, then dug into the ground as the front end surged and dipped through the brush.

The undercarriage creaked and clanked. Springs groaned. A mule deer ran in front of us and froze momentarily before bolting off into the darkness. Here and there, half hidden in the grasses, the hulking forms of rusted cars loomed like rhinos.

Once over the first rise, the land stretched out for miles in a dizzying profusion of ebbs and draws. The silver moonlight washed away all detail, leaving only great splashes of dark and light upon the earth.

Grover drove without fear. Once or twice I thought he was going to get stuck in a hollow. But he revved and roared and spun his way across every obstacle. Here and there a side path would break off, yet he never slowed, never wavered. The sedate caution of his highway driving had disappeared; in its place was a relentless certainty. He was the captain, plowing through grassland seas.

The nose of the car rose and fell, rose and fell. We were buffeted around in our seats like men on a carnival ride. Bottles clinked in the grocery bag. Somewhere in the trunk a jack or tire iron had become dislodged and was thudding and chunking off the wheel wells and trunk lid.

We ground our way to the top of a long hill and Grover brought the car to a stop. There, at the bottom of the next hollow, nestled among a few scrubby trees, stood a solitary structure. From our vantage point, still a half a mile away, it seemed uninhabited. But a close look revealed a dim glow from a tiny window.

The building was not much bigger than a chicken coop. Objects were scattered on the ground around it. There was no car anywhere.

"Well, we made it," Grover announced.

Dan nodded.

A small figure appeared in the yard. The sound of barking filled the evening quiet. Three dogs raced up the rise toward us. Fatback bolted in her seat and started whimpering. Grover reached behind and flipped open the rear door so she could slip out.

She rushed to the front of the car. The charging dogs lapped and panted up the rise and almost overran her. They began a wild frenzy of wagging and growling and sniffing.

Grover blinked his headlights several times. The figure by the house waved, and we proceeded down the hill.

When we reached the trees I could see that the figure was a woman. She was heavybreasted and old, almost as old as Dan. She wore a baggy print dress cinched around the waist with a man's belt. A thin dark sweater was draped over her shoulders like a shawl.

Her hair was white or silver — I could not tell in the moonlight — and was pulled together in back. It hung down almost to the bottom of the sweater.

She was standing with her hands on her hips, like a stern mother awaiting the late arrival of her daughter from a date. As the car lights swept across her, I could see that she was smiling. It was a mother's grin, full of knowing mirth.

Grover shouted something out the window in Lakota. She clasped her hands in front of her and rocked back onto her heels several times. Her smile got even broader. Some more words were exchanged, and Grover told us all to get out.

The old woman turned back toward the house. The dogs moiled behind her, including Fatback. She walked bent over, on heavy ankles.

"Come on," Grover coaxed. "This is Annie," as if that were sufficient to make all things clear.

Now that the headlights were off, the stars burst forth like crystals. As my eyes adjusted I surveyed the surroundings. The house was indeed not much bigger than a chicken coop. It was made of rough, uneven squared logs, chinked between by a heavy layer of concrete or mud. The roof was tarpaper held down by thin wood batting strips and old car tires. Off behind I could barely make out the form of a tall thin outhouse set against a clump of trees. To its left was a tiny humpbacked house trailer with its tongue resting on a section of log.

The yard itself, if indeed it could be called a yard, contained a small garden plot that was fenced in by chicken wire. Some low vegetables seemed to be growing in its rows. A metal bedframe and mattress stood near the house for no apparent reason.

On the opposite side, away from the car, wood was stacked almost as high as the roof. A bucket hung from the neck of an old crook-handled pump near the front door.

All of this stood huddled, like a tiny outpost of human habitation, in the center of this great bowl of land that stretched for miles in all directions.

Grover nudged me. "Does she live here alone?" I asked. The sea of stars seemed to flow on forever.

"Bring the bag of groceries," was all he answered. Dan had walked ahead and had already entered the house.

Inside, the house seemed even smaller. It was divided into two rooms, each no bigger than a large closet. The floor was made from wood planks and there were small windows cut into each of the heavy timber walls. A red and green striped blanket served as a door between the two rooms. The only illumination was a tiny yellow light flickering from a kerosene hurricane lamp that stood on a table next to the door.

Because of the rug divider, I could only see the first of the rooms. It contained only four pieces of furniture: the square pine table on which the lamp was placed; a massive grey-and-white enamel wood cook stove that took up almost an entire wall; an old overstuffed easy chair shoved in the corner just to my left; and a single ladderback wooden kitchen chair pushed in against the table. The sheer size of the objects made the room claustrophobic; there were places to sit and stand, but no place to move.

Pots and dishes lined a shelf above the table, along with jars of beans and flour. Pieces of dried meat hung from a rack above the shelf.

Though the windows were open, I felt like I might suffocate. The smell of something burbling on the stove mixed with the acrid reek of kerosene. The heat from the stove was immense, and not at all mitigated by the dry breeze blowing through. Everything was too close.

I heard Dan's voice from the back room. He was laughing with another man. Their conversation was all in Lakota, and I could recognize no word other than *wasichu*.

I had no sense of protocol. The woman had not acknowledged me beyond smiling warmly in my direction. I did not know whether I should introduce myself, or even if she spoke any English. I stood silently by the front door and watched her take the groceries out of the bag and place them in various shelves and corners around the room.

She was obviously a kind woman. Her face was creased with deep furrows that flowed gracefully from the edges of her eyes and the corners of her mouth. She wore the perpetual expression of one withholding a humorous secret.

Since there was no graceful place to stand, and nothing had been said about where I should sit, I stayed in the open doorway, smiling warmly whenever the old woman looked at me. Grover had pushed aside the blanket between the rooms and was involved in the conversation that Dan was having with the unseen man.

Outside the dogs continued to tussle and tumble in mock battle under the star-filled sky. I considered going back out to sit with them, but the woman gestured me in. It was a warm, come hither gesture — the universal welcome of a grandmother with food. "You want to eat?" she said.

The English surprised me. She gestured me toward the single ladderback chair. "Come on. Sit down."

I had enough sense not to refuse hospitality. I had made enough errors in etiquette to last for a while.

I wedged my way in to the table. The old woman took a bowl from the shelf and ladled something from the cast-iron skillet. I had no idea what it was, but I knew I had to eat it. Memories drifted up of the Ojibwe kids at Red Lake joking about the Lakota, or "Sioux" as they called them, being "dog eaters." Most of them were merely mouthing stories they had heard. But the stories had to have come from somewhere.

I looked hard into the gruel. I saw nothing demonstrably canine, though chunks of some kind of meat floated half submerged in an ominously dark gravy. They were surrounded by reassuringly round objects of vegetable or grain origin. I took the dented metal spoon and lifted a bit of the liquid to my lips.

The old woman was grinning.

It was surprisingly good. There were tastes of pepper and corn, and a lingering aftertaste of berries. I bit into one of the balls. It was some kind of dumpling, and quite tasty in its own right. I worked my way through the liquid, skirting the meat as best I could.

Grover turned and saw me. He looked at my bowl full of meat chunks, then looked at Annie. "Didn't you used to have four dogs?" he said in English.

♦ ♦ ♦ ♦

It wasn't long before my exhaustion overcame me. "You sleep on the bed in the yard," Annie said. I remembered the strange iron frame with the faded striped mattress. If we didn't have a late-night thunderstorm, it seemed like a fine choice.

I grabbed my sleeping bag from the trunk and curled up on the creaking springs of the old bed. Despite the comings and goings of the dogs, and the occasional bursts of laughter from inside the house, I was soon fast asleep.

I must have slept soundly. I had no recollection of Dan and Grover or anyone else walking by me on the way to the trailer or the outhouse. When I opened my eyes the sun was creeping over the horizon to the east. The sky was a symphony of violets and purples, and a sparkle of dew covered the grass. I lay in silence, listening to the movements of the insects and the animals.

Sounds of life came from the other side of the house. I climbed out of my sleeping bag and went to the car to get my toothbrush and some clean clothes.

Annie was in the yard by the pump. She was pushing the rusty metal handle up and down in short, powerful bursts. Her outfit was the same as yesterday, but she now wore a dark headscarf against the wind. She waved at me and smiled.

In the daylight I could get a better sense of where we were. The house sat alone in the middle of a bowl that must have been twenty miles across. There were no other structures in any direction;

only a few stands of trees broke the unending dip and roll of the brown grassland hills.

The trail we had driven in on stretched up and over a rise to our rear. Other than that, no roads or pathways were anywhere to be found. A man walking, or riding on a horse, would have been seen for miles.

The sky dominated all. Like the land, it was too large, too singular, to be absorbed. The sunrise was swathing the east with colors of golds and oranges and purples. They dripped and streamed across the entire horizon, backlighting the clouds and shooting rays of yellow sunlight across the land. The sun was slowly pushing into view. As it rose, it drove the shadows deep into the valleys and the draws. I felt like I was in an amphitheater of the gods.

Annie had returned to the house with her basin of water. I walked over to the pump and worked the handle until a small stream came from the spout. Holding my breath against the anticipated cold, I shoved my head under the flow and slapped a handful of shampoo onto my hair.

The water was anything but cold. The smell was putrid and sulfuric; the temperature, tepid; the color, brackish. I quickly finished washing and tried to towel myself free of any residue from the vile substance.

Annie was standing in the door. Memories of the soup rose up inside me. "Don't drink," she said. "Here." She held out a cup. "Use this." I took it from her hand and looked down at the clear liquid. It was water, but it had come from someplace other than the pump. "Thank you," I said, and finished brushing my teeth.

While I was washing, Annie had pulled the wooden chair outside and placed it next to the front door. She was working something in her lap, either shucking some kind of vegetables or making some kind of craft. I paid no attention and finished dressing. Neither Dan nor Grover had emerged from wherever they had spent the night, nor had the mystery man whose voice had come from the back room last evening.

I could sense Annie watching me. I was badly in need of coffee, but was afraid to ask. Perhaps they were tea drinkers. Perhaps they were too poor to have coffee. Perhaps they had coffee but made it with water from the pump.

Annie gestured me over with a flick of her head. Her hands remained busy in her lap. Their movement was swift and automatic. I smiled and approached.

"Sit," she said, nodding toward the stoop. I glanced at her hands. She was working a rosary.

The shock was almost as great as when she had first spoken English. It was not that it was improbable, just that it was so unexpected.

"Catholic?" I said, for no reason at all.

She smiled and nodded, as if I had acknowledged something important. "Oh, yah," she said. Her hands worked their way down the beads with practiced ease. I expected something more — an explanation, perhaps, or a question about my background. But nothing further was forthcoming. She rocked in her seat to some inner melody.

We sat in silence as the sun rose. From the yard behind I heard the metal creak of the trailer door, then the banging of the outhouse. Soon Dan made his way across to the car. He was wearing his quilted undershirt. His stained khaki pants were buttoned but not yet zipped. The suspenders hung in loops down his sides. His old deerskin slippers half covered his sockless feet. He looked like someone who had wandered away from a nursing home.

He went directly to the car without acknowledging either of us. After some rummaging in the trunk, he extracted a crinkled brown paper bag and disappeared again behind the house. Annie kept rocking and working her hands. The sounds of insects began to fill the morning air.

I wanted to talk but had no idea what to say. By bidding me to sit, she had locked me in place for no apparent reason. I heard the low whisper of her prayer litany: "Hail Mary, full of grace." She was speaking in English.

She worked her way down the beads as the sun worked its way into the sky. The day was going to be a hot one. I sat in silence as she fingered each bead until she arrived at the crucifix that hung on the end. She lifted it to her mouth and kissed it in a ritual fashion, then put it in the pocket of her dress. Having finished, she arose. She held up one finger to indicate that I should pay attention, then walked into the house.

She emerged shortly with a black-and-white photograph mounted on a piece of heavy cardboard. It was old and faded. The picture was of a group of children posed in front of a porch. There were about fifty of them, arranged in rows, boys separated from girls, all about seven or eight. The girls were wearing white dresses and the boys had on little men's suits. Most of the boys were wearing floppy pork-pie hats or snap-brim fedoras. Behind them, off to the right, stood a single adult: a white man, wearing a Roman collar.

Annie pointed to one of the poker-faced little boys. "Dan," she said, using his Indian name. She moved her finger to a cute little girl in pigtails sitting with her hands demurely in her lap. "Me."

I laughed with pleasure. Dan's leathery old scowl was immediately recognizable in the tough little expression on the boy in the photo. Annie put her hand to her mouth and giggled like a girl.

"Oh, yah," she said. "He was always in trouble. Ran away all the time."

I looked at the stern-faced priest. "Oh," I said.

"I liked it there," she volunteered. "I got to work in the kitchen with the nuns."

"Did they ever talk about the Ghost Dance?" I asked.

She chortled and made a dismissing gesture with her gnarled hand. "Oh, that was just silly Indians," she said.

I wanted to ask more, but the sound of barking interrupted me. The dogs had taken off up the ridge behind the house. Within seconds the hum of an engine could be heard, followed by a dusty cloud in the distance. Soon a white pickup poked its nose over the ridge and clanked its way down toward the house with the dogs circling and barking at its front fender.

Annie got up to meet it. It bounced into the yard and pulled to a halt. There were four people in the front seat — a man, a woman, and two children. Another boy in his early teens rode in the back.

They stepped out one by one. The man was in his late thirties, wearing the standard range outfit of jeans, white T-shirt, and cowboy boots. His hair shone like a blackbird's wing from beneath a white cowboy hat. His mouth was locked in a gambler's grin.

The woman, who was somewhat younger, had on a Hard Rock Cafe T-shirt and jeans. She was skinny and tough, with the hard hollow-cheeked beauty of a bar queen. She guided the children out like ducklings.

The children were scruffy but scrubbed. They ran toward Annie, who had bent over and stood with arms outstretched. The two older children were dark-haired and round-faced. The third, who was no more than five, had blue eyes and a long, shaggy mop of blond curls.

Annie grabbed them each and spoke to them in Lakota. They spoke back to her in English. Forgetting the picture in my hands, and making no introduction, she led the children inside where I heard screams of "Grandpa, Grandpa."

There was scuffling and scraping. A figure appeared in the door, pushed in a wheelchair by two of the children. It was the man whose voice I had heard the night before. He, too, was almost as old as Dan. His face was brown as a chestnut and his hair was pushed to the side in a shock of white. He was wearing a white long-sleeved shirt buttoned at the neck and a pair of blue trousers. He had no legs below the knees.

I smiled clumsily at the man and woman who had emerged from the pickup. Much to my surprise, the man reached to shake hands with me. Reverting to form, I introduced myself. "Kent Nerburn. I'm a friend of Dan's and Grover's."

"Delvin," he said, offering no more, and took my hand in a lazy grip. The woman reached out more formally: "Danelle." She held my hand with authority, like someone trying to assay its value. They both looked me in the eye as they introduced themselves. They had lived somewhere among white people.

The name "Danelle" aroused my curiosity. It could just be a co-incidence, I told myself. But the woman bore a striking similarity to Wenonah in both looks and manner. I wondered what the connection might be, but did not feel comfortable pursuing it. I was happy enough just to be in the presence of some people who seemed to operate by some of the ground rules of white society.

Like a man overseas who had just met someone from home, I wanted to start chattering. But I held back. The woman's stern formality and the great silence of the open space did not encourage idle words.

Danelle saw the picture and warmed a bit. "Grandma talking about the old days?" In the glancing sunlight I could see the harsh textures of a case of childhood smallpox written on her skin.

"Not much," I said. "We just got started."

"Grover's here, huh?" she said.

"You know him, I assume?"

Her expression clouded. "Yeah, I know him."

The children had pushed the old man out into the yard. Danelle went over and kissed him on the cheek. Delvin was unhitching the tailgate of the pickup truck. I went over to help him. The bed was filled with boxes of groceries and a big corrugated steel tank about the size of a fifty-gallon drum.

We brought the boxes into the house. Then Delvin climbed in the truck and drove it around the side. Thankful for something to do, I followed him. He backed up to the wall and hopped into the truckbed. He took a green garden hose and snaked it through a small opening in the wall. "Okay," he hollered.

Danelle's voice answered from somewhere inside. I watched from the side of the truck. "Water," he said, sensing my curiosity. "Can't drink this shit." He grinned in the direction of the pump.

"Do they live out here all winter?" I asked.

"Used to. Not any more. Diabetes got the old man. He'd stay out here now if we'd let him."

"Pretty tough to survive in their condition."

"Don't take bets."

Delvin leaned against the cab of the pickup. "You writing a book or something?" I had no idea how he knew. He saw my surprise. "Just figured. White man hanging with the Skins."

"It's for Dan," I explained.

"Shit. If we had a dime for every book someone is writing about us we could buy back the Black Hills."

There was no malice in his voice. Still, the comment stung.

"Dan asked me," I explained, protesting too much.

Delvin defused my fears. "You're going to have to be a hell of a liar to turn that old duffer into a wise man."

"I don't want to write a 'wise man' book."

"No 'Black Elk Speaks'?"

"Maybe, 'Black Dog Speaks'," I said, nodding toward Fatback, who was lazing in the shade under the bedframe.

"Now, that's a book we could use," he grinned. We shared a skeptic's sympathy.

"The water's not flowing," Danelle shouted from inside the house. Delvin adjusted the hose. "That's better," she hollered.

Delvin gestured toward the wall. "He's her grandfather, you know."

"Who, Dan?"

My stunned response pleased him. "Yeah. You didn't know that? His kid was her dad."

I didn't know what to say. In a few sentences I had discovered more about Dan than I had learned in being around him for several months. It made me realize how closed-mouthed he had been.

"You mean the son who got killed? Who went to Haskell?"

"Yeah. You didn't know that?"

"I don't know anything," I said. "I just ride."

He laughed a bit. It was a warm, friendly, natural chuckle. "That's what we all do, man. Just ride." He tipped the tank on edge so the hose would have a chance to siphon all the water.

"So, Wenonah's her sister?" I asked.

"Yeah. She's the good one. Stayed home with Grandpa after Mom and Dad were killed."

The revelations were mind-boggling. In themselves, they were nothing — just fragments like the notes in the shoe box. But they started to fill in the background of an old man I had come to respect and even love. I realized how much I longed to know these things. But I was unsure how far I should go in asking. Still, I decided to pursue. I was still completely confused, and I wanted to sort things out in my mind. Maybe, I thought, I could find a mainspring that would help me understand Dan and the mission that he seemed intent upon sharing with me.

"Do you mind talking about this stuff?" I asked Delvin.

"Hell, no. I'm surprised the old man never told you these things."

"He doesn't tell me much. He's mentioned his dad and his grandparents several times, and I saw some pictures on his wall. But that's all."

"So you don't know about his wife, or any of that stuff?"

"I don't know anything," I said, almost desperately.

"Yeah," Delvin said. "I can see. He's a crafty old devil. Likes to keep the upper hand."

"What about his wife?" I said. "I've wondered why there are no women anywhere around him."

"It's a funny story. The old man married some white churchy social worker who came out to the rez back during the war. World War II. He couldn't get in because of his eye. I think it really bothered him. He really wanted to go. Those old Indians, you know, they really take that army stuff seriously.

"He tried to do some work on the reservation, but they wouldn't let him. Wrong family. You know the bullshit. He and his wife had a kid. She sort of flipped out and split. Couldn't take the prairie. Went back East somewhere. I don't think he ever got over it."

The mention of a white wife who was a social worker made me smile. It explained a lot of his vitriol at the cafe the day before.

Delvin was enjoying himself. He could see how hungry I was for this information. He doled it out in tantalizing chunks.

"Bobby — that's his kid — had a tough time, I guess. All that 'halfbreed' shit. Really wanted to do it right for both his mom and dad. Went off to Haskell. Wanted to be a teacher or something. I don't know what happened, then. I guess Bobby ended up back on the rez. Got hooked up with AIM, or at least that's what people say. That's when he married Dannie's mom."

"Dannie?"

"Danelle."

"And . . . Dannie's mom is Annie's daughter?" I tried the name out on my tongue. It felt clumsy and confused.

"Yeah."

"So what happened? How did he get killed?"

"Don't know. They both did. Bobby and Katherine — Dannie's mom. Police said they were killed in a car accident. But that was bullshit. There were bullet holes in them. They weren't even on their own reservation. Maybe they killed themselves, I don't know. But then why would the police say they were killed in a car accident? Reservation police — you know how it is."

"Okay," Danelle shouted through the wall.

Delvin snaked the hose back out and curled it neatly next to the tank. There would be water enough to last another few days.

I could hear Danelle's footsteps moving across the floor to the door. She would be out with us in a few seconds. I decided to let the matter drop.

Apparently Delvin thought it best to change the subject as well. He leaned back against the cab of the pickup and pulled the brim of his hat down like a cowboy taking a siesta. He started whistling some tuneless melody and drumming something on the truck body with his hands. It was a gesture of calculated nonchalance, too studied to be believable, too blatant to be ignored. He looked like the bad kid in the back of the classroom pretending he had done nothing wrong.

Danelle came around the corner.

"Did we get it all?" she asked.

"Every drop," Delvin said, thumping the empty tank as evidence.

"How long do you think it will last?"

"Oh, a week, maybe, unless these guys are staying." He nodded toward me.

"I don't know," I said. "Nobody tells me anything."

Danelle looked at me with a shade of a scowl. I was an interloper, taking up precious resources. She looked into the growing sun. "It's going to get hot," she said. There was concern in her voice. "Maybe we should take Grandma and Grandpa home with us until it cools down."

Delvin shrugged and jumped to the ground. "You ask them."

I stood silently by the side of the truck. There were bigger issues at stake here than my curiosity about Dan's background. But I couldn't keep my eyes off Danelle now that I knew she was Dan's granddaughter. It was as if by watching her I might gain some clues into the old man.

She noticed my attention and caught my eyes in a hard stare. It was not a challenge so much as a measuring. She was not someone to trifle with.

She swung herself onto the tailgate with a cowgirl's grace. "Well, mister. What's your story? How come you're out here with Dan and Grover?"

Her schoolgirl directness caught me off guard. I didn't know how much familiarity I should assume, or how much about her relationship to Dan I was supposed to know. The fact that she called her grandpa "Dan" made me think she didn't want me to know about it. "Nothing, really. I write. I used to work on Red Lake reservation in northern Minnesota. Dan's granddaughter — Wenonah — called me."

"Wenonah?" she said. She sounded surprised, but offered no more explanation.

"Yeah. Said Dan wanted me to come out and help him put together a book. I said I would."

It was a short answer, but good enough, I thought. She chewed her bottom lip and looked at me hard. "A book?"

"Yeah."

"What kind of book?"

"I'm not sure. Dan had this shoe box of notes that he wanted me to put into some kind of form. But we decided to junk that and just write a kind of a story, where I watch and record and try to give some of his views on life and the world."

"What was in the shoe box?"

"Fragments. Hundreds of them. Written on scraps of paper. A few newspaper columns. Some letters. A real strange collection."

She sat quietly for a minute. "White people shouldn't write books about Indians."

"I'm not writing a book about Indians," I said, suddenly defensive. "I'm writing a book for an Indian. That's what he wants. I asked him what he wanted and how he wanted it and that's what I'm trying to do." My apology was too long.

"Why didn't he ask an Indian?" Her responses were as direct as mine were excessive. I tried to reign myself in.

"I don't know. I've wondered that myself."

"He must think pretty highly of you," she said. It was almost a challenge. She looked at me strangely, as if trying to see a clue as to why her grandfather would have chosen me. Then, deciding to pursue it no further, she slipped off the tailgate and shut it with a slam. "Well, don't blow it, mister *wasichu*. Working on a reservation doesn't make you an Indian. Let's go, Delvin."

Delvin gave me a knowing smile.

I should have let things lie, but, unaccountably, I spoke up again. I wanted to connect with her on some level. I cast about for something to keep her talking.

I took a chance. "I'm doing this for your grandpa," I said. "Not for me."

She whirled. "Every *wasichu* is doing it for himself. He just doesn't always know why." It was my intentions she challenged, not my knowledge of her relationship to Dan, so I pushed a bit further.

"I'm going to do it, Dannie," I said. "Your grandpa asked me. I wish you'd help me." At my use of her nickname her eyes flashed a quick fury. Then she subsided and stared hard at me.

"And what sort of help can I give you? You seem to know exactly what you're about." The bitterness and sarcasm fairly dripped from her voice.

"Can I tell you the truth?" I said.

"I wish to hell you would," she said. Delvin was grinning from ear to ear. He had obviously been on the receiving end of her anger before.

"I'm scared of this one. I really am."

"And I'm scared of you doing it."

"And you should be. I could really blow it. I wanted to give it back to him so he could find an Indian to help him. But he really wants me to do it. He really does. I don't know why."

She sat motionless and surveyed me like an animal. You could almost read the inner conversation on her face. When she spoke it was in grave tones. There was to be no mistaking her seriousness.

"My grandpa is one of the most important people in the world to me. He's all I've got left of my dad. If my sister called you, I'll trust you. But I don't like it. I don't like *wasichu* writers coming to the reservation. Nothing good comes of it. But if Grandpa wants you to do it, you do it. But you do it his way."

"Believe me, Dannie, I'm trying."

She bit her bottom lip again and tensed her shoulders. She was a woman in a private turmoil.

"Did you know my dad?"

"No. I never even heard of your dad until I saw his picture on your grandpa's wall."

"He was murdered, you know."

I glanced at Delvin. He nodded his okay. "Delvin told me," I said.

She looked at Delvin. He flashed his teeth from behind his sunglasses and held up his hands like a man showing he had no weapons.

"You talk a lot, Delvin," Dannie said.

He grinned again and said nothing.

"My dad was a really good man. He really cared about people. He was going to do something good for the Indian people. Then he got killed. Along with Mom."

I remained silent. This was her talk. I would let it go where she wanted. She sniffed once, then continued.

"He wanted to build a bridge to Grandma. That's what he always said. He wanted to build a bridge to Grandma."

"What did he mean?" I asked as gently as I could.

"Grandpa and Grandma . . ."

"Your grandpa, Dan?" I clarified.

"Yes. Grandpa and Grandma didn't get along very well, I guess. She was *wasichu*. I don't think Grandpa understood her very well. They split up and she went back East where she came from. My dad was still pretty little, like twelve or something. I don't know the whole story. Just what Grandma Annie told me. She knew them both.

"I guess my dad was really sad. He always blamed Grandpa. He said he was going to build a bridge for his mom to come back. That's what he told me when I was just little.

"He was such a good man, my dad. He used to take me on walks up on the hill by our house and say that we had to learn to forgive, like the land forgives. He would show me places where the land had been destroyed and say that the earth would cover it with new grasses, and that's what Indian people had to do with the white people."

"But he stayed on the rez with your grandpa?"

"He went back East to be with his mom a couple of times. But he hated it. She had remarried to a white man. They had some other kids, and those kids didn't like him. Called him Tonto and were really mean to him. He really wanted those kids to be his brothers and sisters. Even when he grew up he used to write them. I remember seeing him sitting at the kitchen table writing letters to them. They never wrote him back. He even tried to go to college back there, but he just couldn't. He went to Haskell instead."

She was crying now, small tears that came from deep in her childhood memory. She quickly wiped them away.

"He was going to write a book that explained things to Grandma, about the Indian way and how it really was. He was going to build a bridge between Grandpa and Grandma."

I felt a deep flush go through my entire body. I exhaled audibly.

"How much did he ever get written?" I asked.

"I don't know. Grandpa said he used to write letters from Haskell. I know Grandpa saved some of them."

Delvin turned toward me and smiled a close-lipped smile. He moved his head up and down as if to say, "There you are." I was almost shaking.

"Don't take advantage of him," she said. Her eyes were pleading, rimmed with tears. "This is bigger than you understand."

"I'm starting to," I said. "This is the hardest thing I've ever tried. But I'll do it right. I promise you."

"God, I hope so. It's really important."

We could see Grover and Dan puttering over by the trailer. Dan still had his suspenders hanging from the side of his pants while he washed up. There was no more I could say to reassure her.

"He really is a wise man," I offered.

"I know," Dannie answered. "That's where my dad got it. He taught my dad in the old way. He took him out, made him look at nature. He really was good. My dad learned it all, too."

Neither of us could bear to say the obvious.

"What sort of things is he telling you?" she asked.

"Sometimes he gives what he calls . . ."

"'Little talks,'" she broke in.

"Right." She smiled knowingly. "Other times he just goes off on a subject and bangs around in it."

"Are they good?"

"Do you want to hear?" I said. "I've been recording them."

She nodded, and I went to the car to get the tape recorder. Fatback saw me and came wagging after. She followed me back to the pickup where Dannie and Delvin had taken seats side by side on the tailgate.

"Fatback, you old hound," Dannie said as we approached. Seeing the dog seemed to lift her spirits.

Fatback wagged vigorously and tried to rise up on her hind legs. Dannie slid off the tailgate and got down nose to nose with the dog. She made huffing sounds and ruffled the old dog's ears. Fatback squeaked and whimpered like a happy puppy. "She's my dad's old dog," Dannie said. "He trained her just before he died."

"Trained her?"

"Yeah. He wanted to. Said he didn't want her to be just a rez dog. Show him, Fatback. Roll over."

The old dog sat down slowly, then dropped to the ground, curled her lip, and rolled onto her back.

"She can't get all the way over any more," Dannie explained. "But she used to be able to do all sorts of tricks."

"I've seen some of them," I said, remembering the episode on the hilltop.

"He's really close to her." Fatback pulled playfully at the cuff of her jeans, an old gesture of friendship stored somewhere deep in their shared memories. "He thinks my dad's spirit is in her."

"That dog's old as shit," Delvin said, inappropriately. "I'm surprised she could make a trip this far." I was doing some mathematical totting in my head even as he spoke. As near as I could figure, Fatback had to be almost twenty. I thought of Dan telling me she had just shown up on his porch one day, then of Grover telling me I had to watch out, because the old man would try to trick me. Things indeed were not what they seemed.

"Play the tape," Dannie said.

I had grabbed a tape at random from the box in my aviator's bag. It turned out to be Dan speaking about the land. Dannie's face lit up as the tinny voice spoke of white men planting a flag and claiming all the land up to that point.

"Those are the same stories he told me when I was little," she smiled. The tape went on. Dan was expounding on the difference between land and property.

Delvin picked at his teeth with the edge of a jackknife. "That old duffer's pretty smart."

"Grandma Annie said he was the smartest Indian she ever knew," Danelle said proudly. "He really is good, isn't he?"

"I think he is," I said. "I really do. That's why I'm doing this."

Over by the trailer Dan had finished washing up. He was pulling his suspenders up over his ribbed long-sleeve undershirt.

"A long-sleeve goddamn shirt," Delvin said in mock astonishment. "It's goddamn ninety degrees already, and he's wearing a long-sleeve shirt." Danelle had clicked off the tape and handed the machine back to me.

"There's one thing you've got to promise me," she said.

"If I can help you, I will."

"Just don't listen to them about women. Especially Grover."

It seemed a strange comment.

"What does Grover have to do with it?" I asked.

She spat her answer. "He thinks he's still in the Navy."

"She doesn't like the way he treats women," Delvin interpreted.

"I don't like anything about him," she corrected.

"You know him pretty well?" I asked.

"I only met him once, but I understand him perfectly," she said.

"We went up on a visit," Delvin explained. "He slapped her in the tailfeathers once when she walked by. Didn't sit too well with her."

"The hand speaks the truth of the mind," she observed.

Delvin laughed. It was not a serious offense to him.

"It doesn't seem to be Dan's kind of subject," I said.

"It's not. But it's Grover's. Grandpa listens to Grover too much, at least that's what my sister says. Remember, Grandma was a *wasichu*, like you. Grandpa never got over her. He doesn't know a whole lot about Indian women and the way things are today. If he says anything it will probably just be Grover talking."

She touched my arm with her fingertips. It was a surprising and powerful gesture; firm, without intimacy, like a nurse's. It held me in place. "Listen," she confided. "Grandpa's doing what he has to do. I'm sure you're doing your best. But you don't understand. You can't. We women are the hope of our people right now. I don't want Grandpa saying stupid things that are all wrong."

"I don't understand," I said.

"That's just the point. No matter how much you care, Indian culture is just a game to you. Maybe it's something important. Maybe you think it's the most important thing in the world. But if we're gone, you'll still survive. It's not that way for us. If our culture goes, we go. Everything our old people starved for and our ancestors died for will be gone. Look at Grandma and Grandpa. That's what's left. Her sitting with those rosary beads all day. Him without any legs. They stole his body and they stole her spirit."

"I know," I answered. "That's why I'm here. I want people to know. You've got to believe me."

"I believe you, but it doesn't make what you're doing right. You could just get it all wrong in your own way. See, the men like my grandpa Dan, they are still fighting. You're helping them fight. That's good. But it's our turn now — Indian women. The men are tired. They fought for almost two hundred years. Now it's our turn."

"Tell me about it," I said. Hers was the voice I needed to hear.

"They were warriors. They went out and struggled for us. But there were too many of you. They lost, and now they are defeated. They're angry and they're full of shame. It's in their blood. They keep trying. But their war is over.

"If honor had mattered, they would have won and we would still be strong and healthy as a people. But honor didn't matter. Numbers mattered. They fought and lost. Now they still try to fight, like my grandpa is doing, with words. But they are the defeated.

"It was taken from them. Everything. Your people did it. That's the way it was planned, and it worked. You took their spirits and left them with shame. But no one paid any attention to us women. We kept things alive in our hearts and hands."

She smiled knowingly and looked out over the rolling landscape, like a person caressing a secret in her mind.

"They ignored us. We were just women. But we were always the ones to keep the culture alive. That was our job, as women and mothers. It always has been. The men can't hunt buffalo anymore. But we can still cook and sew and practice the old ways. We can still feed the old people and make their days warm. We can teach the children. Our men may be defeated, but our women's hearts are still strong."

Dannie was speaking beautifully and eloquently. I did not want to cut her off. But there was a hard question I wanted to ask. This seemed the right time.

"Dannie," I said. "Can I ask you a tough question? I hope you won't take offense."

"That's why I'm talking to you. So you don't get things wrong."

"When I worked on Red Lake it seemed to me that the Indian women were strong — stronger than white women in a lot of ways. But they were strong apart from the men, as mothers, as grandmothers. A lot of times, when they were with the men, they were walking around with black eyes, or raising kids with some guy who wasn't their dad. Something was out of whack."

"At least you're honest," she said. "But it's like I said. You just don't understand. Sure, there's a lot of violence. You can usually trace it back to alcohol. But there are good families, lots of them, a lot more loving than most of your white families, with the grand-parents living there with the fathers and mothers, and everyone re-specting everyone else.

"This is what I mean about it being our time — the Indian woman. We have always been at the center. The Indian family has been like a circle, and the woman has been at the center. White families have been like lines, with the men standing in front.

"That's why white women haven't been able to understand us. They talk about sisterhood and liberation, but their struggle is not our struggle. We don't need to get free. We need to free our men."

She glanced to see if I was paying attention. Her fingertips were pressing hard on my arm.

"Things are different for us. We know who we are. We are mothers. We are the bearers of our race. It gives us status to do other things. We are honored for what we are. If our men are treat-ing us poorly, it is because they are shamed. Why should we want to set ourselves against them and call that liberation? Until they are free in their hearts again, none of us Indian people will be free."

I had found a subject dear to her heart. "This is good for you to know," she continued. "Maybe this will help you understand. We women can go out and get a job with the *wasichu*, and we're still okay. We can come home at night and not feel like we've sold our skin. We are still honored.

"But the men can't. If they go to the *wasichu*, they are shamed, even though they won't say it. The only way to lose that shame is to give up their blood and become white. They don't want to do that. But if they stay on the reservations, among their people, there is no work. And where there is no work they can't provide for their families. When they can't provide for their families they leave, or drink, or get angry. Maybe all of those. They get mad at us, even while they love us.

"All you see is the violence and the alcohol. All the white women see is the silence and the bruises. What we see is a broken circle, and we're going to make it whole. This isn't about men and women. This is about our whole culture and our ancestors and our children. White people always think of themselves first, and how to get your individual rights. We don't. We think about the culture and how to make the people strong within it.

"That's what we're doing. We're building the culture. That's our job. That's why it's our turn, now."

She released her grip on my arm and slid off the tailgate. "See? It's easy," she said over her shoulder, with just a hint of irony in her voice.

Delvin grinned and picked at his teeth with the tip of a jackknife. He held up his hands in a knowing shrug. Danelle took several steps toward the yard, then turned to face us. "Well, I should go see Grandpa," she said breezily. She walked off toward the trailer. After about twenty feet she turned again and looked at me. "Here's something for you," she said with a lilt. "If we're so repressed as women, how come all the white sisters come to our old ones to find wisdom? I dare you to write that."

I pulled my pen from my pocket and waved it at her to show that I would. She gave a clever little smirk and skipped a schoolyard skip.

"She's no one to mess with," Delvin laughed.

"None of them are," I said.

Delvin pointed at Danelle's receding form with the tip of his knife. "They've held our people together," he said, a tone of admiration shading into his voice. Danelle was herding two kids toward the trailer, gesturing instructions with one hand and adjusting a collar with the other. "Should've sicced them on the white man. You guys would've gone home in rowboats."

Chapter 21

Half-breed

We didn't leave Annie's place until well after noon. Dan had immersed himself in a long conversation with the legless man and Grover was doing something with the kids under the watchful eye of Danelle. Most of the talk was in Lakota, so I made myself as unobtrusive as possible by performing mechanical tasks like checking the oil and undercarriage of Grover's Buick. I had enough to think about to keep myself occupied.

Annie had retreated to the shade of the chair by the door, where she had surrounded herself with an array of vegetables that Delvin and Dannie had brought from the store. It was a treasure to her of almost religious significance, and her hands worked the ears and pods with the same private devotion they had lavished on the rosary beads.

I crawled under the car to check for a rattle I had heard in the exhaust system. Even if I found it, there was not much I could do without tools. But I wanted to stay out of the way. This was family — even Grover in his way — and I was not. I preferred the solitary comradeship of mufflers and shock absorbers to forced conversation or idle hanging about.

Before long, however, a pair of eyes peered in at me. They

were followed by another, then another. The three children had made their way over from Grover to see what the *wasichu* was doing.

I slid out and said hello. The kids stood silently with their hands in their pockets. A burst of laughter came from across the lawn. We all turned in time to see Dan doing a strange gigue in the dirt. Puffs of dust rose from his feet and blew off across the yard.

"What's your name?" I asked the boy with the blond curls. His appearance fascinated me and I wanted to know something of his story.

"Eugene," he said shyly.

I gestured toward Danelle. "Is that your mama?"

"Yes."

"Who are your brothers and sisters?"

He pointed to the others, proud of knowing the answer. "Myron and April."

The little girl covered her face and giggled. The older boy just stared. He would reveal nothing.

The little blond boy licked his lips. His correct answers had given him courage. He could talk to the *wasichu*.

"Are you Grizzly Adams?" he asked. The observation made me smile. Whether it reflected my actual appearance, or some mythology that everyone around here wanted to play out, it was becoming a familiar refrain.

"No," I said. "Do I look like him?"

The little girl giggled again and shook her head up and down.

The blond boy pressed forward. "What's your name?"

I thought for a second before answering, "Kent." "Mr. Nerburn" seemed too formal; "Nerburn"— the choice of most of the older Indians — was ridiculous in this situation. "Kent" was what I was left with when I ran out of alternatives.

"Do you have kids?" the boy in curls asked.

"Yes."

"Where are they?" He was running down his own list of children's concerns.

"At my house in Minnesota."

"Are you a white man?"

I laughed at his openness.

"Sure am."

"So's my daddy. He lives in California."

"Have you ever been there?" I asked.

"No," he said. His lower lip thrust out momentarily. My heart flooded toward the boy, then back toward my own son almost a thousand miles away. I wanted to grab this little fellow and give him a hug.

The other children stood behind Eugene watching the conversation. The little girl was shy and demure, as if waiting for a gift. For no apparent reason I reached in my pocket and gave her a quarter. She ran off toward her mother squealing with delight.

The older boy didn't move. I fished out another handful of change. Because he was older it seemed I should give more. I took an assortment of coins and held them toward him. He looked unsmilingly at them, then took them in a crisp gesture and thrust them quickly into his pants pocket. He did not leave.

The little blond boy was staring wide-eyed toward my pocket, anticipating a treasure of his own. I had backed myself into a corner where anything I gave him would be either too much or too little.

"How old is your sister?" I asked.

"Eight."

"Then you should have a quarter, too." I hoped the absolute lack of logic would serve as an irrefutable explanation. I dropped the silver coin into his hand like a precious stone. The dark-eyed boy just stood and stared.

"So you're Myron?" I said, trying to engage him. The boy said nothing. Expressions moved across his face like reflections on the surface of a lake.

"Where do you live?" I persisted. Still no answer.

"Do you like coming to visit your great grandma?" The boy turned his back to me and walked away swiftly. He had seen me, judged me, conversed with me, and rejected me, all without a word on his part.

I looked back at the blond boy. His eyes met mine, then turned toward his departing brother, then turned back to me. He wrestled for a moment with some private indecision, then quickly stuffed his shirttail back into his belt and took off in the direction of the house.

The sun had lost all gentleness by the time we were ready to leave. It hung in the sky like an angry wound, barely visible through an arid haze so dry that it hurt the lungs. Even the dogs had given up their jumping and chasing and had taken refuge in small dusty hollows they had carved out for themselves in the tiny patches of shade beneath the trees.

Shimmering waves of heat rose from every object. A shrub became a man walking toward you; a man became a willowy spectre with putty limbs and melting face. The great bowl of land that only hours ago had seemed blessed by the gentleness of the morning wind was now a tortured, desiccated cauldron.

The children had gathered in a copse of trees out by the outhouse. They were sitting together, talking occasionally, drawing in the dirt with bent sticks. Delvin, Danelle, and the legless man had retreated to the thin sliver of shade cast by the overhanging roof of the tiny log house. Annie still held her post in the stiff wooden chair by the door. The work of her hands had to continue even in the harsh brittle heat. Every once in a while she lifted her head to see if we were done loading and packing. I sat protected in the shade of a wheel well of Grover's Buick; I just wanted to get in the car and get going.

Grover was walking back and forth from the trailer to the car loading various bags into the trunk. Dan was saying some final words to the legless man. They were obviously very good friends. Their exchanges, all in Lakota, had been marked by outbursts of shared laughter — two people taking pleasure in common memories.

Grover slammed the trunk. "Saddled up," he hollered toward Dan from beneath his cowboy hat. I envied him its broad brim and the circle of shade it provided.

"Just a minute," Dan shouted from the doorway.

He disappeared into the dark interior, only to reemerge seconds later.

We watched him move slowly back across the yard. His form shimmered and shifted in the heat. I could not decide if his long-sleeved shirt was a protection or just added to the pain. He was like an animal that paid no attention to its skin.

Grover fired up the car. Dan got in and slammed the door. No one in the house or under the trees moved. The horizon wavered in the heat. One of the young kids picked up a hunk of clay and threw it half-heartedly in our direction. We drove out of the dusty yard with no waves or good-byes.

When we reached the top of the rise, Grover honked twice. I twisted in my seat to get one last look at the cabin. Everyone was in the yard, watching, with their hands at their sides. The wind blew their clothes hard against their bodies. Grover honked once more, and we drove off over the hill, out of their view, out of their world, out of their lives.

The miles passed quickly on the empty highway. The landscape on either side of us was beginning to change. Rock outcroppings began to jut like broken bones through the grasslands. It was as if the earth's skeleton were being revealed, and the thin skin of soil that had so recently been a grassland sea was now no more than a fragile layer of protection from the prehistoric geological forces that groaned beneath our feet. Buttes and mesas rose up through the earth and towered in the distance. Table rocks and flat-topped cones like extinct volcanoes dotted the horizon. This was the true "west river", as the locals called it — the western side of the Missouri — where the monster Rockies started to break and rise like a slumbering giant through the extinct seabed of the Dakota high plains.

The heat was stifling. We rode with the windows down, silenced by the roar of the wind rushing past. The sky had gotten heavy and pregnant with meaning. Clouds massed and raced on the horizon. A flush of birds rose from the roadside like leaves in a windgust. There was a storm in the air.

I stared idly out the window at the looming clouds. The little blond boy and his family had filled my mind with thoughts of home. I felt alien, disconnected, alone. Delvin's and Dannie's revelations about Dan's past had made me feel distant. These were things he could have told me.

Dan seemed to be reading my mind. "You liked the little blond kid, huh?" he shouted over the rush of the passing air.

"Reminded me of my boy," I answered absently. "I miss him."

"You talked different to him than to the others."

The observation irritated me. I didn't feel like having my actions scrutinized by someone who had hidden the motivations behind so many of his own. And besides, I wanted to stay inside my own thoughts. "He reminded me of my own kid," I answered sharply. "I told you."

"It's good to be reminded of your kid," he answered cryptically. Everything he said now echoed with a double meaning. "But I don't think that was it."

"Dan," I said testily, "He was standing in the front. He was the only one who talked. I just did the natural thing."

"I don't think so," he persisted. "The other kids noticed it. They always do." He rolled up his window. He wanted to talk.

I gave in. There was no sense denying him when the urge to speak overtook him. I rolled up my window, too. "Okay, what are you driving at?"

"He wasn't an Indian to you. That's why you talked to him more."

"Jeez!" I said. This was not a subject I wanted to pursue. "He wasn't anything. He was a kid. His dad was white." I almost added, "like your wife." But that would have been petulant, and would have opened up a conversation I didn't feel like having. "That's what he told me."

"So he wasn't an Indian."

"He was half Indian and half white."

"A half-breed, then?"

"What do you want me to say?" I answered. The heat had given me a headache and my shirt was sticking to the back seat of the car.

"He was a half-breed, right?"

"If you say so."

Dan was getting excited. He had an idea he was stalking. "You didn't call him that, maybe. But that's what he's called. He's a 'breed'. The other kids — the older kids — they lived in Denver around white people for two years. The little guy, Eugene, he's never been as far as Rapid City. He speaks Lakota. He's never even seen his white dad. But to you the other kids are more Indian."

I thought of their silent mahogany faces and their straight, shining hair. "Racially, I guess they are."

"And that's what matters to make them an Indian to you?"

"I guess. I don't know." This conversation was far too loaded. I wanted out of it. But Dan was anxious for more. He was obviously pleased with my admissions.

"See, that's the way it is with you white people. It's like race is the biggest thing."

"Well, you sure as hell want it to be."

"No, it's not me," he said. "But this is something I think about a lot. Seeing you with Eugene reminded me."

"Oh?"

"Yeah. It's something you should think about. Here, let me tell you something. It wasn't forty years ago they still divided kids in school into groups. Full-bloods, half-bloods, and quarter-bloods. Made them hold up signs. Then took pictures. Those were just kids, and they were divided up like they were some kind of damn recipe or something."

"That was forty years ago, Dan," I said.

"So you think it isn't going on anymore? Look at you, the way you talked to Eugene."

"I told you, he was the one who talked to me."

Dan was not to be deterred. "Yeah. We see it all the time. It's one of the things that surprises white people when they first come to a reservation. A lot of the kids don't look like Indians. Some of them are blond, like Eugene, or redhead. Some have blue eyes. That bothers white people. We can see it. You talk different to those kids. They aren't real Indians to you.

"Every Indian notices this. Those kids are Indians to us, but not to you. Since your people first came over here we have been taking white people and letting them live with us. They have become Indians and we think that's fine. But it drives you crazy.

"In the old days, during all the fighting, people would be captured, or we'd find someone without a home—you know, there were a lot of kids without parents—their parents were killed in accidents or maybe in the Civil War."

"Maybe by Indians," I said. I was getting irritable.

"Yeah. Maybe by Indians," Dan answered. He would not take the bait. "We took those kids and those other people and let them live with us. We made them Indians. When they had children with one of our people, the children were Indians. Nowadays it's more like some woman having a kid with a white man . . ."

I couldn't resist. "Or a man having a kid with a white woman."

"Right," he glared, "or a kid having a white grandparent." We were jousting now. "But they're still our people. They're still Indians to us."

I kept hearing Delvin's words that Dan's son had "had a tough time" because of his mixed race background. I wondered what that had meant — if the trouble had been with other Indians, or with the whites, or about self-identity.

Dan seemed to anticipate my question. "But if one of those children went back with your people, they're not white either. You don't see the white half and claim them. Then you see the Indian half and call them a half-breed. They get teased in school. Called 'Tonto' or 'Pocahantas'. We know. The kids come back and tell us."

I imagined Dan's son returning to the reservation after trying to live back East with his mother.

"Think of that!" Dan said. "All we cared about was the way they were raised and the people they became. You looked at the color of their skin and the color of their hair and you started dividing them up to see how much white they had in them! You called them half-breeds. Wouldn't let them be white and wouldn't let them be Indians."

Even in the heat, and filled as I was with a foul mood, I couldn't help but feel the pain of the old man's private memories. I kept seeing the picture of that solemn young man in the mortarboard hanging on his livingroom wall. The serious expression, the sense of purpose: the face of a youth who was going to "build a bridge" to his mother.

"That's just the way it is, Nerburn," Dan continued. "Race is the biggest thing to white people. You can see it yourself. All you have to do is watch white people talk to people who aren't white. Sooner or later they're going to bring up race.

"Wenonah's one little girl, she's like Eugene. She doesn't look like an Indian, so no one ever talks about it, except maybe to say, 'Oh, you don't look like an Indian'. But me or Wenonah or even old Grover, we look like Indians. Pretty soon after we start talking with a white person, that white person will bring up Indians, sure as anything."

"It's true, Nerburn," Grover chimed in.

Dan kept on. "They might talk about some other Indian they knew or they might talk about some movie or something to do with Indians. Probably it's to show us how much they claim to like Indians. But you sure know that they're going to bring up Indians. It's like that's the biggest thing when they meet me. I could be the president or have a cure for cancer, but before anyone could talk about it, they'd have to say something about Indians.

"Black people have told me it's the same for them, too. You white people just seem to see race first, no matter what.

"Then the really funny thing is that you pretend you don't see race. Like the other night, I was sitting with Grover. We were watching a boxing match on TV."

He turned toward Grover for confirmation. "You remember that?"

"Sure do. Lousy fight."

"Anyway, the announcer kept talking about the one guy in black trunks with a white stripe and the other guy in black trunks with a gold stripe. Hell, I couldn't even see the difference. But that was how he kept talking about them. And you know what? One guy was white and the other guy was black! But the announcer couldn't say, 'the white guy' and 'the black guy' because you're not supposed to see that. It was the damndest thing I ever saw.

"It's all part of a big lie you live. It's like race is the biggest thing you see, but its the hardest thing for you to talk about."

"I guess I kind of touched a nerve, eh?" I said. I was still hoping he might mention his son.

"It's not my nerve," he said. "It's the white people's nerve. I'll tell you what's really going on. White people are afraid of everyone who isn't white. Look at how you define black people. If a person had one black ancestor back somewhere, and you can see it, you tell them they are black. Everybody for the last thousand years might have been white, but one grandparent was black, then you tell that person they are black. You don't do that with Italians or Irish. You don't say they're Italian if they have one old grandma somewhere who came over on a boat a hundred years ago. But one black grandma? Bingo, you're black. Think about it, Nerburn. If your wife was black, and you had a kid, you'd lose that kid. He'd be black. But the thing is, you're not really saying they are black. You're saying they're not white.

"See, white is a weak color. Think of paint. You add one drop of something else and it's not white. You can add white and white and white and white and you're never going to overcome that one drop of the different color. That paint will never be white again. That's what you're afraid of.

"But at least with blacks, you let them alone once you decided they weren't white. You just threw them all in a barrel — black, brown, tan, whatever — and called them black. But us Indians, you couldn't even leave us alone to be Indians once you decided we weren't white. You start dividing us up, calling us half-breeds, full bloods. Try calling a black person with some white blood a half-breed. See how that goes over."

He steepled his hands up like a preacher making a point. "See, we do it the other way. One Indian, and you're an Indian if you want to be. For white people, you've got to have all white people to be white. One person who's not white, and that kid is an outsider forever. We only need one Indian to be an Indian. Do you see what I mean?"

"Yeah, I see what you mean."

"Then think about it. You've got all sorts of rules that you don't even know. Like, it's okay for white people to adopt Chinese kids, but it's not okay for Chinese people to adopt white kids. Or when different races go out together, the men are always supposed to be white."

He looked to me for confirmation. I said nothing.

"It's true," he continued. "If a white man is with a black woman, then he's liberal. But if a black man is with a white woman, he must be a pimp. It's the same with Indians. If a white man is with an Indian woman, it might be okay. That's the way they like to do it in the movies. But if an Indian man is with a white woman, there's something wrong with her that she would choose to be with one of 'those people'.

"I think it has to do with conquering. The white man has to be in control. If there is a man of a different color who is in control of a white woman, either there has to be something wrong with her or there is something bad about him. She's a captive or a renegade. I mean, why would a decent white woman ever want to be with an Indian man? Right?"

I couldn't help but smile. He was right on target.

"It's the same about kids," he went on. "If a white person marries someone who's not white, and they have children, it's okay if the kids are raised like white people, at least while the kids are still small. But if they're raised as Indians or blacks or something else, you say, 'Oh, that poor kid. He doesn't really belong anywhere.'"

"Well, if that kid has an Indian parent, they belong with us. We believe that. We don't give them any tests or put them in groups according to how much Indian blood they have in them.

"Admit it. If little Eugene was with white people you would think it's more okay than him living with Indians. Admit it." He was proud of his reasoning. Without waiting for an answer, he continued, "But if that little fellow went back to live with white people, other kids would call him Tonto and half-breed and would make war-hoops when he went by. That's the damn truth."

"The kid was talking to me," I said simply. "That's all there was to it."

"Tell that to April," he answered, reaching into his pocket. He pulled out a piece of lined paper that had been torn from a school notebook and handed it to me. On it was a meticulously rendered child's drawing of four people. There was a big round figure outlined in pink with a scrawly beard, standing next to a smaller round figure with yellow curliques hanging from its head. The two were facing forward and had watermelon smiles, large circle eyes with dots in them, and stick arms that ended in bird-foot hands. Next to them, with a slight separation in between, were two other round figures, smaller, one with legs and one with a triangle dress. The one with a dress had a silver coin in her bird hand. Her face, like that of the figure next to her, was colored in a dark brown. Both had little dots like raisins for eyes. Neither had a mouth.

On the bottom was scrawled, in careful Catholic-school hand, "For mister kent. from April. Thanks. Bye."

I flushed a bit as I stared at it. "It's okay, Nerburn," Dan said. "You gave her a quarter."

Chapter 22

The Song of History

We drove onward into a darkening sky. Signs began appearing along the side of the roadway. Most touted some desperately conceived attraction or artificial reason for a traveler to stop: "Live Bears." "Reptiles." "World's Largest Car Collection." "See Elvis' Motorcycle." "Shortest Route to the Black Hills."

Others demanded that we renounce abortion or make a commitment to Jesus.

Grover took great pleasure in reading their messages out loud as we passed. He was a town crier at work, making no commentary, but merely repeating what was before him.

Occasionally he would chuckle if one struck his fancy, though there was no apparent logic in his choices.

Dan, as usual, was smoking cigarette after cigarette. Whatever anger and agitation had gripped him as we left Annie's house seemed to have dissipated. I wasn't sure whether it had just been my perception or whether he had actually been feeling anguish about his son, but he had a less wistful, more analytical air about him now. He was watching the passing landscape with a renewed interest.

Approaching cars now had their lights on. Far up on a hill

some rancher had erected a cross. It stood in whitewashed naked-
ness against the grey backdrop of the impending storm.

"The land of Jesus," I said, idly.

"The land of *Wakan Tanka*," Dan corrected.

"A land of faith, at any rate," I said, trying to embrace all possi-
bilities.

"Yep. It'll do that to you."

The heat was stifling and foreboding. Dan was relaxed in his
seat with one arm draped out the window. His old plaid shirt
flapped around his elbow.

"What do you think of Jesus, Nerburn?" he asked.

It was a question I did not want to touch. I said nothing.

"I mean, do you think he is alive today?"

"Like the Second Coming?"

"That might have already happened," Dan said slyly. "I mean, is
his spirit alive?"

I started to launch into some academic dodge. Dan stopped me.

"No, I don't want to hear that. I got you figured already. It's
that rancher I want to know about. The one who put up that cross.
What does he think?"

I cast about for an answer. Grover broke in to read us some billboard about Mount Rushmore.

"That's what I mean," Dan said. I hadn't a clue what he was
talking about.

"Those presidents. I've thought about this a lot. Let's take those
two guys."

"What two guys?"

"The two guys I'm talking about. Jesus and Abraham Lincoln."

I thought perhaps he had lost all grip on reality. "You're not
talking about them, Dan. You must be thinking about them. I think
the heat's got you."

He pushed on, undeterred. "Those missionaries come around
the reservation. Three, four ladies in a car, all dressed up. They

come out and try to talk to you about Jesus. Now, Jesus has been dead for a lot of years. Why do they come and try to talk to us about Jesus?"

He was on the trail again. All I could do was go along. At least the ghost of his son did not hang over this conversation. "Because they believe if you believe in him he will be alive in your heart and you will be saved," I said.

"Right!" Dan was excited. "Now, why don't they get all dressed up and come and talk to us about Abraham Lincoln?"

The image was so bizarre that I didn't even hazard an answer.

"It's because Abraham Lincoln is dead. But, now, Jesus is dead, too. But he can come alive if you bring him into your heart. That's what they always say. Here's the question: Why can't Abraham Lincoln come alive if you bring him into your heart?"

I felt like a contestant on a surreal quiz show. "I don't know."

Dan was triumphant. "It's because Abraham Lincoln was part of white man history."

"And Jesus wasn't?"

"No. He's part of a different kind of history. The kind Indian people understand. Where things have power because they are *wakan*. That's why so many Indian people believe in him."

For all its fragmented logic, there was something significant percolating in Dan's mind. I sat up and took interest.

"Good," he said. "You've decided to listen. I was getting ready to give up on you."

"I'm all ears." I switched on the recorder and settled myself into a comfortable position against the sweaty green vinyl. Fatback chuffed at being disturbed, but quickly settled back to sleep.

"Now. Your Abraham Lincoln kind of history, the kind you teach in schools, is not good for Indian people. It is a funny kind of history, where the most important thing is what happened. You want to know everything about what happened, like how many people were somewhere, what they wore, what they were thinking. That's all important to you. The more you know the more history you think you have.

"This isn't good history. It isn't Indian history. It's like studying all the parts of the body and then saying you understand about life. It is just facts.

"This has really hurt the Indian people. You had a bad kind of history, then you got that bad history all wrong."

"What do you mean, we got it wrong?" I interjected. I wanted to make sure I was following him.

He breathed a deep sigh of resignation. "Am I talking or are you? I thought you wanted to learn something."

"Sorry."

He shook a crooked finger at me. "That's why we always beat you white guys in a fair fight! You only know how to go in a straight line. We knew how to move around and come in on you from all sides. Now, just be quiet and listen."

Grover slapped the steering wheel in pleasure.

Dan continued. He was his old, cantankerous, exuberant self.

"Look at what your way did to our people. When you came among us you didn't care what was alive in our hearts. You wanted to know facts.

"If you asked us when something happened, we might tell you it was in the year when all the buffalo froze. Then you'd get mad and ask us, when was that? So maybe we'd tell you it was the year the stars fell. That's how we kept track of years.

"But that wouldn't be a good enough answer for you. You would want to know what year it was by a number. As if it made any difference to know a number of a year. You got mad when we couldn't give you a day with a number on it and said we didn't remember.

"So you made our history from the things your people could remember. And all you remembered were the things the traders wrote down, or the things the missionaries wrote down, or the soldiers. When we fought with you, you wrote down what weapons we used and how many people got killed.

"If you could find some Indian who would work for you, you

made him a chief so he could sign papers giving away our land, then you wrote down what he said. If he didn't say anything, you wrote down something for him and had him sign it, then that was the history.

"Do you see what this did? Think about it. The traders wrote down numbers about how many furs they got. Maybe they wrote something about what the Indians lived like. The missionaries wrote down why we weren't civilized and maybe about our ceremonies, and how strange they seemed. The people who fought us wrote down whatever they wanted in order to make themselves look good.

"Do you think they wrote, 'The Indians had a better battle plan and were better fighters'? Do you think they wrote, 'We killed a lot of babies today'? I don't think so.

"And those false chiefs, you wrote whatever you wanted to make those false chiefs seem like our leaders. And they would say anything you wanted because then you would give them houses and money. You even had them sign things they couldn't even read, and because it was written down, you said it was true, even though there wasn't an Indian in the world who knew what it said.

"Then later, when you tried to divide our land up and give us little pieces, you tried to make us have last names and marriage certificates, like we were white people. You wrote it all down. Some of our people thought it was so stupid they would give you different names every time they talked to you. So you got everything confused and wrong.

"By the end, everything was wrong and a lie. But it was all written down, so you said it was true and you taught it to your children like it was true.

"That's what your white history did for us."

He sucked triumphantly on his cigarette. The signs for Mount Rushmore, with their bad line drawings of the four presidents' heads, were becoming more frequent. They looked absurd and miniature against the looming dark of the western sky. I thought he was finished. But he exhaled hard, expelling a long stream of smoke, and began again.

"But it did something worse, too. It took away all of our history from before the time you came here to our country. It's like before you came here, we didn't exist. You won't believe anything we tell you unless you can dig up some pot or an arrowhead. Then you put it in a lot of machines and put chemicals on it so you can know when it was made, and then you say, 'Now we know about it. Now we know what happened.' Then the man who did the tests writes down what he found out and other people write down what they think about what he found out, and you call that history.

"I can come to you and tell you what my grandfathers told me, and that's not history unless the chemicals told you the same things. I can even tell you about power, like *wipoye*, the medicine bag, or how one becomes a double woman — but I wouldn't — and you would just say that is a story.

"See, none of what we know is history to you. Our sacred stories are just legends to you. The powers we were given by our ancestors you think are superstitions. The responsibilities, too. None of that is real in your history.

"All it really means is there wasn't anyone with a book writing things down. It doesn't matter that when your people came with books and wrote things down, they wrote lies. All that is important to you is that they wrote something down. Once it was down then it was truth. Then there was history. The elders used to say, '*Wasichu* builds his house on lies.' That's what they meant."

I couldn't suppress a smile. Dan looked at me and twinkled, his milky white eye glinting in the halflight. A little, low "heh, heh," came like thunder from deep in his chest. He knew he had me.

"This is where Jesus comes in. When they made me go to church and learn about Jesus, nobody asked what year it was. Here he was, the most important person, and nobody wanted to know what year it was when things happened to him. It was just 'when Jesus was alive.' What was important was what happened.

"Like, I was taught that when he was killed there was a big earthquake."

"Yes," I interjected, looking out at the gloaming sky, "A great darkness came over the land."

Dan was in no mood for cleverness. "It was killing him that made it happen. Nobody ever asked how many people were killed in this earthquake, or how many people were standing around when Jesus died. No one needed to know what year it was. That wasn't important. What was important was that an earthquake happened when Jesus died.

"Don't you see? If it was important that an earthquake happened when Jesus died, then why wasn't it important that a lot of stars fell in the year the buffalo froze?"

A far-off blast of lightning lit the edges of the billowing clouds. "I'll tell you why. Because white people wouldn't believe the two things had anything to do with each other. You believed that Jesus and the earthquake had something to do with each other, but you didn't believe that the buffalo and the stars had anything to do with each other. An earthquake could happen because Jesus died. But the stars couldn't fall because the buffalo died.

"Here's another one. There was a star in heaven that led those kings to Jesus when he was born. But there can't be a star that is given to our people as a guide. When our people talk about the seven stars and how they taught us to have seven council fires, you don't believe it is real. You say it is a myth or a legend. Well, maybe the star leading the kings is just a myth or a legend, too.

"I think you should think about this. You have two different stories about how history works. It doesn't make any sense."

"This is a big sucker," Grover interrupted, gesturing across the dashboard toward the sky. "I'm going to try to outflank it." He was once again the captain, guiding his ship away from the dangers of the treacherous reefs and shoals. He took a left down a long ribbon of asphalt that stretched off southward into the hills. The storm lay in wait, grumbling and flashing, along the western horizon.

"Never do it," said Dan.

"Maybe," Grover answered. He pressed the accelerator harder and the Buick surged forward. The wall of dark to the west glinted and flashed at us like dragons' eyes.

Dan went on with his story. "The reason my people listened when you talked about Jesus was because we could understand how you were thinking. It was like what happened to Jesus then is important now, the same as it was the day it happened.

"We could understand that, because that's how we learned about our past. If my grandfather's grandfather made the buffalo turn away from the village one time, then that was how I knew the year. It was the year the buffalo turned away from the village. It was the year my grandfather gave me the power to turn danger away from our people. I still have that power, because he gave it to me by what he did.

"That's how you taught me about Jesus. He was alive a long time ago, but he gave you power to do things today. But when you wanted to learn about my grandfather's grandfather, you don't believe he gave me power. You want to know how many buffalo, and what year it was.

"Well, why don't you go try to find out what year Jesus was born and how many people were there when he was killed, and the scientific reason why there was an earthquake then? Why isn't all that important? That's what you want to know about the buffalo, if maybe they had some disease that made them charge the camp, or if maybe we had the camp in a different place that year. If I talk to you about the power that gave me, you don't want to listen. But you want me to listen all about the power that Jesus gave you.

"It doesn't make any sense. Either it's the way things work, or it isn't. If it's okay for you to not know what year Jesus lived, but just to start numbering the years from then, then it's okay for me not to know what year my grandfather's grandfather lived. If it's okay for what Jesus did to give you power now, then it's okay for what my grandfather's grandfather did to give me power now.

"But your mind lives in two worlds. In one of those worlds, things that happen always have power, like Jesus. In the other world, things only happen once, and they only have power when they happen, and you have to get a perfect picture of it, with how many people were there and all the things that were there and all the things that lead up to it and all the things that happened because of it. That's the only way you really understand it."

He stopped to let me absorb what I'd heard. "What do you think of that, Nerburn?"

I was dazed. I didn't know if I was ten steps ahead of him or ten steps behind. "You know, Dan," I said. "Sometimes I think you're just toying with me."

"Why do you think they couldn't catch Geronimo, or Joseph?" Grover said proudly. Dan just came forth with a few more low, rumbling "heh, heh's."

"Now you will hear about Abraham Lincoln," he said. "I said I was thinking about him, too. To me he was like one of your great chiefs. When I think about him I see how different we really are. To me, he was your greatest leader. He wasn't afraid to do things for people he never saw. He tried to do right. I think he would have been a good Indian.

"But you teach about him like a dead man. He's not like Jesus to you. He's not alive to you any more. So you make children learn when he was born and where he was born and everything about him. You make them learn him like he was a stuffed bear in a museum. This is your mistake.

"Why don't you say that he is still alive today in the hearts of your people? Why don't you teach your history so that your children have to keep him alive in their hearts and make that more important than knowing how tall he was and where he was born?

"You teach your children that Abraham Lincoln freed the slaves. Why don't you teach them that he made you all slave-freers and that you are now his children and must uphold his honor?

"That's what we do.

"But you want your children to pass a test about when Abraham Lincoln signed some paper that freed the slaves. If they know that, then you say they know about Abraham Lincoln. It makes your history thin and ugly because it puts things in boxes on shelves to be taken down and examined instead of keeping them alive. I think our way is better. I really do."

"I can't disagree with you, Dan," I said.

"You'd better not," he laughed. "I was starting to think you were stupid. I'll tell you just a little more, now. Just a little more.

"See, we have always had history like white people history, too. You just wouldn't believe us. We had our stories and our pictures. We had our ways of doing things that were passed down to us from our elders. That was just like white people history. It had facts, too. But they weren't good enough for you.

"If I show you how my grandfather made something, you didn't trust me. But if some white person who didn't even know what he was seeing wrote it down, then that was good enough to be history.

"There is too much to know everything. We Indians just tried to know the important things, so we could live better and understand.

"We had people who could tell us about the old days and why they were important to us. We made our children learn the stories so they could repeat them just as they were told. Our history was alive. But your history was dead, even though it was written down in words.

"I will tell it to you one more way. If you hear a song, is it real? Or is it only real once somebody writes it down?

"Well, for us, the story of our people was like a song. As long as somebody could still sing it, it was real. It never mattered if someone wrote it down. When you came you said that our song wasn't real because it wasn't written down. Then you wrote it down the way you wanted it.

"You are still writing down our story, using your words, and you are still getting it all wrong. Your words are all full of sharp edges that cut us. But we have been bleeding so long we don't even feel it anymore.

"It doesn't hurt me. I am old. I knew the old language and so did my friends. We still speak it. It is still the song in our heart. It is the young people who must learn to sing the song again."

He folded his arms and fell silent.

Grover hit the steering wheel like a baseball fan celebrating the announcement of a home run. "Damn!" he said. "Nerburn? I hope you're learning something."

I was still trying to take in everything I had heard. I rewound the tape recorder and listened to a few words to make sure I had it right.

Dan had returned to sitting upright in his seat and staring straight ahead, as he often did when he had finished speaking. But his mind was still working. "I will tell you one last thing," he spoke up. Once more, it was as if he were hearing a voice, and passing along what it said. "It is why you *wasichu* are in trouble. For you nothing is *wakan*. You have taken the power out of the Earth and the sky and the things that live there. Everything is a fact. You will drown under your facts."

Grover was positively ecstatic. I realized that he, too, had been concerned about Dan's descents into melancholy. This was the old man he knew and revered. He turned at me and grinned like a coyote. "In the old days, people brought gifts to elders who taught them like this," he said.

"Oh?" I answered.

"Yeah. It was a sign of respect." There was a playful twinkle in his eye.

"What sort of thing are you thinking of?"

He looked out at a red-and-white sign mounted on a hillside. "Steaks. Chicken. Ribs," he read.

"Ah," I answered. "I suppose they bought dinner for the man who drove the horse, too?"

"I'm just reading the signs, Nerburn," he said.

Chapter 23

Storm

Grover packed the last of his rib bones into a napkin for Fat-back. I paid the bill and we started out to the car.

One step outside the door and we could feel that the storm had caught us. The air had been moody and unsettled all day; now it was so close and thick you could hardly breathe. The light had taken on an unearthly green hue. Sheets of lightning flapped beyond the horizon.

Grover pulled back on the highway and took a turn directly west. "Got to make some time," was all he said.

"This one's got us," Dan said.

I sat dumbly, transfixed by the drama taking place in the heavens around me. Off to my right the sky was a crucible of darkness. It moved down upon us like a rolling night. Directly in front of us, the clouds were roiling and massing like a towering sea.

The sun was lost as if in the smoke of a prairie fire. Here and there it would find an opening and cut through with sickly shafts of sepulchral yellow light that burst across the hills and valleys for a moment, then were gone. Tiny electrical surges shot within the mushrooming cloud formations. The momentary flashes revealed angry interiors like avalanches or crashing rivers of sulphur. It was nature moving too fast, too large, to be subject to any human control.

A few raindrops hit like gunshots against the windshield.

"Big sucker," Grover intoned again.

A momentary flash of lightning revealed a billboard all written in blood red with a quote from John 3:16 and a huddled form of a fetus. It melted from view as the rain sheeted and flowed down the windshield.

The weather had made Fatback nervous. She rose in her seat and started whining.

"Good dog," I said, and scratched under her neck. She did not relax. Some primitive alarm had been raised in her. It was her duty to remain vigilant.

"I can see why people out here get religion," I said.

"Got the wrong one," Dan observed.

The cracking in the clouds revealed exploding billows of darkness, miles high and miles deep. Orange glows, like from a blast furnace, lit up the edges of the forms.

Lightning flashes cracked the sky and illuminated the tops of distant mesas.

"You going to drive through that?" I said, trying to keep my voice nonchalant.

Dan started chanting something in Lakota.

Rain cut like shards of glass on a diagonal through the pale cones of Grover's headlights. The roof of the car began to crack and ping. Ahead of us loomed a wall of celestial darkness. It was impenetrable, biblical, devoid of all light.

Dan closed his eyes and began chanting in a singsong voice. The air was electric. I expected to be taken up in a firestorm.

Suddenly all rain and movement stopped, as if the heavens were holding their breath. Grover pulled quickly to the side of the road.

Then, like an earthquake, a surge of wind roared across the

land. It swirled and hammered and blasted the car with sheets of rain. The whole car shook; water streamed down the windows. Cutting mists drove in through the cracks. We were cast into total darkness.

Involuntarily I slid down into the corner of my seat. Fatback crawled to the floor. Dan was still chanting, though his voice was hardly audible through the thunderous roar. Grover pulled a cigarette from his breast pocket and began to smoke.

The thick heavy odor of cigarettes and sweat filled the inside of the car. The wind roared like a banshee, a freight train, a herd of ten thousand buffalo. It buffeted us without mercy and clawed at the windows. Once or twice the car was rocked so violently I thought we were going to be blown over.

I was terrified like a child. This storm had a malevolence that seemed almost personal. It tore at the car as if it wanted to get in.

Fatback started whimpering. She pawed, agitated, driven by something unseen. Dan was rocking back and forth, much like Annie with her rosary. His singsong chants were lost in the wind. Grover smoked harder. The air was stultifying.

I imagined us inside some high plains tornado, about to be torn apart and scattered, bone from flesh, across miles of Dakota plain. Wild images of my son, of Eugene, of the legless man inside his room, blended and bled in my mind. "There are powers, Nerburn . . ." A thousand Indian voices admonished me. The storm raged in Lakota, I was convinced of it. Dan's chant was consonant with it, drowning in it, rising to meet it.

A wall of water came from the north and pommeled the car. We bounced and shook like men shipwrecked on an angry sea.

"*Wiyopeyate Wichasha*," Dan said clearly. I looked up. He was holding his hands in the air, beside his face. "The Man from the West. He is here."

I looked at Grover. He was staring intently at Dan. Dan's voice rose higher. He was speaking half in English. "*Yata*, I am your friend." Then something about *Wakinyan*. His eyes were still closed and he was rocking. I glanced at Grover.

"The Winged One," he whispered. The car shook and rattled; water streamed down all the windows.

A great swoop of wind almost tore the roof off the car, then all was still. A few sheets of rain blasted against us. The car shuddered once or twice, then settled. It was over.

The light returned dimly. The shapes of the hills emerged through the streaming water on the windshield. We could see the dark sky receding, moving toward the south. Light filtered through the clouds, catching the running rivulets and glistening in droplets on the grasses.

A shaft of sunlight cut through and raced across the hillsides. The sun peered around the corner of the retreating blackness. The earth was born again.

Grover began speaking to Dan in Lakota. The conversation was low, serious. There was much back and forth discussion, with some apparent disagreement.

I rose up in my seat, drained and exhausted. I wanted to talk about the storm, but I sensed that the discussion going on in front of me was something I should not interrupt. The two men had never talked so much between themselves in Lakota around me. Either they did not wish me to hear what they were saying, or this was a conversation which could not easily be carried on in English. I listened intently in the faint hope that I could understand a word or two.

Abruptly Dan turned and spoke to me in English. "There should not have been wind from the north," he said. "This troubles me."

I didn't know if this was a meteorological concern or something else. I suspected it had to do with larger issues.

"Why?" I said.

"I think it was all the west," Grover interjected. "Hell, you knew it, too," he said, using Dan's Lakota name. He and Dan began discussing again in Lakota.

After a moment Dan turned to me and asked, "Where was the wind, Nerburn?"

During the storm I had been huddling in my corner against a generalized fury. It had never occurred to me to consider the direction from which the wind had come. "I don't know," I said.

"Think," said Dan.

"I wasn't paying attention."

Dan grew angry. "You've always got to pay attention. It's important. What do you think I'm trying to teach you?"

Remembering the moving cloud banks off to our right I said, without conviction, "North, I guess. Though that doesn't make a lot of sense this time of year, so . . . ."

"It doesn't matter what makes sense," Dan snapped. "Did you feel wind from the north or not? I don't mean where did the storm come from. I mean, in the storm, was the wind that beat on the car from the north?"

"Well, yeah, I guess, but . . ."

"Yes or no."

I checked the position the car was facing. Grover had pulled off the road directly into the brunt of the storm, facing west. I felt the dampness on my right shoulder where the rain had forced its way through the cracked weather stripping around the car windows.

"Yes."

"Hnnh," Dan said. "*Waziya*. There is a message."

"What do you mean?" I said, slightly disconcerted.

"*Waziya* is not good. He is cold and cruel."

"*Waziya*?"

"The wind from the north." Dan was pulling a small pouch from inside his shirt. It had been hung around his neck on a leather thong. "The dead must pass his tepee on the way to the spirit land. They must tell him everything. When he comes, it is to bring messages from the dead."

I had always been prone to presentiments and belief in unseen forces. But usually I was able to ignore them. Here, in this open land, in my agitation after the storm, it was not so easy. My mind flashed to my wife and children.

"What do you think it means?" I asked.

He ignored my question. "What were you talking to Delvin and Danelle about?" he said. "I saw you talking to them for a long time."

"They were telling me about your past."

Dan made a gesture of spitting. "Hah," he said. Grover pursed his lips.

"Wait here now," Dan ordered. He opened the door and stepped out. The fresh smell of the drying earth rushed into the car. Fatback squeaked and clamored to get over the seat.

"Let her out," Dan said curtly. I opened the door on my side. She scrabbled across me and almost fell onto the ground. Dan spoke to her in Lakota. She got up and whimpered. Together they made their way across the steaming grass up over a short rise.

"Should have buried that dog with the kid," Grover muttered.

"What?" I said.

"Nothing. Just talking."

"What's going on here?" I said to Grover. "It spooks me when he gets like this."

"Spooks me, too," Grover answered, and pulled out another cigarette.

I wanted to get him talking, to reassure myself. "Does he get like this after every storm?" I asked.

"Nah. He didn't like this one, though. Said it had a message."

"A message?"

"Dan's in touch with a lot of forces," he said, cryptically.

I felt a shiver on the back of my neck. Grover had lit a match and was holding it up in front of him and idly watching it burn.

"I worry about my family when he talks like that," I said.

"Don't worry about your family," he said disinterestedly. The flame was burning down toward his fingers.

"I know. It's just that . . ."

"The old man wasn't talking about your family," he interjected. His voice was weary and slightly disgusted.

"What was he talking about?"

He pinched out the match. "Don't matter. The wind was from the west."

Presently, Dan and Fatback emerged from behind the rise. Dan was still fingering the pouch around his neck. Fatback hobbled behind him with her tongue out.

"We will go now," he said to me in English when he returned to the car. There was a sense of purpose in his manner that had not been there before.

He and Grover had a short discussion in Lakota; then Grover started the engine. He drove through the streams of water that were coursing off into the ditches and got back on the glistening highway. Already the water had begun to dry from the pavement. Willowy pillars of steam and heat rose from the asphalt like spirits. The memory of the great storm was etched into every plant and hill and hollow.

I felt like a man on the waking edge of a nightmare — exhilarated, unsure, still shaken; not sure which side of the dream was real. The dark cloud had moved far to the south and was rumbling and spitting over distant hills and mesas. Lightning flickered like snakes' tongues in the retreating forms. In front of us the prairie stretched and breathed deeply and seemed to come alive with birds and sunlight. Every bit of life seemed fresher, more fragile, more precious.

Dan offered no explanation for either his behavior during the storm or his actions afterward. "You must take me there, now," was all he said. Grover nodded and drove without comment.

A double rainbow arched across the sky. "Ah," said Dan, with an air of understanding. "That's good."

Mile after mile we drove in silence, each of us lost in private thoughts. I wanted to ask him about the wind and what he thought it had meant, but I didn't dare. His was a world in which every action, every movement, had meaning. My ignorance of those meanings felt like naivete. I was better served by silence.

The sun, victorious, lowered itself toward the horizon. It illuminated the bellies of the remaining clouds, creating a tapestry of oranges and silvers. With the wind gone, the sky stood triumphant. It became a landscape in itself — a great ethereal garden in the colors of memories — golden, violet, orange — all proceeding from the sun, as if in ritual procession.

"Here," Dan said, "this way." Grover veered onto another road. We arched over a freeway and made our way southward. The cars on the freeway beneath us seemed from a different world, with different missions. In the distance I could see the coarse sandstone spires of the badlands rising like a city of sepulchres.

The runoff from the furious storm had disappeared, leaving only tiny pools among the red clay glistening on the side of the road. We took a turn and bounced onto a gravel roadbed. Grover never varied his speed. The undercarriage of the car pinged from rocks that the tires threw up as we flew toward the unearthly formations in the distance.

All sense of leisure had been cast aside. We moved like men pursued. On either side of us, table rocks a hundred feet high rose like altars awaiting some celestial sacrifice. Their surfaces stretched out high above us, inaccessible, invisible, a landscape of the gods.

We came to an edge. The earth dropped off before us into a prehistoric seabed of stone pillars and crenelated cones of sand. With no more than a momentary hesitation, Grover plunged the car down the winding gravel path into this lunar landscape. Ancient miniature mountains rose around us like dragons' teeth. Spires of sand like Tibetan temples loomed on all sides. Bands of color cut for miles through the desiccated formations, echoing geological time that dwarfed all human considerations.

"Badlands," Grover said. No one responded. "This is where they came, Nerburn," he continued.

"Who?" I asked. Dan remained in silence, staring straight ahead.

"Sitting Bull's people." The ghost of a full moon was becoming visible in the sky above the valley floor. "Trying to get away from the soldiers."

He looked toward Dan, as if he expected the old man to begin talking. But Dan said nothing.

Grover was forced to continue his explanation. "After he was killed. You know, by the Indian police. His people were terrified. They joined with Big Foot and came south here. They figured the soldiers wouldn't follow them."

I looked around at the savage wasteland of sand and dust.

"They were wrong, though." He gestured out over the waterless terrain. "Look at this! It was December. The Moon of Popping Trees. Do you know what this is like in December?"

"Not very pleasant, I imagine," I said.

"Wind that will kill you. Freeze off your toes and fingers in minutes. Snow that will blind you," Grover went on. "Ice on everything. Temperatures so cold the rivers crack and the trees split. It's time to be indoors, telling stories. But they were outside, running from soldiers in the wind and cold. They had children, women. Babies wrapped in blankets. They'd snuck down a path that the soldiers didn't know. Isn't that right, Dan?"

Dan chewed his mouth, like a man adjusting his false teeth. But he did not speak.

"These were families, Nerburn," Grover said. "With little babies and old people. They had their tepees and cooking pots. They just wanted to live. But they couldn't even build fires to keep their children warm. The soldiers would have found them and killed them. They were starving and freezing."

The car roared through the desolate moonscape without slowing. The sun was disappearing with one last blaze of orange fury. The sand formations caught its brilliant glint and glowed like fire. In the cracks and crevasses the dark began to grow into new and threatening shapes.

"I am too old," Dan said suddenly.

I looked at him with alarm. He was still making that strange chewing action with his mouth.

"I should not throw my mind back," he said, as if to someone unseen. "I should live here in the life I have. I should think about my grandchildren and my great grandchildren. But my eyes see the tracks of the past. I cannot forget the dead." He turned toward Grover. "You should not trick me into talking, *Mitakola*."

Grover gave a faint hint of a smile. "You said you would teach him, *Tunkashila*. Now is the time."

Grover's tires spit up rocks. The shadows were stretching long across the land. Dan's good eye flashed like an animal's. "Now is not a good time for me to speak. My heart is heavy with the past. This is hard land for us. The spirits of our dead fill the skies."

"That's why you should talk," Grover said. "Sometimes when your heart is heavy you speak more truly."

"Hnnh," Dan said.

I looked warily from one to the other. I could not divine what was happening. Grover was clearly pushing the old man, and the old man was clearly listening to some inner voices. Again, their lapse into an almost formal manner of speaking hinted of serious intent.

"I will speak," Dan said suddenly. Grover tapped a cigarette triumphantly on the steering wheel.

"Yes, this was bad here. Babies froze in their mothers' arms. But it was the same everywhere. In Montana with Chief Joseph. With Geronimo. Everywhere. We were a good people. But we were not allowed to live."

The long shadows began to bend around the pillars and cones, enclosing them in darkness.

"You can tell us time has passed. You can say the world has changed. But the bones of my fathers still cry. My son is buried in a conquered land." This was the first he had ever mentioned his son since the first time I had visited him.

He looked at me, through me, beyond me. His face shone like fire in the waning light.

"We are not memories to be lost, like wind in the grass. What I am about to say to you are hard words. But I choose to say them, because this is hard land, and it invites hard words. Hear me. Then I will be quiet for a while."

He squared himself in his seat and began.

"There is no Indian alive who dares to think too much on the past. If we looked too long at the past we would be too angry to live. You try to make it up to us by making us into heroes and wise people in all your movies and books. That's fine for you. But I can still go to a museum and see my grandmother's skull in a case and hear someone talk about it as an artifact.

"Would you want your grandmother's skull to be in a case in my house? Would you be angry then?"

He cast his gaze out onto the shadowy formations. His bad eye glowed like an ember.

"And sometimes I think about all the wars between my people and your people. Those white men that fought us were men without any families, lots of them. They were young men out in the West making money. Some of them were convicts. Some of them were still blood drunk from the Civil War.

"They weren't your best people. Many of them were brutal and stupid. They did terrible things because it was fun. Not all of them, but they were soldiers and it was their job to kill people.

"My people never had a chance. We were families. We were in our homes, with our old people and our babies. And the soldiers attacked us. They attacked our homes and killed our elders and our children.

"The government sent men who didn't have anything or didn't fit anywhere, and gave them guns and put them on horses and told them to go out and attack the villages where we had our women and our old people and our little babies. There were little girls playing with dolls and little boys who were just learning to walk. The soldiers killed them all.

"Then your people have the nerve to talk about massacres by the Indians."

He turned in his seat and stared directly into my eyes. "Do you know why we ambushed the soldiers?"

I sat quietly. There was no answer I could give.

"Because," he said, "we were trying to keep them away from our children and babies and our old people. We had to get to them before they got to our families. We couldn't move fast because we had all our old people and children. All we had on our side was surprise and that we knew the land. We didn't have weapons and we couldn't run. We knew white soldiers always stayed together when they fought and we could outsmart them, so we did."

He paused for a moment to gather himself. The moon had cast off its ghostly aura and taken on a life of its own.

"We did kill innocent people. I know that. It happened when our young men got angry at what was happening to the old people and the children, when they were starving or being killed. The young men would get so angry they wouldn't listen to the old men.

"The old men knew we couldn't win and that more white people would come and there would just be more killing. But the young men were so angry that they attacked anyone."

"What do you think?" he said. His gaze was steady and direct. It left me no escape. "If you saw your father lying on his bed too weak to stand up because he was starving, or you saw your baby crying all the time because she was hungry, and you knew it was because someone took their food away from them, wouldn't you be angry?

"What if some men came through and killed your grandmother and didn't have any reason? They just did it, then they laughed and rode away. And you stood there and looked at her cut up or shot. Can you tell me you wouldn't be angry?"

He emitted a harsh and bitter laugh.

"This is why I shouldn't think about these things. Because, you know, I don't blame my people who ambushed the white soldiers or even raided the homes of the settlers. I don't say it was right. I just say I understand. We lost everything. Your government sent heartltless, greedy men to keep us under control and they lied and raped and stole from us and they could kill us for any reason and it was okay."

He stared me down, an old man, bearing eighty years of pain, speaking his mind to one of the race that had almost destroyed his people. This was personal now. He wanted me to feel his pain and he wanted to see my shame.

"What if someone raped your little sister?" he said. "That happened all the time."

"What if someone took your wife and slit open her belly and pulled out your unborn child, then laid it on the ground like a trophy still attached to her dead mother? That happened, too."

"See, we weren't even people. Did you know that? The Catholic church even held a conference to determine if we were people or not. In their great wise religion they thought they should decide if we were people or animals. That's the way we were thought of and treated. It was okay to do anything to us."

Perspiration had formed on his upper lip. He took a dirty rag from his pocket and swabbed his face. His expression was as dark as the land outside; his eyes as hollow as the moon.

"I think this is hard for you to understand. But our old people were our best people. Nowadays, the world is all for the young people. It wasn't that way for us. We were taught that the old people and the babies were the closest to God and it was for them that we all lived. They were the most helpless and they needed us the most.

"And your people came in and killed them. We couldn't protect them and that was what we had to do. But you were too strong. There were too many of you. We had to do what we could to protect our old people and our families and we couldn't because your soldiers broke into our houses and killed them when they couldn't get away."

His inner turmoil was titanic now. His hands shook and his eyelid twitched. He looked toward the sky as if beseeching some greater power for help. The moon hung empty over the towering spires.

"It wasn't the same when we fought the other tribes. They respected the old people and the children, too. When we fought each other there were some things more important than the fight. The greatest act of bravery was to touch your enemy — to 'count coup' upon him — not to kill him.

"But not for your soldiers. They just wanted to kill us. They were hunting us in that way your people hunt things where they kill as many as they can just to see them die or to count them and say they killed more than anyone else. It's something I can't understand. You even have to have laws saying how much of something you can kill or people would kill everything.

"That's what happened to us. There weren't any laws saying how many of us could be killed. We were treated worse than deer or fish. You could kill as many of us as you wanted, and the old people and the children were the easiest.

"Now there are skulls of my grandparents in museums and sacred blankets and drums on walls of museums for rich people to look at. You go there and talk about how sacred it is. You call it sacred because you don't have anything of your own that's sacred. But it's not sacred because you took the sacred out of it, just like you take the sacred out of everything, and now we can hardly feel it ourselves anymore. You killed our people and you took what was sacred to us and then you told us that's what proved you were better than we were."

I felt a great shame come across me. Dan was sparing me nothing now.

"Sometimes I think I would like to go into one of your cemeteries with a bulldozer and knock over all the headstones and plow up all the coffins. Then I'd take the bones and put them in plastic bags. I'd put them all in the window of a store with a sign that said, 'White People's Artifacts.' Then you could come down and point at a bag and say, 'That's my grandmother.' If you were lucky, I might even have the measurements of her skull on a little card on the bag.

"If you wanted the bones back, I'd just laugh. I'd say they were part of an exhibit and that we were treating them with respect. I might even charge you a dollar to come in and look at them. But I'd let your children in cheaper because I'd say they should learn about their past and how sacred it is. Then I'd take their money and show them the bags."

He stopped abruptly and let out a little sound that was somewhere between a sob and a yelp. He breathed deeply and stared hard at the darkening sky. Far in the distance the faint echo of thunder rumbled from the west.

Gathering himself, he spoke again. His voice was lower, almost contrite. "I am sorry to say these words to you. I shouldn't talk like this. It doesn't do any good. It just makes me feel angry and makes you feel bad. It all happened. I have to learn to forgive you and your people. We have to live together. I have to look to my grandchildren now. Maybe it will be better for them.

"I just wish I knew why it happened this way. I really do. I could be so much more peaceful if I just knew why it happened this way."

He leaned his head forward like a man in prayer. Grover stared at the road and gripped the steering wheel with both hands. The moon sat silent above the jagged peaks, hollow and empty, like the socket of an eye.

Chapter 24

Paha Sapa

We drove in heavy silence. I sat, pensive, chastened, saddened. Dan hunched in front of me, within a hand's grasp, but a thousand miles away. The looming sandstone menhirs and dolmens became fewer, then smaller, then gave way completely to rolling grasslands. The badlands had disappeared as abruptly as they came.

Grover's Buick cut through the night. Here and there we would pass by some tiny shipwreck of a town, devoid of lights, with a huddling cluster of abandoned wooden buildings standing swaybacked against the cold illumination of the moon.

Under the empty lunar gaze the whole world turned to silver. Everything was alive, yet there was no life anywhere. It was a land of phantoms.

Our car seemed a tiny projectile coursing through a silent universe. It was as if we were the observed, not the observer; we had to pass through quickly, benignly, without intrusion or incident.

To our left the hills rose up to meet rocky outcroppings that had pushed through the earth, like bone through skin, to make high grassy ridges that ran for miles along the side of the road.

Carcasses of abandoned cars rested silent on the hillsides.

Where the ridges broke, long draws ran down between them, dry memories of forgotten creeks and streams. Scrub oak clustered against them, like animals gathered to slake their thirst. In the dark they could have been huddled herds of buffalo, or grizzlies, come together under the full moon.

In the distance I could make out the ragged contours of the Black Hills. The outcroppings and draws we were passing were the first hint of their presence.

I remembered the journeys as a child, in a borrowed car, through the seemingly endless spaces and unforgiving Dakota heat, toward those same ragged outlines. But then it was to ride the narrow-gauge trains and visit the reptile gardens and pony rides that had sprung up everywhere to take advantage of the presence of those four gigantic stone faces carved in the side of the mountain called Rushmore.

Now, this tiny outcropping of mountains was something less seen than felt — a home, a presence, a gathering place of spiritual forces — the *Paha Sapa*, the sacred center of the universe for the Lakota people. Their presence seemed active, more like a sentinel than a destination.

For a moment, and dimly, I lost my own eyes and saw with the eyes Dan had given me; saw the huddled people in their blankets, desperately trying to outrun an army that had committed itself to killing every man and woman and child and infant that had dark skin or spoke in a tongue born of this land. I heard the voices of mothers trying to keep track of each other in the swirling snow, slowing to help the old people who could neither walk nor understand why they had to flee, pulling their own clothes from their bodies to wrap their freezing children tighter against the winter night; saw them huddling together in the freezing darkness, afraid to build a fire against the ice and wind of December because the men who were hunting them like animals would see it and come riding in and rip their children from their arms before pumping bullets into their hearts, their legs, their skulls, and then riding off.

But most of all I felt the pain of their confusion that their god had failed.

In a land that as a child had filled me with dreams of pony rides and ice cream cones and four presidents' heads on a mountain, people who had sensed the power of God in every rock and bird and square inch of land had been reduced to dancing crazily in a circle, in hopes that their desperate ecstasy would call forth a savior who would keep them from having to watch one more of their children die hollow-eyed and uncomprehending in their arms.

The last afterglow of twilight had silhouetted the Black Hills against the night. It was easy to understand how they had become the sacred center. They stood mutely, majestically, in the middle of this endless plain, like a cathedral of the gods.

For these mountains, I thought, the Lakota had been willing to give away everything else, only to have them, too, taken away when white people who had trespassed illegally shouted the magic word, "Gold." "The metal that makes the *wasichu* crazy," the Lakota had called it. An ore in the ground.

For that, my ancestors had been willing to lie and steal and kill old people and children, and then spend the next century remaking the story so that all the dead and all the betrayals would effectively disappear from history.

For that, and the hunger to own a piece of the earth, we had destroyed the dreams and families of an entire race, leaving them homeless, faithless, and with nothing but the ashes of a once grace-ful and balanced way of life. And now we had the arrogance to claim to "rediscover" them and to appropriate the very spiritual truths we had tried to destroy, in order to fill the void of our own spiritual bankruptcy.

I was filled with a helpless shame and contrition. My mind moved fitfully across this bleak inner terrain, seeking rest and find-ing none. Dan's motionless form was outlined against the night. I wondered how he could live with such rage, how anyone could live with such rage. His last words, "I just wish I knew why it happened this way," echoed in my mind. The *Paha Sapa* rose ragged against the western sky as Grover's headlights strafed the silent land. I, too, wondered why it had to happen that way, and if this earth, with the knowledge it had, would ever grant any of us peace.

Chapter 25

Wounded Knee

"Let me out," Dan said.

I jumped in my seat. It had been an exhausting day, and under the preternatural moonlight I had given my mind free reign to wander. Dan's voice shocked me back to reality.

"Right here," Dan said.

I looked quickly to Grover. His face showed no emotion. He slowed the car as if the request was completely natural.

Outside the night had grown large. High, thin clouds wisped across the darkness like shadows, hiding, then revealing, the hollow moon and causing the hills and valleys to dance in a spiritplay of ghostly movement.

Grover pulled off the pavement into a rutted path that coursed up a steep rise. I assumed that Dan's anger and grief had caused him to want to speak to the spirits once again. I did not blame him. If one of his personal rituals would help salve the pain he was feeling, such a stop was a small price to pay.

"Get out," he said. He was looking at me.

I stared at him, confused.

"Get out," he repeated. There was no gentleness in his voice. A thousand thoughts raced through my mind: I was being abandoned;

he was so angry he couldn't stand a white man in the same car with him; we had reached a campsite; there was some point of interest he wanted to show me. It could have been anything. But he gave no indication beyond the brusque command.

I shifted uneasily in my seat and opened the door. Fatback clamored desperately across my lap and scuttered out onto the ground. Grover shut off the engine and the night engulfed us.

The moon had risen high in the sky. It was now no more than a hole in the night, revealed sporadically by the parting of the clouds.

Far up on the rise I could make out two brick pillars with a metal arch between them. They formed an entry of some sort; perhaps the remains of an old building or the entrance to an abandoned cemetery.

"Open the trunk," Dan ordered. He was now giving instructions with no explanation.

Grover fiddled with the key and popped the trunk lid. Dan reached in and took a large, beaded, animal skin bag. "Take your pack," he said to me. I dared not ask for an explanation; his manner was too curt and formidable.

"Is Fatback going?" I asked stupidly.

"Come on," Dan answered.

I waited for Grover to get his things out. But he simply slammed the trunk and walked back to the driver's door.

"How about Grover?" I said.

Grover slid in behind the steering wheel and shut his door. He started the engine. "See you later, Nerburn."

Dan said something in Lakota. Grover responded with a few words, then drove off. I stood watching his red taillights grow tiny in the distance, then disappear altogether as he passed over a ridge. In a moment they appeared again, even further away, then disappeared once and for all.

I stared at their afterimage in the darkness. The hum of the engine could still be heard on the edge of the silence. Then that, too, went out, and we were cast into the night.

Fatback snuffled in the grass nearby. Nighttime always made her come alive. Dan spoke several words in Lakota and she panted over to his side.

He gestured up the hill and started walking. The path was deeply rutted. Each step risked a fall or a turned ankle. Dan walked slowly but steadily, keeping his eyes ever on the shadowy columns at the top of the rise.

Somewhere far in the distance a dog barked. I could hear Dan's labored breathing as he lifted one foot, then the other, never pausing, never varying. I stayed several paces behind and said nothing.

The moon cut through the clouds and bathed the hill in empty, phosphorescent light. I could see that the backs and sides of the brick pillars on the hilltop had been painted white. They glowed like bones against the darkened sky. In the front of each was an alcove, a shrine for an absent saint. From this distance they appeared to be empty. The latticework arch between the two pillars reminded me of the tracery over the entrance to the Nazi death camps. I half expected to see "Arbeit Macht Frei" written in forged metal letters in the center of the arch. But instead, a small white cross rose from its top.

Dan stumbled and fell. I reached quickly for him. He pushed me away. I tried to help him with his bag, but he pulled it toward him. He made his way slowly to his feet and continued upward.

It was not an easy climb. The ruts made each step precarious. Our bags became burdens uncomfortable to bear. The straps on mine cut into my hand, and I shifted it clumsily from left to right when the pain became too great.

Fatback sensed that Dan was laboring. She stayed close to him, and even seemed to be charting a path by walking directly in front of him. Dan's breathing became raspy; I worried for his health. But he would not slow or vary his pace. In between the gasps and heaves I could hear him trying to aspirate some kind of a song, but the wind and his heavy breathing made it almost inaudible.

A car whined through the night far in the distance. Its lights moved away like a ship disappearing on the sea. Dan stumbled again but caught himself; we were almost to the top.

I could see the arch clearly now. It was the entrance to a small cemetery that stood forlornly on the top of the rise.

The alcoves in the front of the pillars were indeed empty. They stared like blind eyes out over the landscape and made the whole arch seem like an ancient ruin, long abandoned by those who had once built and tended it.

A flapping caught the corner of my eye. I looked up. All along the steel latticework of the arch were tied ragged pieces of ribbon. They squirmed like minnows in the dark.

Dan led me to the arch. Plastic Pepsi bottles and cellophane candy wrappers littered the ground in front of the entrance. If it was a ruin, it was a ruin that people still visited.

"Come," Dan said.

We crossed between the pillars and under the arch. Inside, directly in front of us, a plot of ground maybe eighty feet long and eight feet wide had been marked off and bordered by cement. It was enclosed by a bent and dented chainlink fence that also was hung with ribbons ripped ragged by the wind.

In the center of the plot, a single monument — an obelisk about nine feet tall — stood grey and austere under the moonlight. Plastic flowers were strewn haphazardly around its base.

Dan walked slowly around the outside of the fence to the left. A dirt path had been worn into the prairie grasses. On either side of the enclosure lay other graves, newer, marked with simple white crosses or low square headstones. They rose in tiny mounds above the surface of the land, providing a ghostly reminder of the bodies that lay within.

A shiver come across me as I followed Dan on the path. The earth was alive here, but there was nothing living. From the graves to the alcoves to the ribbons flapping in the dark, this place spoke of life that had fled. You could almost feel the earth moan beneath your feet.

A plastic flower from one of the graves blew onto the path in front of me. It lay in shadowy isolation in the dirt. I started to reach for it, then backed off. I did not want to touch it. It was part of the dead.

Fatback wandered among the graves, never crossing any of the mounds. It was as if she had a sixth sense. A flying thing swooped in front of me. I could not tell if was a bat or a bird; it moved too fast and quickly disappeared into the shadows.

Dan circled the entire fenced area. He would walk slowly, chanting something under his breath, then suddenly come to a halt and reach into the large bag he was carrying. At each stop he took out a small cloth bundle and tied it to the fence before proceeding. He did this seven times.

Four times he took a pinch of tobacco or something else from a tiny pouch and offered it to the wind. He did not do it casually, like a man scattering seed. Rather, he stopped, faced out from the fence, and held the substance at arm's length before him, raising it up toward the sky, then down toward the earth, and at last speaking some low incantation before releasing it gently, like a man setting a bird free or releasing the ashes of the dead.

I followed behind in silence. Dan's chanting was unearthly. It wove amid the gusts and echoes of the wind as if it were a part of them.

When we had completed our circle, Dan opened the gate to the chainlink fence and walked in. His singing was louder now, more forceful. The winds seemed to sing back to him, to take his song and mingle it with their own. I stood at the gate, uncertain if I should enter. Though the boundary was only a fence, something — maybe the strict formality of the cement border or the monument in the center — made the ground within seem hallowed, a *sanctum sanctorum* that one needed permission to approach.

Dan sensed I was not behind him. He turned and saw me at the gate. He jerked his head to tell me to follow. I stepped in, meekly, uncertain, a man treading on foreign ground. Fatback stayed outside the perimeter.

"Come," Dan spoke. His voice, in English, sounded stilted and distant, like a man not speaking his own language. Turning away from me, he joined his voice once more with the chorus of the wind.

I walked gingerly along the cement border. Its formality and echoes of city spaces were alien and intrusive here on this windswept hilltop.

"Come," he said again. He was standing by the monument.

He reached deep into his bag and took out a long roll of chamois-like leather. Meticulously he unrolled it and removed a small red pipe bowl. He took the wooden handle that had also been in the roll and fitted it onto the bowl. All the time he continued the chant.

I glanced at the slate-grey monument behind him and tried to read the inscription in the moonlight. Shadow obscured most of the words, but I was able to make out the first sentence: "This monument is erected by the surviving relatives and other Ogallala and Cheyenne River Sioux Indians in Memory of the Chief Big Foot Massacre December 29, 1890." There was more writing, then the sentence, "Many innocent women and children who knew no wrong died here."

A sense of utter desolation came across me. What was this place and what was the effect it was having on me?

Dan had filled the pipe and was attempting to light it. The match flared in the darkness and quickly went out. In the short burst of illumination I was able to read another side of the monument. "Horncloud. The peacemaker died here innocent."

There was a sense of outcry in all these words, all protesting innocence. What had happened here?

Dan had lit the pipe and was facing toward the west. He held the pipe outward, with the stem pointing at the dark horizon. He then turned it back and smoked from it, lifting the smoke around his head with a cupped hand. He walked around the monument and repeated the action to the north, the east, and the south, while speaking a private incantation in each direction.

When he was finished, he handed it to me.

"Smoke," he said. "You must pray, too."

I took the pipe and tried to mimic his actions, holding the stem toward the west.

"No," he stopped me. "You must clear your heart." The wind blew hard across me. Sparks jumped from the bowl of the pipe and shot into the darkness.

"I'm trying."

"You must forget yourself. You are not here for yourself. You are not here for me. This is Wounded Knee. You are standing on the grave."

At those words the earth seemed to heave under my feet. I looked at the concrete border. Dan saw me. "That's right. This is the grave. The bodies of two hundred murdered Lakota people are buried here. The old ones and women and children. Children like your son. They were killed running from your soldiers. They were dumped here after they were killed. Thrown in on top of each other and covered with dirt. This is their grave."

I moved further back onto the concrete border, as if standing on that would protect me from the forces rising up from the ground beneath my feet. Dan pointed through the arch back down the hill across the road. A dark mass of trees coursed along a draw. "There," he said. "They were running. They tried to hide in that creekbed. They huddled together and the soldiers on horses shot them down. They left them dying and freezing in the snow. When our people found them there were little babies all covered with blood and half frozen trying to nurse on their dead mothers' breasts." He turned and locked me in his gaze. "Little boys like your boy, Nerburn," he said again. "Their spirit is still crying."

I gazed off over his shoulder at the shadowy hills. Forms danced wildly in the moonlight. The image of my son, running, rose up before me. It was more than memory. It was like he was there, alive. He was running hard, like a young boy does, full of energy but not making much progress. He was running up the hill to me, yelling to me, reaching toward me, with his crooked smile and his dancing blond hair. His voice was in the wind; I heard it. Then he exploded, covered with blood, and I couldn't reach him.

"The pipe," I heard Dan say.

I held it up. I started to shake. I didn't want this image. I wanted it to go away. But I didn't have control.

"The pipe," Dan said again. The wind was like a chorus, a thousand voices blended into one.

I took the pipe and sucked in. The warm heat of the tobacco and *kinnikinic* filled my mouth. The sweet, acrid aroma surrounded me like a cloud, taking me away from the hill, away from the stars, away from the wind and the night. It was like a wall that protected me from the awful image of my son torn apart.

I inhaled again. The warmth comforted me. I cupped my hand and moved the smoke around me, like a protection, a shield, a blanket of peace. I did not want that vision to return.

I held the pipe to the west. The smoke curled out from the stem and rose into the sky.

"Pray," Dan said. "I know you can. I've seen you." It was not a request, but something more — an order, an entreaty. "Pray. To the west." I was shaking hard. The image of my boy was before me again.

"To whom?" I stammered. "I don't know what to . . ."

"The west, Nerburn. Talk to the west," Dan coaxed.

The image of my son would not leave me. He kept coming toward me, smiling, reaching. I tried to pray as I had seen Dan do. "To you, the west, where dreams take wing and day comes to a rest, hear me, keep this image from me." I drew in the sweet smoke and inhaled it into the wind.

"Don't ask for things, just pray," Dan said. "It is not yours to say what comes. Now, the north."

I turned to the north. The image would not leave. I did not

know how to pray to a direction, or even what words to use. All I wanted was to stop this image. "Dear north," I said, in clumsy invocation, like a child, "You are the direction of my spirit, the direction of caution and great darkness, the giver of winter, of phantoms, of the snow that covers us in oneness, I offer this to you." I puffed hard on the pipe and smoke billowed out.

"Good," I heard Dan say.

"The east."

The rich, heavy aroma of the tobacco mixture surrounded me. I turned my back to the wind and held the stem of the pipe out into the darkness. "To you, the east, the direction of the sunrise, where hope is born and every day begins anew, I offer this." I puffed again and cupped the billowing smoke around my head with my hand.

"Now the south."

I turned. The pillars loomed before me with their tracery arch and tiny white cross. Through their opening I could see the draw and the trees, alive with shadows and movement. The smoke and wind burned by eyes, causing them to tear. Through the blur the moving forms became running children and screaming women. I blinked my eyes. The hills were alive with silhouettes of old men hobbling desperately toward the trees, stumbling like Dan on the frozen earth.

Above me the ribbons flapped like gunshots in the wind. Clouds raced before the moon. The little children all ran like my son; the old men, frail, with brittle bones, moved like Dan or my father, while old women, frantic and heavy legged, huddled together to protect the young women and the babies with their bodies.

The wind wailed around me. I closed my eyes to chase the image away. My son ran toward me, reaching.

"No," I shouted. "I don't want this."

"The south," Dan said. "The south."

"To the south, from where warmth comes, and rest, and growth and color and life, I offer this pipe."

I puffed and blew the smoke out. The wind grabbed it and rushed it away. There was a sound of moaning and keening, perhaps from the wind singing in the wires in the chainlink fence. The ribbons snapped and cracked.

"To the sky. To *Wakan Tanka*," Dan ordered.

I thrust the stem of the pipe upward. I did not know what I was doing or why. "*Wakan Tanka*," I blurted. "God. Creator. Father. I do not know what to call you, or if you are my God at all. Hear me. Take this smoke that rises to you."

I opened my eyes. The smoke was streaming out the mouthpiece of the pipe and twisting sinuously, urgently, toward the moon. I closed my eyes again and turned the pipe back to me and smoked.

"Now the earth," Dan said.

I held the stem downward. For a moment it felt like something tugged on it. I jumped backward. "To the earth, the mother of us all, from which all life comes and to which it must return, I offer this pipe. Please hear me." I smoked the last embers and stood silent. The pipe seemed to lighten in my hand. The images still flooded before me, but were quieter and more distant.

I felt Dan's hand upon the pipe. He withdrew it gently from my grasp.

"Now sit," he said, softly. "Talk. Tell the truth. What is in your heart."

I slid down to the ground with a sigh. My back rested against the monument to the dead. I was still shaking. "I'm scared," I said. "There is too much pain, too much fear. I see images of my son, trying to get to me, dying, being shot, expoding; of old people — I don't know if it's my imagination, or guilt — running for that ravine.

"I feel so awful, so guilty, like it's real and I have to do something and there's nothing I can do. And I can't stop it but I don't want it to happen . . . to have happened. I don't want any of this to have happened. I want there to have been a different way."

"Keep talking," he said, and started a low chanting. I was like a boy in a confessional, huddled over, with my eyes closed, pouring something out into the darkness while the priest incanted some distant absolution. I clasped my hands around my knees and rocked back and forth.

"I don't know what I'm doing here. I don't know why I'm doing this. I don't know what to believe, if I am making this up or if there are powers I can't even fathom. I want to believe, but I'm afraid, and I don't want to anger anything or disturb anything sacred. I just want do what's right, and protect my family, and do some good in this world."

Dan sang louder. I felt his hand on my shoulder. I opened my eyes and looked up. He was standing above me, with his left hand on my shoulder, his eyes closed. He was looking toward the moon and singing something in Lakota. He kept his hand there, gently holding me, like Danelle had, while he sang and spoke toward the sky. The pipe was cradled in his right arm, like an infant.

"What hurts the most?" he said quietly, in English, without opening his eyes or looking down.

"The children and the old people. That they were killed. That they had so much faith. That their world was destroyed."

"What else?"

"That maybe my heart isn't pure. That I might be doing this for the wrong reasons."

"What else?"

"That there are reasons for this that are too far beyond me, and that maybe I am the thing I fear most, one more white person with good intentions who will end up doing harm." A gust of wind blew harshly across my face. The strange, keening sound came again. "And that the earth is crying," I said, "and that nothing can wash away her tears."

Dan stopped his singing. He slowly lowered himself to the ground across from me. I sat huddled against the monument for the dead. He made a lengthy prayer in Lakota, then changed to

English. "I will talk again, now," he said. He took a small leather bag from inside his shirt and removed a round stone from it. He held this in his hand and began to speak.

"You have spoken well. Your words could have been my words. I, too, am afraid for what I am doing, and I, too, fear that there are powers that will be angry. But the children are dead. The old ones are dead. It is a hurt too great to bear in silence. We must speak. We must speak together."

He directed his words at me, but they were formal and precise.

"I see the old ones and the children every night when I lay down. I see them here. I see them at Sand Creek. I see them in a hundred villages that are now forgotten. I, too, will join them soon. I want to know why they had to die running. I want to know why our land was cut and scarred and we were not allowed to stand against you to protect the land and the children and the old ones. I want to know why the Creator let his happen. For my whole life I have wanted to know this.

"But I am just a man, like you. I can see to the edge of my life and no further. I can walk to the edge of my land and no further. I cannot see beyond the horizon. That is how the Creator made us all.

"But now I am old. Different voices speak to me. And here is what they say.

"They say that perhaps it is not by love, but by blood, that land is bought. They say that perhaps my people had to die to nourish this earth with their truth. Your people did not have ears to hear. Perhaps we had to return to the earth, so that we could grow within your hearts. Perhaps we have come back and will fill the hills and valleys with our song. Who is to know?

"There may be greater truths than ours. The Creator hears and sees far over the horizon. I must cry my tears and sing my songs for my people, so that they will always be honored and will never die. But I cannot try to know the Creator's ways. Perhaps we may someday see; perhaps not. Perhaps there is a new truth, larger even than the Lakota's, larger than all the Indian peoples', larger than the truths your people brought to this land, larger than all our truths combined, and that now we are coming to find it together.

"Here is what I say.

"There is no more time for fighting. Our anger must be buried. If I cannot bury mine, it will be for my children to bury theirs. And if they cannot bury theirs, it will be for their children, or their children's children. We are prisoners of our hearts, and only time will free us.

"Your people must learn to give up their arrogance. They are not the only ones placed on this earth. Theirs is not the only way. People have worshipped the Creator and loved their families in many ways in all places. Your people must learn to honor this.

"It is your gift to have material power. You have much strength not given to other people. Can you share it, or can you use it only to get more? That is your challenge — to find the way to share your gift, because it is a strong and dangerous one.

"It is my people who must stand as the shadow that reminds you of your failures. It is our memory that must keep you on the good road. It does you no good to pretend that we did not exist, and that you did not destroy us. This was our land. We will always be here. You can no more remove our memory than you can hide the sun by putting your hand over your eyes.

"I am sad that the Creator saw fit to destroy us to give you life. But maybe that is not so bad, for is that not what your religion teaches you that he did with Jesus? Maybe it was the power of our spirit that made us able to accept our physical death.

"Maybe it was the power of our spirit that made the Creator see that we, alone, could save you, who cared so much about things that should not matter.

"Maybe it is we who are the true sons and daughters of God, who had to die on the cross of your fears and greed, so that you could be saved from yourselves.

"Is that so strange? I do not think so. *Wakan Tanka*, the Great

Mystery, the Creator, He who you call God, knows that our people were always willing to die for each other. It was our greatest honor. Maybe the greatest honor of all is that we as a people were able to die for the whole human race. *Wakan Tanka* alone knows these things."

He reached his gnarled hand across in the darkness and took my wrist.

"Here," he said. "Give me your hand. We are brothers. You are my son. I pass to you my vision, even though I cannot pass to you my knowledge. There lies in the ground not far from here one who truly was my son. He could not bear the pain of knowing two truths. And so I give my vision to you who knows only one. Perhaps it will be easier to bear. Perhaps it will be easier to share.

"There are spirits to help you. There are spirits to help us all. If only your people would learn to listen to them, to go into the sunlight and give thanks for the day, they would find them. Then they would not be so quick to do harm, or so able to rest at night when they spent the day working only for themselves.

"The earth is deep, Nerburn, and its knowledge is great. Listen to the stones, and listen to the wind. Do what you must do to find the voices that will speak to you. They are there. They are calling. Do what you must do to find them, and share their words.

"I will pray now."

He let go of my wrist. I felt an unbearable weariness come over me. My eyelids drooped.

"Sleep," he said. "But watch."

I barely heard him. I was receding from his words like the clouds in the sky.

I cannot remember much about that night. I fell into a fitful sleep full of howlings and hauntings. Images fractured and shattered and rose reconfigured. I would pop to the surface, open my eyes, panic for a moment until I remembered where I was, then drop again, even deeper, even further, to places where fears combined with memories, and presentiments of future dangers loomed like the ghostly brick pillars standing sentinel outside the gate.

I remember the cold of the concrete beneath me, and how I kept pushing myself back onto it, as if the earth itself were a darkened sea that lapped, dangerous and unfathomable, at my feet.

Once I awoke and sat bolt upright. Dan was outside the enclosure. He was standing with his arms out, facing over the hills. The moon had withdrawn far into the sky — a distant empty orb that cast neither light nor warmth.

I watched him for a moment. He did not move. I thought he might be chanting, but I heard nothing. I wanted to go to him, like a child to a father, but my limbs were too heavy. I fell again into the abyss of fitful dreams.

I remember tumbling. It was a palpable sense, head over heels, dizzying in its descent.

Far down somewhere I came upon a place. It was not a real place, but it somehow seemed real, because when I arrived there the whole world became completely still, as if before a storm, and the twisting images and turbulent memories suddenly disappeared.

I was standing in a valley. I had never been there before, but I knew I was supposed to wait. I was to wait for a burning orange hawk that would come flying over the hill behind me.

I stood in silence surveying the sky overhead until the brilliant orange bird flashed across my vision at a heavenly speed. It swooped down upon another brown-and-white hawk that I had not seen before.

I shielded my eyes from the sight, and when I looked up again I saw a majestic multi-colored bird with feathers of many hues. I cannot remember all the colors — I see yellow and red and orange and gold — but its presence was radiant. He dominated the sky and the light shone through his outstretched wings like sunset through stained glass. He seemed oblivious to the other hawks, who were off to the left, toward the hill. They became insignificant dots in the sky while he floated, magnificent, suspended directly above me, between me and the sun.

The dream stayed on, unaffected by time. It was a space I in-habited, like a memory of infinite breadth. But more than that, it didn't seem like my dream. It was as if it were already there, and I had just come upon it, as one comes upon a valley when cresting a hill.

When at last I emerged, I was like a man emerging not from a sleep, but from a trance. I opened my eyes with total clarity and consciousness.

The morning had broken. Thin wisps of purple clouds were fin-gering across the eastern sky. The dawn birds had begun their cho-rus and the hills were basking in the growing sun.

Dan was standing at the edge of the graves facing east. An old weathered shack with several junk cars stood off in the distance. Written on it in white paint was, "Wounded Knee is not for sale."

In the daylight I could see the graves with their crosses and headstones and plastic flowers. Some were covered with small stones that seemed to have been arranged with a purpose. The pit area bordered by the concrete was trampled and worn, no different from the miles of grasslands that spread out around us.

I stood up to get my bearings. Dan was facing into the morning sun. Fatback was lying by his side with her head on her paws. About a foot from her was the large hide bag Dan had brought up the night before.

The morning breeze was fresh. It hinted of heat. I shielded my eyes from the growing sun and looked again at Dan. He was wear-ing the same clothes as the night before. It was impossible to know if he had slept or if he had stayed up all night.

He did not turn to face me, but he must have sensed my move-ment. "Did you watch?" he said, as if no other thought had inter-vened from the time I had fallen asleep.

I did not feel right speaking loudly from within the fenced enclo-sure. I pushed open the gate and crossed to where he was standing.

"Yes," I said. "I think I did."

"What did you see?"

I told him about the strange quiet hillside and the translucent multi-hued bird. He sucked his lips and mulled it over for a minute. "I think you are ready to write," he said. He picked up his bag and started walking. I thought perhaps he was beginning some private ritual. But he walked directly through the pillars and started down the hill.

I ran back to the monument and grabbed my bag. Dan was already navigating the rutted gumbo trail that led to the parking area. On the road below traffic had begun to pick up. The sweet smell of morning was everywhere.

I hurried to catch up to him.

"What does it mean, Dan?" I asked.

"It was a good night," he said.

"I mean, the dream. What does it mean?"

He gave me a wicked grin. "Hell, I don't know. I can't interpret dreams. You've got to find a *wichasha wakan* for that kind of stuff. They don't work cheap. Probably have to trade in your truck."

The wind was blowing warm and dry by the time we got to the bottom of the hill. It was going to be a hot day.

In a nearby pull-off area Indians were setting up open air stands to sell earrings and dream catchers to the few tourists who might pass this way. In the morning sunlight, the gully where the killings took place seemed benign and full of light. It was almost impossible to imagine that cold winter night with the screams and the slaughter.

Someone over by the earring stands was playing powwow music on a boom box. Dan reached in his bag and fished out a bottle. The sweet whistlings of larksong floated from the rustling grasses. "Want some water?" he said.

I gratefully took a swig and swished it around my mouth. He squatted down and pulled out a cigarette. There was a peace and contentment over the entire land.

I left Dan to his thoughts and walked over to a large wooden sign that described the events of the massacre. It was a long and detailed recounting painted on a large white board and bolted to two utility poles sunk into the earth.

The story seemed sad, but distant. The fleeing Lakota, the winter camp, the soldiers, the attack, the confusion, the dead. It was one more string of words chronicling the tragedy and injustice of American history. People could drive by, read it from their cars, buy a dream catcher, and move on. The Black Hills and Mount Rushmore were only an hour away. There were still narrow-gauge trains and giant water slides to visit — maybe even the recreation of the shooting of Wild Bill Hickock or the Black Hills Passion Play.

Dan squatted placidly in the middle of the gravel pull-off area. The rising plume of smoke from his cigarette was quickly grabbed by the morning breeze. Far up on the hill the two pillars with their joining arch stood empty against the sun.

"Seems different in the daylight," I said, returning to his side.

"Yep," he answered. "Grass grows over everything."

In the distance the low sound of a powerful motor cut through the morning heat.

"Right on time," Dan said as Grover's Buick came nosing over the hill. How they knew what time it was and how they arranged the meeting, I did not know. The rumbling car pulled up beside us and Grover leaned out into the sun. He was freshly washed and cleanshaven. He had on a crisp white T-shirt that looked almost blue in the brilliant morning light. The smell of aftershave wafted across us.

"Want some coffee, Nerburn?" he said. He took a styrofoam convenience store cup off the dashboard. The heat from the coffee had steamed a small circle of fog on the inside of the windshield. "Know you need the stuff."

I took the cup eagerly and lifted it to my lips. A thick stream of heavy, frothy coffee, dark with flavor, coursed into my mouth.

"Grover!" I said. "This is real. Where did you get it?"

Grover tamped a cigarette on the dashboard and flipped it adroitly up to his lips. "Got connections, Nerburn."

Dan had wandered over. "Try that stuff, old man," Grover said, pointing to the styrofoam cup in my hand. Dan took a sip and spit it out in the dirt.

"Tastes like tar," he said. "Damn hippie junk."

"That's the stuff Nerburn likes. Capistrano, they call it."

Dan was still trying to spit the last vestiges out of his mouth. "Where'd you get that crap?" he asked. "They sure as hell don't sell that in Pine Ridge."

"Made a deal," Grover answered.

"With the devil?" Dan said.

"No. With the old hippies. Remember the ones in the restaurant?"

"The ones with the green bus?" I asked.

"Yeah. Saw them in Pine Ridge, getting gas."

Dan was already muttering and shaking his head.

"Smelled some bad shit coming from their bus," Grover continued. "Thought maybe it was on fire. But when it didn't explode I just figured it was their coffee. So I made a deal with them."

"You made a deal for that crap?" Dan said. "You're dumber than those Indians that sold Manhattan."

"I told them you'd tell them about the Great Spirit and give them all handshakes," Grover answered without cracking a smile. "They should be here any minute."

Dan snorted in disgust.

"Really, Grover," I said. "Where'd you get it?"

"That's the truth," he said. "Would I lie to you?"

He leaned back comfortably into his seat and blew smoke rings toward the rearview mirror. No matter what Dan or I said to him, he would not say another word.

Chapter 26

The Promise

The trip back took almost two days. Grover drove steadily but leisurely. He never once left the road or even suggested it; the "little trip" had ended when we got to Wounded Knee and whatever mysterious destination had claimed Grover for the night Dan and I had spent on the hill.

Grover had tried hard to convince Dan that we should go on to Mount Rushmore, but Dan would have none of it. "Those damn heads are the worst thing that the white man ever did," he snapped. "Blowing up the sacred mountains to put a bunch of white faces on them." He carried on at some length about how Indians should be allowed to sell tacos on the altars at white churches in exchange for what had been done to the Black Hills, and threatened to die right in the Mount Rushmore parking lot if we made him go there, so Grover eventually gave up the idea and headed for home.

We managed to shower and wash at a public campground in a little farm town somewhere off the highway. That took some of the edge off the cheap cologne that Grover had splashed all over himself during the mystery night in Pine Ridge. He never volunteered any more information about that night, and Dan never asked.

We drove in contented silence through the late summer heat.

Fatback slept most of the way with her head on my lap. The lyrical roll of the landscape reduced me once again to reverie. The time and the miles passed quickly.

Late on the second morning, Grover turned off the main highway onto the road to the reservation. Fatback became more alert and agitated. She sensed she was close to home.

Dan cupped his hand over his eyes and squinted off into the distance. "Looks like a buffalo up there," he said.

Grover bent over the wheel and stared hard into the sun. "Sure as hell does," he seconded.

I tried to look where they were staring. The sun burst in rainbow haloes through the windshield as I tried to focus on a black spot moving across the ridge.

"Moves too fast for a buffalo," Dan observed.

My eyes adjusted slowly and the ridgetop came into view.

"That's my truck!" I shouted.

Far up on the rise my black Nissan pounded across the prairie. A plume of dust rose behind it like a cloud.

"By God, you're right," Dan said. "Thought for sure it was a buffalo."

"Looks like Jumbo got it running," Grover added.

The truck bounced and bucked over the ridgetop and disappeared.

"Want some lunch?" Dan asked, turning to face me. I was still staring at the dissipating dust cloud.

"What's my truck doing up there?" I said.

"Looked like it was running pretty good," Grover said.

"Yeah, Jumbo can fix stuff," Dan added.

I was caught between elation and outrage. I had figured my truck would never run again, and now it not only was running, but someone else was driving it. "I didn't tell anyone else to drive it," I said.

"Someone else might be driving your wife, too, Nerburn,"

Grover cracked. "You don't seem too worried about that."

"Let's get some lunch," Dan said. "A man's got to eat."

"How about getting the truck first," I argued. "Jumbo or whoever that is could be on his way to Seattle, for all we know."

"Yep. Could be," Dan said.

"Why are you doing this to me?" I pleaded.

"An old man needs his food, Nerburn."

I didn't have any choice. I could be angry at them, but they would just laugh. I could beg, but they would just do what they wanted, anyway. The cloud of dust had settled. The ridgetop was clear. The truck was gone.

"Need some soup," Dan said.

"It's Saturday. Must be poodle noodle," Grover observed. They both laughed heartily; it was an old joke.

Grover took a left turn and headed down a side road. Before long we came to a low building with a tarpaper roof and a collection of cowskulls hanging from the entryway. A red-and-white sign in the window said, "Closed." But there were cars and trucks outside.

We pulled up next to an old Volare with no hubcaps and a broken grill. The rear window on the passenger side had been smashed out and replaced with a piece of cardboard that was held in place by duct tape. The muffler was held on by a bungee cord that was hooked into the tailpipe on one end and the trunk lip on the other.

I glanced over into the back seat. A filthy air filter canister and a pair of jumper cables lay on top of a little girl's pink sweater amid a pile of tinfoil fast food wrappers.

"Must be one Jumbo fixed," Grover observed.

"There's got to be a special place in hell for people like you," I said.

"No Indians there," Grover answered. "Too full of white people."

We walked into the darkened cafe. On the far side a vast mass hulked on one of the stools.

"Jumbo!" I blurted, almost ecstatic.

Jumbo nodded. I looked out the window behind him. My truck was parked out back behind the building.

Jumbo was working over a platter of fried chicken. A pile of bones sat in a napkin near the side of the plate. He held a cigarette in one hand and a drumstick in the other.

"Truck's fixed," he said, as if he had been sitting there waiting for me. "Runs good." He was in a talkative mood.

I wanted to ask him why he was driving it, but I knew better.

"What was wrong?" I asked instead.

"I'm eating," Jumbo replied, leaving no doubt that there were more serious issues on his mind.

"Come on, Nerburn, sit down," Dan said. "Worry about your truck later."

I followed them hesitantly to a table. My truck gleamed outside in the afternoon sun.

Jumbo swivelled on his stool and rose up. He gripped the oval platter of chicken parts in his right hand and tottered toward us. A cigarette ash dropped onto the plate and disappeared among the wings and thighs. He lumbered to our table and lowered himself into a vacant chair.

"Twenty bucks," he said.

I thought he was telling us the cost of his chicken platter.

"Twenty bucks," he repeated. He was looking straight at me.

"For the truck?" I asked, suddenly realizing what he was saying. He nodded.

"For a head gasket?" I said.

"Wasn't a head gasket." He glanced at Dan. "Blew a hose. Had it fixed before supper." He measured his time by the space between meals.

"I wonder why a hose went?" I said. I had just had the hoses changed in the spring.

"Aw, don't worry about it, Nerburn," Grover said. "It's done."

Something in his tone caught my attention. Instead of jabbing at me for my concern, he was trying to move me away from the subject. "Do you know something I don't know?" I asked.

"I know a lot of things you don't know," Grover said.

"I mean, about my truck, about why it broke."

"Don't know nothing about that," he answered tersely. He stared intently at the cup of coffee the waitress had just placed in front of him. Dan was intricately involved in tearing open a small cracker package with his stiff, arthritic hands.

"Dan?" I said. "Do you know anything about what happened to my truck?"

"Goddamn!" he said. "An old man can't even eat in peace anymore."

I glanced from Dan to Grover to Jumbo. None of them would look at me.

"You sons of bitches," I said. "You did it. You set me up."

Dan freed his crackers from their cellophane wrapper and they tumbled onto the table. Grover stirred his coffee. Jumbo was parsing his plate of chicken parts with his index finger, trying to isolate the cigarette ashes.

"You never learn, Nerburn," Dan said.

"What?"

"You always blame the Indians."

"Blame the Indians! Who the hell should I blame? You guys look like Indians to me."

"Wasn't us," Dan said.

"Nope," said Grover.

"Then who was it?" I said.

Jumbo ripped a piece of chicken flesh off a leg bone. "Great Spirit," he answered. Dan nodded. So did Grover. They sat quietly for a moment, then all burst into laughter.

The waitress came over and dropped a white greasy bag on the table in front of Jumbo.

"What's that?" Grover said. "You just ate half the chickens on the rez."

"Got to gain some weight," Jumbo answered, corkscrewing his cigarette out in the ashtray. "Had to go on a diet. Ain't a lot of room in them Nissans." Then, rising, he added, "Got to get back to work."

I was not about to let my truck out of my sight again. I left Dan and Grover to their poodle noodle soup and told them I would meet them back at the garage.

Jumbo led me through the back door of the restaurant to the parking area. My truck gleamed like a black diamond in the sun. Jumbo threw the keys across the roof of the cab and dropped himself into the passenger seat. The truck creaked and settled. I brushed a few pieces of pie crust off the seat and slid behind the wheel.

The ash tray was overflowing with cigarette butts, and the cab stunk of grease and body odor. But the truck ran like new. The idle was smoother and it seemed to have more power.

"Did a few other things, too," Jumbo said proudly. "Timing was off. Bad plug wire."

"You really did work on it, then," I said.

Jumbo nodded. "Pain in the ass, too. Pretty good tape deck, though."

Three young boys on dirt bikes rode out of their driveway and started hollering, "*Wasichu* truck! *Wasichu* truck! Give us another ride!" Jumbo waved from the passenger window and the boys did skid stops in the dirt along side us.

"Ain't mine no more," Jumbo shouted. He tossed a chicken bone off into the brush on the side of the road.

I smiled and shifted up into third gear. The truck pulled out with ease and galloped across the gravel.

"You did a good job," I said.

Jumbo gave a toothless jack-o-lantern grin. "I can fix stuff," he answered.

I let him out in front of his building. I tried to give him some extra money for his work, but he refused. "Twenty's good," was all he said, and stuffed the bill into the front pocket of his bib overalls. The idea of a receipt or a guarantee was unthinkable.

Another gaggle of young boys had gathered alongside the truck and were climbing in and out of the pickup box as if it were a jungle gym. I tried to get them to stay out by claiming I was leaving soon, but they paid no mind. By now this truck was as much theirs as mine.

Jumbo had already turned his back to me and was working on the sprocket of a bicycle that was balanced upside down on its seat and handlebars in the dusty shadows in front of his shop.

"Thanks again, Jumbo," I said. His head nodded once or twice in acknowledgment, but that was all. He was on to other tasks.

Soon the young boys drifted over to the bicycle that was undergoing surgery. They stood like interns around Jumbo, offering advice and falling silent as he pointed out the intricacies of chain tension and bearing lubrication.

I was left alone in the noonday sun. The heat was relentless. I could not even lean against the truck without getting burned. Far down the street some trees twitched listlessly in the stagnant breeze. A skeletal dog moved slowly across the road and dug into a hollow of shade near a culvert. The only sound was the clicking of Jumbo's ratchet and the distant empty thunk of some machine that rose and fell indifferent to the burning heat.

Before long I heard the crunch of tires. Grover's green Buick came crawling around the corner like a great, lazy reptile. It pulled up beside me and Dan climbed out.

"Truck okay?" he said.

"Works great."

"Jumbo can fix stuff."

"He sure can."

We stood silent, measuring the space between us. I expected him to invite me out to the house, but no invitation was forthcoming.

"Well," I said finally, "I might as well get started. It's a long drive."

"Hot, too," Dan added. Then, "Got something for you." He reached through the window of Grover's car and into the animal-skin bag he had carried up the hill with him that night at Wounded Knee. He dug around a bit and pulled out a flat piece of red stone carved into the stylized shape of an eagle. It was strung on a cord for hanging around the neck.

He pushed it casually toward me; there was no ceremony in the giving. I took the carving from his chestnut hand. He held onto it for an instant before letting go, then it was mine.

He did not withdraw his hand immediately. It hung out there like a tree root, exposed, unearthed, revealed. He was thinking.

Finally, he shook his head. The thought, like a storm cloud, had passed. He opened his hand and held it forward. This was good-bye.

I took his hand in mine. The whiteness of my grip against his mahogany gnarls and knuckles made me seem effete and un-formed. He squeezed hard. A promise was being passed.

I looked at him. He was looking away. The meaning was in the hand, not in the eyes.

"I'll do a good job," I said.

He nodded.

"I'll send you drafts," I continued.

He nodded again.

I wanted to talk, to pour things out, to hug him, to thank him, to do something. He dropped his hand and turned away. I started to talk again. He raised his hand up level with his shoulder and waved it slightly: "You have said enough," it said. "Be quiet."

I stood in the baking heat, watching him fumble with the gleaming chrome door handle on Grover's car. Fatback was panting and drooling in the back seat. She was home again, and excited. Grover bent down a little in the seat so he could see me where I stood. He touched his hand once to the brim of his hat — a tiny salute — before Dan opened the door and slid in beside him.

The car clunked into gear and rolled down the street with a low rumble. I could see the backs of two men's heads as they drove away. Only Fatback had turned to watch me. Her eyes drooped and her head rested on the back window ledge.

I lifted my hand and waved at her, half pretending, and half believing, that she could understand. She raised her ears and gave me a baleful look. The car rumbled forward over the rise and was gone.

The trees had fallen completely still in the midday calm. Slowly I reached up and dropped the necklace over my head. The stone eagle was cool; it lay heavy against my chest. I stood in the dust in the empty street, listening to the deep throat of Grover's Buick grow dim in the distance. The old dog down by the culvert got up and circled three times, then settled back into the dirt. I remained there, motionless, listening, until long after there was anything left to hear.

About the Author

Kent Nerburn is an author, sculptor, and educator who has been deeply involved in Native American issues and education. He developed and directed an award-winning oral history project on the Red Lake Ojibwe Reservation in Northern Minnesota. He has served as a consultant in curriculum development for the American Indian Institute in Norman, Oklahoma, and has been a presenter before various groups including the National Indian Education Association and the President's Blue Ribbon Panel on Indian Education.

Nerburn has served as project director for two books of oral history — *To Walk the Red Road* and *We Choose to Remember*. He has edited three books on Native American subjects: *Native American Wisdom*, *The Wisdom of the Great Chiefs*, and *The Soul of an Indian*. He is currently developing the Ohiyesa Prize for Native Writers, to be administered by New World Library.

He is the author of the highly acclaimed book *Letters to My Son: A Father's Wisdom on Manhood, Women, Life and Love*.

Nerburn holds a Ph.D. in Religion and Art and lives with his wife and two children in Bemidji, Minnesota.

New World Library is dedicated to publishing books and cassettes that help improve the quality of our lives. If you enjoyed *Neither Wolf nor Dog*, we highly recommend the following books:

Native American Wisdom edited by Kent Nerburn and Louise Mengelkoch. Taken from speeches and writings of peoples from all tribes, this book presents the best of Native American wisdom on topics such as the land, the ways of living, and the ways of the heart.

The Soul of an Indian and Other Writings from Ohiyesa (Charles Alexander Eastman) edited by Kent Nerburn. Ohiyesa has been described as "the Native American Thoreau." This sensitively edited new edition presents the profound and beautiful reflections of this important writer on nature, the education of children, and a life of honor.

The Wisdom of the Great Chiefs: The Classic Speeches of Chief Red Jacket, Chief Joseph, and Chief Seattle edited by Kent Nerburn. These speeches reveal the broad panorama of the Native American experience and also eloquently reveal that the spirit of the native people, the First People, has never died.

Native Heart: An American Indian Odyssey by Gabriel Horn (White Deer of Autumn). This is a celebration of the great heritage of the Native American people, and moves us to consider our own sacred path. With a sense of childhood yearning and wonder that has never waned, Gabriel Horn reflects upon his relationship with the Great Mystery, the stars, birds, trees, and Mother Earth.

If you would like a catalog of our fine
books and cassettes, contact:
New World Library
14 Pamaron Way
Novato, CA 94949
(415) 884-2100 or call toll-free: (800) 972-6657